D0138449

DISCRETE
SYSTEM
SIMULATION

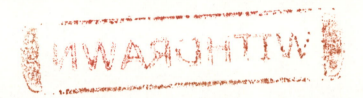

DISCRETE SYSTEM SIMULATION

WILLIAM G. BULGREN

University of Kansas

PRENTICE-HALL, INC., Englewood Cliffs, New Jersey 07632

Library of Congress Cataloging in Publication Data

Bulgren, William G. (date)
Discrete system simulation.

Bibliography: p.
Includes index.
1. Digital computer simulation. I. Title.
QA76.9.C65B84   001.4′34   81-21062
ISBN 0-13-215764-0   AACR2

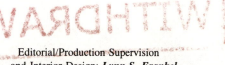

Editorial/Production Supervision
and Interior Design: *Lynn S. Frankel*
Cover Design: *Edsal Enterprises*
Manufacturing Buyer: *Gordon Osbourne*

Printed in the United States of America

10 9 8 7 6 5 4 3 2 1

ISBN 0-13-215764-0

Prentice-Hall International, Inc., *London*
Prentice-Hall of Australia Pty. Limited, *Sydney*
Prentice-Hall of Canada, Ltd., *Toronto*
Prentice-Hall of India Private Limited, *New Delhi*
Prentice-Hall of Japan, Inc., *Tokyo*
Prentice-Hall of Southeast Asia Pte. Ltd., *Singapore*
Whitehall Books Limited, *Wellington, New Zealand*

CONTENTS

v

9

EXAMPLES

187

A

APPENDIX: PROOFS FOR CHAPTER 4

207

B

APPENDIX: SEMESTER PROJECTS

210

C

APPENDIX: TABLES

213

INDEX

225

PREFACE

The purpose of this book is to introduce the art and techniques of discrete-system simulation. The book contains all the necessary tools for learning discrete-system simulation, including statistics, discrete-system simulation languages, elementary queuing theory, advanced programming techniques, random-number generation, generation of various random variates, and elementary modeling techniques.

A belief that the best learning situations involve the student personally and subjectively in the subject matter has guided the preparation of this book. Simulation courses lend themselves particularly well to laboratory work. The exercises, examples, and problems in this book lend themselves to this goal. These can be best utilized while learning specific skills or concepts. The important concepts of simulation are not easily learned by hearing someone talk about them or by reading about them in a textbook. One learns these things best, it seems, by doing the work.

The instructor will find this book so arranged that it may be used in a one-semester course. It is the author's intent to emphasize problem solving on a computer, which can be conveniently divided into nine phases or parts: formulation, modeling, algorithm selection, programming, debugging, verification, production of results, analysis of results, and feedback. The reader will find that each of the chapters addresses some portion of problem solving on a computer.

I appreciate the helpful suggestions and criticisms offered by many students, especially Jerry Place, Greg Wetzel, and Norm Smothers. I am also indebted to the University of Kansas for granting me a sabbatical to go to Trinity College in Dublin, Ireland to finish the book. I am also indebted to Kevin Ryan, Trinity College, Dublin; Victor

Wallace, University of Kansas; and Steve Cline, formerly of Prentice-Hall. I would like to acknowledge the support and understanding of my wife, Janis, whose multiple contributions made the book possible.

I have received from many and return this book to those who find an interest or need.

WILLIAM G. BULGREN

1

INTRODUCTION

Simulation consists of replicating to some degree a real process. The construction of the model is a process that is basically intuitive, but the intuition is derived from careful insight into the problem being simulated. To construct a model, a person must extract from the real system being simulated all the essential characteristics to give similarity without necessarily duplicating the process in its minutest detail.

If the model is a good one and has not been simplified too much, the results of the simulation can tell us a great deal about what will happen in the actual process. For example, the process might involve the optimization of the flow of customers through a bank, and the simulation will enable us to experiment with different strategies to determine which is most likely to succeed.

Another important application is to develop several different models of something we are planning to build, hence enabling us to determine which model is best before we start to build.

Simulation is the only method for estimating performance of new systems before they actually exist. In this type of situation, the complexity of the system is usually such that description by a mathematical model is beyond the capabilities of the model designer. Simulation is used as a technique to extend mathematical analysis.

Simulation is a combination of modeling and measurement. The process of simulation can be viewed as developing a model of a system, developing a model of a work load, and developing a simulator.

TERMINOLOGY

We define *simulation* as a numerical technique for conducting experiments on a digital computer that involves certain types of mathematical and logical models that describe the behavior of a system (economy, business, engineering, etc.) over extended periods of real time. *System* is defined as an aggregation or assemblage of objects joined in some regular interaction or interdependence.

Table 1-1 lists examples of terms of interest for a number of systems. In looking at these systems, we see that there are certain distinct objects, each of which possesses properties of interest. There are also certain interactions occurring in the system that cause changes in the system. The term *entity* will be used to denote an object of interest in a system; the term *attribute* denotes a property of an entity. There can, of course, be many attributes to a given entity. Any process that causes changes in the sytem will be called an *activity*.

In the description of the traffic system, the entities of the system are the cars. Their attributes are such factors as speed and distance. The activities are the driving of the cars. Table 1-1 does *not* show a complete list of all entities, attributes, and activities for the systems. In fact, a complete list cannot be made without knowing the purpose of the system description. Depending upon that purpose, various aspects of the system will be of interest and will determine what needs to be identified.

A system is often affected by changes occurring outside the system. Some system activities may also produce changes that do not react on the system. Such changes

TABLE 1-1
Terms of Interest

System	Entities	Attributes	Activity
Traffic	Cars	Speed	Driving
Bank	Customers	Balance Credit status	Depositing
Communications	Messages	Length Priority	Transmitting
Supermarket	Customers	Shopping list	Checking Out

occurring outside the system are said to occur in the *system environment*. An important step in modeling systems is to decide upon the boundary between the system and its environment. The decision may depend upon the purpose of the study.

As an example, consider the bank system. In this system there may be a limit on the maximum interest rate than can be paid. This would be regarded as a constraint imposed by the environment. In a study of the effects of monetary laws on the banking industry, however, the setting of a limit on the maximum interest rate would be an activity of the system.

The term *endogenous* is used to describe activities occurring within the system, and the term *exogenous* is used to describe activities in the environment that affect the system.

To further illustrate the terms previously defined, let us consider the supermarket example in more detail. *Shoppers* needing *several items* of shopping *arrive* at a supermarket. They *get* a *basket*, if one is *available*, carry out their *shopping*, and then *queue* to *checkout* at one of the *several counters*. After checking out, they *return* the *basket* and leave. Certain words have been italicized because they are considered key words that point out some feature of the system that must be reflected in the model. This description is summarized in Table 1-2 to identify the entities, attributes, and activities. Notice that the term supermarket does not appear as an entity. Supermarket defines the boundary of the system and hence distinguishes between the system and its environment. The arrival of a customer into the system will be regarded as an exogenous activity affecting the system from the environment.

Many processes that we attempt to simulate involve some randomness. For example, the arrival of a customer at a checkout counter is at least partly random, as are the arrivals and departures of cars at an intersection. Where the effects of the activity vary randomly over various outcomes, the activity is said to be *stochastic*. For example, the service of various jobs in a computer system is a stochastic activity.

To simulate randomness, we will need to have a method of producing sequences of numbers that are random or that at least appear to be random. Most program libraries have subroutines available for the production of suitable sequences of numbers so that the programmer need not be concerned with the details. One of the most widely used and most effective methods of generating random numbers is the congruential method.

TABLE 1-2

Supermarket System

Entity	Attribute	Activity
Shopper	No. of items	Arrive Get
Basket	Availability	Shop Queue Check out
Counter	Number Occupancy	Return Leave

It should be emphasized that we have been talking loosely about the term *model*. In this context, the term model is the body of information about a system gathered for the purpose of studying the system. There is *no* unique model of a system, since the purpose of the study will determine the nature of the information that is gathered.

The actual task of deriving a model of a system can be classified into two very interrelated categories. The first is that of establishing the model structure. This determines the system boundary and identifies the entities, attributes, and activities of the system. The second category is that of supplying the data, which provides the values that the attributes can have and defines the relationships involved in the activities.

APPLICATION

Simulation and its application can be understood best by considering the problems encountered and how they may be overcome. One of the first problems in modeling is the lack of flexibility. The attribute is of course needed in either simulation or analytical evaluation. Essentially, the flexibility of a model allows the experimental manipulation of the model without resorting to the real item itself to give an evaluation. Manipulation of model parameters could be simply the coupling of various components of a real system to evaluate them in a real-time environment, for instance.

A second problem in modeling is the inherent approximations the modeler must make. Again, this is the case in both simulation and analytic evaluation. The simplest simulations constructed on digital machines have at least the approximation of discrete time existing in the system being modeled. The important problem to be recognized here is not the approximation just mentioned, but rather that the modeler must be careful not to approximate away by oversimplification the situation he or she was attempting to model. The appropriate problem analysis is also important. Too much detail can be included in a model and cause the model to utilize excessive time to obtain results or even obscure the desired results by unnecessary complication. The level of detail, as previously described, is a decision the modeler must make early in structuring the model, and this decision must be correct or the implementation of the model will be rather useless. Intuition and experience with the system being modeled enter here and are not to be ignored in initial planning of the model.

EXERCISES

1-1. Name three or four of the principal entities, attributes, and activities to be considered and their interactions if you were to simulate the operation of a multiprogramming computer system.

1-2. Name three or four for each of the principal entities, attributes, and activities to be considered if you were to simulate the operation of (a) a gasoline filling station, (b) a cafeteria, (c) a barber shop.

1-3. Name three or four for each of the principal entities, attributes, and activities to be considered if you were to simulate the operation of (a) a bank, (b) a computer system, (c) a post office.

1-4. Name three entities, two attributes for each entity, and three activities for each of the systems to be considered for simulation: (a) a newspaper, (b) an airport, (c) a stop-light intersection.

2

INTRODUCTION TO SIMSCRIPT II.5

SIMSCRIPT II.5 is a language used in discrete-system simulations. The SIMSCRIPT II.5 has many features that help reduce the programming time required for simulation. These include English-like problem formulation, very high level model description, and logical modular development. SIMSCRIPT II.5 contains many automatic features, which include all timing routines, all statistics-gathering mechanisms, dynamic storage management, and flexible report generation.

SIMSCRIPT II.5 requires that the world to be simulated be structured in terms of the following concepts: event, entity, attribute, and sets. An *event* is any process that causes changes in the system. In SIMSCRIPT II.5, an event is a routine to be executed when the event "occurs." An event contains all the decision flow and updating that relate to the change of state in the system during execution. Since time elapses between events and *not* within an event, one can regard a simulation as the execution of events ordered chronologically on desired execution times.

An *entity* is an object of interest in a system. In SIMSCRIPT II.5, an entity is used to model objects that move through the system. These objects are characterized by their attributes and may be permanent or temporary in nature. A *set* is a collection of entities. In SIMSCRIPT II.5, a set is used to collect entities. This collection is ordered by various disciplines (e.g., FIFO) as new entities are added. In SIMSCRIPT II.5, sets are owned by an entity or the system.

The following outlines the program structure of SIMSCRIPT II.5:

Preamble: Defines all modeling elements such as events, entities, and attributes. Variables defined in the PREAMBLE are global and are not to be defined again.

Main: Execution starts with the first statement in the main routine. It is the entry point for restarting the simulation.

Timing routine: This routine is furnished automatically by the SIMSCRIPT II.5 compiler. It acts like a coroutine in synchronizing the event routines.

Event routines: These are routines scheduled (called) by the user. These scheduled routines are executed by the timing routine, which acts like a global routine scheduler.

Subroutines: They are treated like FORTRAN. Arguments are passed by value and not by name.

One important aspect of the program structure is the event routine. Table 2-1 lists the SIMSCRIPTS II.5 statements that will be used in programming the event routines. Examples will be given throughout the chapter.

LANGUAGE ELEMENTS

Events must be defined in the PREAMBLE and must be supported by an event routine. Events are scheduled by the modeler. The following is a partial example of two SIMSCRIPT II.5 events, named ARRIVAL and DEPARTURE.

TABLE 2-1

SIMSCRIPT Statements (Geoffrey Gordon, *System Simulation, 2nd ed.,* ©1978, page 251.
Reprinted by permission of Prentice-Hall, Inc., Englewood Cliffs, N.J.)

CREATE   *temporary entity* or *event notice* (CALLED *variable*)

DESTROY

SCHEDULE AN   *event notice* (CALLED *variable*) $\begin{matrix} \text{IN} \\ \text{AT} \end{matrix}$ *expression*

LET *variable* = *expression*

FILE *variable* IN *set*

REMOVE $\begin{matrix} \text{FIRST} \\ \text{LAST} \end{matrix}$ *variable* FROM *set*

FOR *variable* = *expression.1* TO *expression.2* BY *expression.3*

FOR EACH *permanent entity*

FOR EACH *variable* OF *set*

WITH *expression.1 comparison expression.2*

OR

AND

UNTIL

IF *expression.1 comparison expression.2, statement*

IF *set* $\begin{matrix} \text{IS} \\ \text{IS NOT} \end{matrix}$ EMPTY, *statement*

GO TO *statement label*

DO

LOOP

FIND THE FIRST CASE, IF NONE *statement* ELSE

Example

```
PREAMBLE
EVENT NOTICES INCLUDE ARRIVAL AND DEPARTURE
END

MAIN
SCHEDULE AN ARRIVAL IN TIME EXPRESSION
```

```
START SIMULATION
STOP
END

EVENT ARRIVAL
SCHEDULE AN ARRIVAL IN TIME EXPRESSION
.
.
.
SCHEDULE A DEPARTURE IN TIME EXPRESSION
.
.
.
RETURN
END

EVENT DEPARTURE
.
.
.
RETURN
END
```

The syntax for defining the event within the PREAMBLE IS

```
EVENT NOTICE INCLUDE. . . . .
```

The event names may be separated by a comma instead of AND. Each event routine must begin with the syntax EVENT and end with END. The event routine contains all decision flow and updating that relate to the change in state the execution of the event requires. Since time elapses between events, one can regard a SIMSCRIPT II.5 simulation as the execution of a sequence of events ordered chronologically on desired execution time. However, no time elapses within an event.

THE SCHEDULE STATEMENT

To execute a specific event routine at a specific time, the programmer must include the following statement:

$$\text{SCHEDULE AN } event\ notice\ (\text{CALLED } variable)\ \begin{matrix} \text{IN} \\ \\ \text{AT} \end{matrix}\ time\ expression$$

The time expression will be explained later in this chapter. The CALLED portion is optional and will be explained later.

SIMSCRIPT II.5 makes a notice of the event, including (1) the type of event, and (2) the time at which the event will occur, and places the notices in a list of future events ordered by time of scheduled occurrence. SCHEDULE acts like a delayed call. Simulation begins with the statement START SIMULATION and ends with a STOP statement (in some event routine) or by running out of events.

Figure 2-1 illustrates the execution cycle of a SIMSCRIPT II.5 program. Every time an EVENT is SCHEDULED, it is placed in an *event notice list* according to what time it is to be executed. Figure 2-2 illustrates how the timing routine selects an event from the event notice list and starts execution.

REPRESENTATION OF TIME

The *clock* is a system-defined, real variable called TIME.V. It is dimensionless and considered as *time units*. Initially, TIME.V = 0.0. In the expression SCHEDULE AN ARRIVAL AT TIME.V + 15, an arrival will be 15 time units from "Now". The time units, unless otherwise specified, are DAYS. A relative time expression is given for the SCHEDULE statement as

> SCHEDULE AN *event* IN *expression* DAYS
> HOURS
> MINUTES
> UNITS

DAYS are implicit units for TIME.V. The expression SCHEDULE AN ARRIVAL IN 15 is the same as SCHEDULE AN ARRIVAL AT TIME.V + 15. An expression in hours or minutes will automatically be converted to days using system defined variables

> HOURS.V (default value 24)
> MINUTES.V (default value 60)

Example

> PREAMBLE
> DEFINE MILLISEC TO MEAN UNITS
> DEFINE SECONDS TO MEAN *1000 UNITS

An event may be scheduled immediately by the statement

> SCHEDULE AN *event* NOW

which is the same as

> SCHEDULE AN *event* AT TIME.V

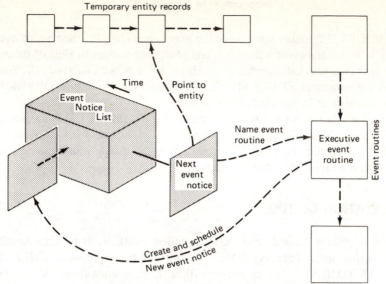

FIGURE 2-1 SIMSCRIPT execution cycle

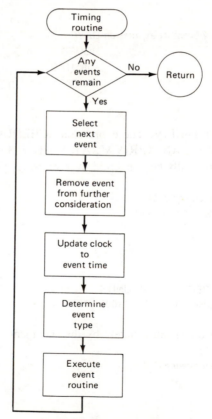

FIGURE 2-2 Timing routine

SIMSCRIPT ARITHMETIC

FORTRAN-like operators and precedence rules are followed. The syntax LET denotes that an arithmetic assignment statement follows.

Example

LET A = (B * C)/ (D + E/F)

NAMING VARIABLES

Any combination of letters, digits, and periods that is not a number may be used for variables

Valid	Invalid
ABC	3.
NO.QUE	123
5D	4 + 5
8.7.37	D/E

MODE OF VARIABLES

Default: All variables are real mode but may be changed (in the preamble) by a NOR-MALLY statement:

NORMALLY MODE IS INTEGER

Individual variables may be defined as INTEGER, REAL, and ALPHA.

Example

DEFINE K AS AN INTEGER VARIABLE

SIMPLE DECISION LOGIC

GO TO statements are allowed, and receiving labels are enclosed in apostrophes and may be either alphanumeric or numeric. The IF statement differs from FORTRAN. The IF syntax is presented in Table 2-1.

13

Examples

```
IF STATION = BUSY
LET NO.QUE = NO.QUE + 1
GO TO NEXT
ELSE
LET STATION = BUSY
'NEXT'
IF STATION = BUSY
LET NO.QUE = NO.QUE + 1
JUMP AHEAD
ELSE
LET STATION = BUSY
HERE
```

Note: JUMP AHEAD transfers control to next HERE. JUMP BACK transfers control to previous HERE. If no alternatives are needed in IF, use ALWAYS (or REGARDLESS) instead of ELSE.

```
IF STATION = BUSY
LET NO.QUE = NO.QUE + 1
ALWAYS
```

ELSE must be preceded by an unconditional transfer such as

```
GO TO
JUMP
RETURN
STOP
```

or the alternative will be executed regardless of the test.

The following example consists of a simple one-queue, one-server model. Figure 2-3 illustrates the simple model. New arrivals enter the system (to the queue) with a mean rate L. If the service facility is not presently in use, then the new arrival (entity) enters the service facility; otherwise, it must wait in the queue. When the entity leaves the server (after a random time with mean t), it leaves the system. Figure 2-4 gives a flow chart of the two important event routines needed to implement this model. Figure 2-5 is a SIMSCRIPT II.5 program for a simple single-queue, single-server model. All variables defined in the PREAMBLE are global to all event routines. The function UNIFORM.F(12.0,24.0,1) generates a value from the uniform distribution (Chapter 8) in the interval (12.0,24.0). The parameters of the uniform func-

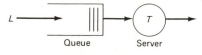

Queue   Server

FIGURE 2-3

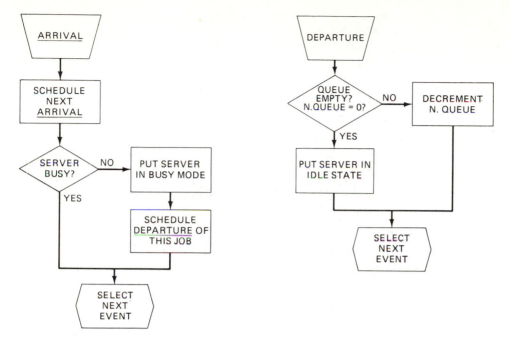

FIGURE 2-4 Simple Single-Queue, Single-Server Model


```
"SINGLE SERVER, SINGLE QUEUE SYSTEM
PREAMBLE
EVENT NOTICES INCLUDE ARRIVAL, DEPARTURE, AND
      STOP.SIMULATION
DEFINE N.QUEUE AND STATUS AS INTEGER VARIABLES
DEFINE IDLE TO MEAN 0
DEFINE BUSY TO MEAN 1
END

MAIN
SCHEDULE AN ARRIVAL IN UNIFORM.F(12.0,24.0,1) MINUTES
SCHEDULE A STOP.SIMULATION IN 8 HOURS
START SIMULATION
END

EVENT ARRIVAL
SCHEDULE AN ARRIVAL IN UNIFORM.F(12.0,24.0,1) MINUTES
IF STATUS = BUSY,
LET N.QUEUE = N.QUEUE + 1
RETURN
ELSE
```

FIGURE 2-5 Simple Single-Server SIMSCRIPT II.5 Program

```
SCHEDULE A DEPARTURE IN UNIFORM.F(12.0,24.0,1)
      MINUTES
LET STATUS = BUSY
RETURN
END

EVENT DEPARTURE
IF N.QUEUE = 0
LET STATUS = IDLE
RETURN
ELSE
LET N.QUEUE = N.QUEUE − 1
SCHEDULE A DEPARTURE IN UNIFORM.F(12.0,24.0,1)
      MINUTES
RETURN
END

EVENT STOP.SIMULATION
STOP
END
```

FIGURE 2-5   *(continued)*

tion are (1) lower limit, (2) upper limit, and (3) random number stream (defined later in this Chapter). In this example, $L = T = 18$. The statement DEFINE IDLE TO MEAN 0 specifies a symbolic substitution for IDLE, that is 0.

TEMPORARY ENTITIES

An *entity* is a program element, much like a variable, that exists in a modeled system. It is like a subscripted variable in that it has values, called *attributes,* associated with it that, when assigned specific values, define a particular configuration or state of the entity. Entities and their attributes are declared in a program preamble by statements of the general form

> EVERY *entity name* HAS AN *attribute name list*

Example

```
PREAMBLE
EVERYMAN HAS AN AGE, SOME DEPENDENTS AND A
      SOCIAL.SECURITY.NO
```

This declaration states that the value of AGE is to be found in word 1 of a MAN record, the value of DEPENDENTS in word 2, and so on. Each MAN record can be pictured as

```
MAN
value of AGE
value of DEPENDENTS
value of SOCIAL.SECURITY.NO.
```

and the form AGE(MAN) can be translated into "the value found in the first word of the record indexed by the value MAN."

Each time a temporary entity is needed in an event routine, the CREATE statement must be used (Table 2-1). For example, CREATE MAN or CREATE MAN CALLED A creates a specific instance of the preceding data structure. Attributes are given in the following ways:

```
LET AGE(MAN) = UNIFORM.F(21.0,78.0)
LET DEPENDENTS(MAN) = 3
LET DEPENDENT(A) = 3
```

The subscript is the entity reference. The entity reference MAN and A point to the same entity. The difference is that MAN is a global reference (defined in old event routines), whereas A is defined locally (can be referenced only in the event routine where it was defined by the CREATE). When a temporary entity is no longer needed, the copy is removed and the space it occupies is freed by the statement DESTROY MAN or DESTROY THIS MAN. If CREATE MAN CALLED A was used, then DESTROY MAN CALLED A must be used.

PERMANENT ENTITIES

When the number of "copies" of an object is (relatively) constant, use permanent entities.

A predetermined number of entities are "created" en masse.

Storage is allocated for each named attribute as an array.

Example: Bank Facility

It might be reasonable to represent CUSTOMERS as TEMPORARY ENTITIES, but there is no need to model the fixed number of TELLER as TEMPORARY.

```
PERMANENT ENTITIES
EVERY TELLER HAS A STATUS, A CAPACITY, AND OWNS A
      QUEUE
TEMPORARY ENTITIES
EVERY CUSTOMER HAS A DOLLAR AND MAY BELONG TO A
      QUEUE
```

To allocate storage for the tellers,

> READ N. TELLER
> CREATE EVERY TELLER

N.*entity* is a system-defined variable that contains the number of entities in the class, or

> CREATE EVERY TELLER(5)

where N.*entity* never varies.

Access is done as with temporary entities:

> LET CAPACITY(I) = X

where I could be assigned previously by a LET statement. For example, LET I = 4.

A system variable is provided with the same name as the permanent entity (e.g., TELLER) and may assume values from 1 to N.*entity*. This may be set by assignment statements but more commonly is done in loops.

> FOR EACH *entity*

is equivalent to

> FOR *entity* = 1 to N.*entity*

The FOR may also be exercised over members of a set

> FOR   EACH   ALL   *variable*   IN ON OF AT   *set*
>   EVERY

SETS

A SET is a logically ordered collection of entities organized through a set of pointers.

Examples of Sets

Customers waiting for a haircut

Airplanes waiting for a runway

The destinations of a scheduled flight

Computer jobs to be scheduled

Each SET must have a declared owner and declared members

1. Set ownership is unconditional.
2. Set membership is potential.
3. Entities are placed in and removed from sets at will during execution.

A SET is defined by declaring its owner and its member(s) in the PREAMBLE.

Examples

```
EVERY CUSTOMER BELONGS TO A QUEUE
EVERY BARBER OWNS A QUEUE
EVERY JOB OWNS A ROUTINE AND BELONGS TO A
      WAITING.LINE
EVERY TASK BELONGS TO A ROUTING AND HAS A
      SERVICE.TIME AND A ID.NO
EVERY MACHINE OWNS A WAITING.LINE
```

When only one copy of the set exists, it may be ascribed to the "system."

Example

```
EVERY CUSTOMER MAY BELONG TO THE QUEUE
THE SYSTEM OWNS THE QUEUE
```

To add an entity to a set in an event routing, one must

```
FILE CUSTOMER IN THE QUEUE
```

The default set discipline is FIFO and new members are placed at the end.

Sets are initially empty.

An entity may belong to several different sets simultaneously but only one set of a given name.

To remove an entity from a set, specify the one to remove *NOT* by name, but by location within the set (first or last).

Example

```
REMOVE FIRST CUSTOMER FROM QUEUE
```

1. The first member of the set QUEUE is logically disconnected from the set
2. The variable CUSTOMER "points" to this newly removed entity.

Caution!

1. An entity that has been removed from its sets may be "lost" if care is not exercised.
2. A removal operation of an empty set causes a terminal error.
3. An entity cannot be DESTROY(ED) if it is in one or more sets.

tests on sets

IF *entity* IS NOT IN *set*
IF *set* IS NOT EMPTY

more on sets

An entity's attributes and set relationships can be declared in one or more EVERY statements using *attribute name clauses, set ownership clauses,* and *set membership clauses:*

attribute clause	HAS *attribute name list*
	HAVE *attribute name list*
set ownership clause	OWNS *set name list*
	OWN *set name list*
set membership clause	BELONGS TO *set name list*
	BELONG TO *set name list*

The items in an attribute name or set name list must be separated by both a comma and one of the words A, AN, THE, or SOME.

Example

```
TEMPORARY ENTITIES
EVERY CUSTOMER HAS A ARRIVAL.TIME, A SERVICE.TIME
    AND MAY BELONG TO THE QUEUE
THE SYSTEM OWNS THE QUEUE
```

defines QUEUE to be permanently ascribed to the system and the temporary entity CUSTOMER as a potential member of the set QUEUE.

Example

```
PERMANENT ENTITIES
EVERY TELLER HAS A STATUS AND OWNS A QUEUE
TEMPORARY ENTITIES
EVERY CUST HAS A ARRIVAL.TIME AND MAY BELONG TO
     THE QUEUE
```

defines TELLER as a permanent entity, each owning its own set called QUEUE. The number of TELLERs is determined by the CREATE statement for the permanent entity. A CUSTOMER is a potential member of any of the TELLERs' sets.

Example

```
TEMPORARY ENTITIES
EVERY CHILD HAS A SIZE AND BELONGS TO THE FAMILY
     AND THE SCHOOL
THE SYSTEM OWNS FAMILY AND THE SCHOOL
```

defines the system having two permanent sets called FAMILY and SCHOOL. The temporary entity CHILD may potentially belong to the FAMILY and the SCHOOL.

Example   [3, pp. 196–200]

```
PERMANENT ENTITIES
EVERY CHAMBER HAS A STATUS AND BELONGS TO THE
     LOCK
TEMPORARY ENTITIES
EVERY TOW MAY BELONG TO AN UP.Q AND A DOWN.Q
THE SYSTEM OWNS THE UP.Q, THE DOWN Q. AND THE
     LOCK
```

defines the sets UP.Q, DOWN.Q, and LOCK to be permanently ascribed to the system. Membership in the LOCK is potentially that of a CHAMBER, while the temporary entity TOW may potentially belong to the set UP.Q or DOWN.Q.

To group together entities, we use the following in the preamble:

```
EVERY COMMUNITY OWNS A MASONS, AN ELKS, AND A
     BOY.SCOUTS
EVERY MAN MAY BELONG TO THE MASONS, THE ELKS, AND
     THE BOY.SCOUTS
```

The first statement declares that each entity of the class COMMUNITY *owns* a set called MASONS, a set called ELKS, and a set called BOY.SCOUTS. The statement does not specify which men belong to the particular sets; rather, it establishes a system of *set pointers* and *set attributes* for the *owner entities* that enable *set memberships* to be constructed. Each COMMUNITY is given a logical entity record with the following attributes automatically defined:

COMMUNITY

F.MASONS
L.MASONS
F.ELKS
L.ELKS
F.BOY.SCOUTS
L.BOY.SCOUTS

The attributes starting with F. are set pointers that point to the *first* member of the respective sets. The attributes starting with L. are set pointers that point to the *last* member of the respective sets.

The second statement declares that each entity of the class MAN may belong to sets called MASONS, ELKS, and BOY.SCOUTS. The statement automatically defines set attributes for member entities:

MAN

P.MASONS
S.MASONS
P.ELKS
S.ELKS
P.BOY.SCOUTS
S.BOY.SCOUTS

The attributes starting with P. are set pointers pointing to the *predecessor entity* in the indicated set; the attributes starting with S. are set pointers pointing to the *successor entity* in the indicated set (Figure 2-6).

EXAMPLE

PERMANENT ENTITIES
EVERY NODE HAS A TYPE, MAY OWN AN UP.Q, A DOWN.Q AND A LOCK

EVERY PORT OWNS A ROUTE
EVERY CHAMBER BELONGS TO A LOCK
TEMPORARY ENTITIES
EVERY TOW MAY BELONG TO AN UP.Q, A DOWN.Q
EVERY LINK BELONGS TO A ROUTE

defines permanent sets UP.Q, DOWN.Q, LOCK, and ROUTE. Permanent entity CHAM-BER has potential membership in the permanent set LOCK, while temporary entity TOW may belong in UP.Q or DOWN.Q, and temporary entity LINK may be a member in the permanent set ROUTE.

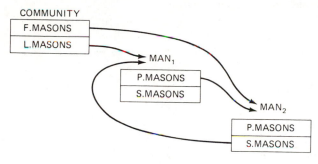

FIGURE 2-6

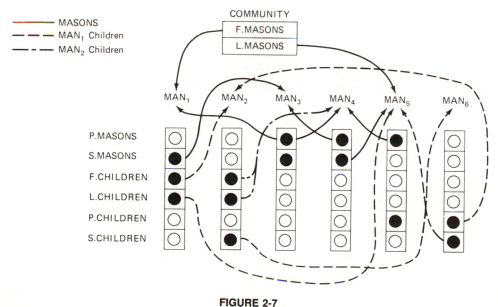

FIGURE 2-7

23

Example

```
PERMANENT ENTITIES
EVERY COMMUNITY OWNS SOME MASONS
TEMPORARY ENTITIES
EVERY MAN MAY BELONG TO THE MASONS, OWN SOME
        CHILDREN AND BELONG TO THE CHILDREN
```

Figure 2-7 shows MAN_1, MAN_3, MAN_4, and MAN_5 as members of the set MASONS. MAN_4 belongs to and is the only member of MAN_2's set called CHILDREN. MAN_2, MAN_6, and MAN_5 are members of MAN_1's set called CHILDREN. It also shows MAN_3, MAN_4, MAN_5, and MAN_6 to be *childless*.

OUTPUT

PRINT statement.

Example

```
PRINT 2 LINES WITH X AND X**2 THUS
THE CURRENT VALUE OF X IS *.***
AND THE SQUARE OF X IS *.******
```

1. Must be a one-to-one correspondence between expressions and "formats."
2. Formats are composed of asterisks and periods (blanks extend format to left only).
3. Interspersed text is copied verbatim.
4. The amount of text is determined solely from the line count (e.g., PRINT 2 LINES . . .).
5. Blank lines are introduced with SKIP *n* LINES statement.
6. The expressions to be printed follow the WITH in the PRINT line (e.g., WITH x and x ** 2 THUS).

FREE FORM INPUT

```
READ A,B,C,D
```

Simscript I/O is not record oriented.

Simscript I/O is field oriented.

Data fields are separated by blanks.

Data conversion is automatic.

ACCUMULATE AND TALLY

A statement of the form

> TALLY *compute list* OF *name*

may be used for time-independent statistics gathering. Each time *name* changes value in an event routine, accumulations are made to collect the statistics requested in the *compute list*. *Name* is the name of an unsubscripted global variable, unsubscripted system attribute, or an attribute of a permanent or temporary entity.

Example　Using an unsubscripted global variable,

```
PREAMBLE
DEFINE X AS A REAL VARIABLE
TALLY M AS THE MEAN AND V AS THE VARIANCE OF X
END



    .

    .

    .

PRINT 1 LINE WITH M AND V AS FOLLOWS
MEAN = **.***     VARIANCE = ***.***
```

In this example, M will contain the current mean and the current variance of the global system variable X.

Example　Using an attribute of a permanent entity,

```
PREAMBLE
PERMANENT ENTITIES
EVERY WOMAN HAS SOME DOLLARS AND OWNS A CAR
    .

    .

    .

TALLY AVE.CASH AS THE MEAN AND MAX.CASH AS THE
        MAXIMUM OF DOLLARS
END
```

.
.
.

      FOR EACH WOMAN, LIST AVE.CASH(WOMAN) AND
            MAX.CASH(WOMAN)

In this example, AVE.CASH will contain the current mean and MAX.CASH will contain the current maximum value of the attribute DOLLARS.

    Example   Using an attribute of a temporary entity,

      TEMPORARY ENTITIES
      EVERY JOB HAS A NUMB
      .

      .

      TALLY TOTAL AS THE SUM OF NUMB
      END
      .

      .

      .

      FOR EACH JOB IN QUEUE(MACHINE) DO
      IF TOTAL(JOB)> MAX.ALLOWED, GO LOOP
      ALWAYS

In this example, TOTAL contains the current sum of the attribute NUMB.

TABLE 2-2

Statistical Keyword	TALLY	ACCUMULATE
NUMBER	N	N
SUM	X	$X*(TIME.V-T_L)$
SUM.OF.SQUARES	X^2	$X^2*(TIME.V-T_L)$
MEAN	SUM/NUMBER	$SUM/(TIME.V-T_o)$
MEAN.SQUARE	SUM.OF.SQUARES /NUMBER	$SUM.OF.SQUARES/(TIME.V-T_o)$
VARIANCE	MEAN.SQUARE-MEAN	MEAN.SQUARE-MEAN
STD.DEV	SQRT.F(VARIANCE)	SQRT.F(VARIANCE)
MAXIMUM	Largest X	Largest X
MINIMUM	Smallest X	Smallest X

T_L, the simulated time and ACCUMULATED variable was set to its current value.
T_0, the simulated time at which ACCUMULATION starts.

Statistical computations where time is introduced into the average, variance and standard deviation are collected using the word ACCUMULATE instead of TALLY. See Table 2-2 for the definition and use of ACCUMULATE and TALLY.

Example

```
PREAMBLE
PERMANENT ENTITIES
EVERY TELLER HAS A STATUS AND OWNS A QUEUE
TEMPORARY ENTITIES
EVERY CUST BELONGS TO A QUEUE
ACCUMULATE AVE.Q AS THE MEAN AND MAX.Q AS THE
     MAXIMUM OF N. QUEUE
ACCUMULATE STAT.TELLER AS THE MEAN OF STATUS
END
```

In this example, AVE.Q will contain the current time-weighted mean and MAX.Q the current maximum value of the global system variable N. QUEUE.

Notice that ACCUMULATE statement gathers statistics on N. QUEUE is not defined. This is because certain attributes are AUTOMATICALLY defined for SETS.

N.set specifies the current number of members of the set

M.set specifies whether a potential member is currently a member of the set (1) or not (0).

CANCELING EVENTS

To cancel an event that has been scheduled to occur,

```
CANCEL
```

will remove the event from the events list (event must have been scheduled).

Example

```
EVENT ARRIVAL
SCHEDULE AN ARRIVAL IN 20 MINUTES
.
.
.
IF TIME ≥ 500
CANCEL THE ARRIVAL
ALWAYS
```

.
.
.

An event may be canceled in order to change the time at which it is scheduled to occur.

Example

CANCEL <u>THE</u> ARRIVAL IN 5 HOURS

THE is imperative to avoid creating a new event notice. Events may be scheduled immediately:

SCHEDULE AN ARRIVAL NOW

LOOP EXAMPLES

In the following, TELLER and CUST are permanent entities:

```
(1) FOR EACH TELLER
    FOR EACH CUST IN QUEUE (TELLER)
    ADD DOLLAR (CUST) TO CAPACITY (TELLER)

(2) FOR EACH CUST IN QUEUE (TELLER) IN REVERSE
        ORDER
    DO
    ADD DOLLAR (CUST) TO SUM
    IF SUM > MAXIMUM GO OUT
    ELSE
    LOOP
    'OUT'
```

Iteration may be forward or backward.

By any increment (integer or real).

Over any range (positive or negative).

May be nested to any depth.

Testing is done before the loop is executed.

When a loop includes more than one statement, use DO-LOOP statements as delimiters.

```
FOR EACH TELLER
DO
```

```
LET STATUS = FREE
LET CAPACITY (TELLER)
LOOP
```

In addition to GO TO statements, two statements are available within LOOPS:

LEAVE: transfers to next executable statement after LOOP.

CYCLE: transfers (effectively) to LOOP statement for next iteration.

SELECTIVITY

Selectivity is specified by

```
WITH (or WHEN)
UNLESS (or EXCEPT)
```

Selectivity is useful in finding values of an attribute that satisfy a predefined condition.

Examples

```
(1) FOR EACH TELLER WITH CAPACITY (TELLER)
(2) FOR I = 1 TO 100 EXCEPT WHEN X(I) = 0
    LET X(I) = Y(I)/X(I)
```

A search technique is presented to find a particular case:

```
FOR EACH TELLER WITH STATUS (TELLER) = 0
FIND THE FIRST CASE
IF NONE
.

.

.

ELSE
.

.

.
```

The search will stop when status of zero is found.
    Phrases may be combined in the loop structure

```
FOR EACH TELLER WITH SALARY (TELLER) LESS
THAN MAXIMUM UNTIL COUNT IS EQUAL TO 50
```

```
DO
ADD 1 TO COUNT
.
.
LOOP
```

Also, logical connectives may be compounded in tests.

```
AND
OR
Parentheses

FOR EACH TELLER WITH STATUS (TELLER) = 0 AND
CAPACITY (BERTH) = DOLLAR (CUST) FIND THE
FIRST CASE

IF 5 < X < 15 AND (D = 1 OR C = 5) AND Q > 0
```

A search may also be done for maximum or minimum of all cases. For this the COMPUTE statement is used.

```
FOR EACH BERTH
COMPUTE .QUEUE.LENGTH AS THE
        MINIMUM OF N .QUEUE
```

After this statement executes, .QUEUE.LENGTH will contain the length of the shortest queue.

The following statistics may also be computed in the COMPUTE statement

NUMBER	SUM
MEAN	SUM.OF.SQUARES
MEAN.SQUARE	VARIANCE
STD.DEV	MAXIMUM
MINIMUM	

The COMPUTE statement must be under control of at least one FOR statement.

RANDOM PHENOMENA

Simscript provides a real function called RANDOM.F, which produces a sample from the uniform population (0, 1). There are 10 sequences of random numbers. A sequence may be chosen by passing a parameter to RANDOM.F.

```
LET A = RANDOM.F(5)
```

will select a sample from stream 5. The 10 sequences are useful in order to guarantee that different random events that use RANDOM.F are independent.

NONUNIFORM DISTRIBUTION

One very common distribution used in modeling is the POISSON process. Its assumptions are as follows:

The probability that an arrival occurs during a small time interval is proportional to the size of the interval.

The probability of more than one arrival during a small time interval is negligible.

The time intervals between arrivals are independent.

Poisson is modeled using the EXPONENTIAL.F function, because interarrival times are exponentially distributed.

Simscript provides these distribution functions:

BETA.F	LOG.NORMAL.F
ERLANG.F	NORMAL.F
EXPONENTIAL.F	UNIFORM.F
GAMMA.F	WEIBULL.F
BINOMIAL.F	POISSON.F
RANDI.F	

These distributions are discussed in detail in Chapter 8.

DISCRETE DISTRIBUTIONS

A function that takes on discrete values could be described as follows:

x	Probability $P(X = x)$	Cumulative Probability $P(X \leq x)$
1	0.20	0.20
2	0.25	0.45
3	0.33	0.78
4	0.22	1.00

In this example, the function is described by four points and hence is discrete. To declare such a distribution function

```
PREAMBLE
THE SYSTEM HAS AN X RANDOM STEP VARIABLE
DEFINE X AS AN INTEGER VARIABLE
END
```

Before X is used, it must be initialized with a free-form READ, and the data must be terminated with an asterisk (*). The preceding example would be

```
READ X
```

where the data to be read are

```
0.2 1 0.25 2 0.33 3 0.22 4 *
```

or a cumulative probability may be used:

```
0.2 1 0.45 2 0.78 3 1.0 4 *
```

To sample from the distribution

```
LET Y = X.
```

In this example, X will take on the value 1, 2, 3, and 4 with the respective probabilities.

CONTINUOUS DISTRIBUTION FUNCTIONS

```
PREAMBLE
EVERY CUST HAS A SERVICE.TIME RANDOM LINEAR
VARIABLE
DEFINE SERVICE.TIME AS A REAL STREAM 3 VARIABLE
END
```

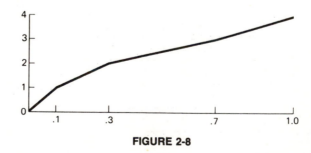

FIGURE 2-8

The input for this *must* describe a cumulative distribution function (see Figure 2-8).

```
READ SERVICE.TIME (LOCK)
```

where the data to be read are

```
0.0 0 0.1 1 0.3 2 0.7 3 1.0 4
```

when the following statement is executed:

```
SCHEDULE A DEPARTURE IN SERVICE.TIME (CUST)
    MINUTES
```
SERVICE.TIME (CUST) will take on a value in the interval 0
to 4. For more details, see Chapter 8.

DATA-DRIVEN SIMULATIONS

A possibility is the introduction of the sequence of events directly as data to the model.
This is done by EXTERNAL EVENTS. An external event differs from other events in
(1) method of scheduling, and (2) passing of attributes (parameters). External events are
scheduled from external event records (cards). An external event record (card) contains
the following:

Name of the event.

Absolute time at which the event is to occur.

Optional data to be read when the event does occur.

The order of the records determines the order of event occurrence. Event notices for
external events are automatically created and filed in the event set.
    To use external events.

1. Declare the intention of having external events:

```
PREAMBLE
EXTERNAL EVENTS ARE FIRE, FAILURE AND END.SIM
.
.
.

END
```

2. Declare where the data to schedule the event are to be found:

EXTERNAL EVENT UNIT IS 2

Note: If no unit is defined, the standard system input device becomes the external
unit.

3. Finally, prepare data to describe the events. The cards are free-form.

event name   event-time   OPTIONAL DATA *

event name is one of the names listed in the EXTERNAL EVENTS statement.
event time is one of several formats.

Decimal   ARRIVAL 11.125 *
Day-hour-minute   ARRIVAL 11 3 10 *
Calendar date   (month/day/year   hour   minute)
          ARRIVAL 5/11/80 3 10 *

The event records must be in ascending time order.

Before using calendar date, an origin date must be established. This is done by a
call to ORIGIN.R.

CALL ORIGIN.R(1,1,76) or CALL ORIGIN.R(MMV,DDV,YYV)

Internally, TIME.V records elapsed time since this origin date.

	System Functions
DATE.F	converts (month,day,year) to time relative to origin
YEAR.F	
MONTH.F	extract the respective portions of an internal time expression
DAY.F	

Example

CALL ORIGIN.R(7,1,68)
LET YY = YEAR.F(476.2)
LET MM = MONTH.F(476.2)
LET DD = DAY.F(476.2)
PRINT 1 LINE WITH MM, DD AND YY THUS
DATE IS **/**/****

Output:

```
DATE IS 10/20/1969
```

SUBROUTINES

Major differences from FORTRAN are as follows:

Input GIVEN and output YIELDING arguments must be segregated.

Each call to a subroutine automatically initializes local variables to zero.

Calls may be recursive.

Example

```
MAIN
.
.
.
LET TELLER = 5
CALL ASSIGNMENT GIVEN TELLER
.
.
.
END

ROUTINE ASSIGNMENT GIVEN P
.
.
.
CALL SELECT GIVEN P YIELDING MONEY
.
.
.
RETURN
END

ROUTINE SELECT GIVEN C YIELDING D
.
.
.
LET A = X+5
LET D = A*100
RETURN
END
```

USER-DEFINED FUNCTIONS

To write user functions to be called in the same manner as system functions,

> Define function in PREAMBLE.
>
> Write routine body.
>
> Terminate routine with a special RETURN WITH statement.
>
> Reference the function in the usual function access method.

Example

```
PREAMBLE
DEFINE FACT AS A FUNCTION
END

MAIN
LET X = FACT (3)
END

FUNCTION FACT GIVEN X
IF X = 1 RETURN WITH 1
ELSE RETURN WITH FACT (X−1)
END
```

Example 1

The accompanying SIMSCRIPT II.5 (Figure 2-10) program illustrates a single-queue, single-server system as described briefly in Figure 2-4. Figure 2-9 illustrates the model.

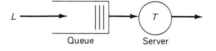

Queue   Server

FIGURE 2-9

New arrivals enter the system (to the queue) with a mean rate L. If the service facility is not presently in use, the transaction enters the service facility; otherwise, it must wait in the queue. When the transaction leaves the server (after an exponential random time with mean T), it leaves the system. In the SIMSCRIPT II.5 program (Figure 2-10), L = 0.2 and T = 0.1. The simulation uses the predefined system distribution function EXPONENTIAL.F. The first parameter of this function is the mean and the second is the random number stream (for more detail on this function, refer to Chapter 8).

    The output statistics of concern are the average queue length (ANIQ), the utilization

```
LINE   CACI SIMSCRIPT II.5   RELEASE 8H

  1    PREAMBLE
  2      EVENT NOTICES INCLUDE ARRIVAL, DEPARTURE AND STOP.SIM
  3      TEMPORARY ENTITIES
  4        EVERY CUSTOMER HAS A TIME.OF.ARRIVAL
  5           AND MAY BELONG TO THE QUEUE
  6      THE SYSTEM OWNS THE QUEUE
  7      DEFINE ARR, SVC, WAIT.TIM AS A VARIABLE
  8      DEFINE NCUST, TIMES, STATUS AS INTEGER VARIABLES
  9      DEFINE IDLE TO MEAN 0
 10      DEFINE BUSY TO MEAN 1
 11      ACCUMULATE ANIQ AS THE AVERAGE OF N.QUEUE
 12      ACCUMULATE XBUSY AS THE AVERAGE OF STATUS
 13      TALLY MAT AS THE MEAN OF ARR
 14      TALLY MST AS THE MEAN OF SVC
 15      TALLY MWT AS THE MEAN OF WAIT.TIM
 16    END
```

C R O S S - R E F E R E N C E

NAME	TYPE	MODE	LINE NUMBERS OF REFERENCES	
ANIQ	ROUTINE		11	
ARR	GLOBAL VARIABLE	DOUBLE	7	13
ARRIVAL	EVENT NOTICE		2	
BUSY	DEFINE TO MEAN		10	
CUSTOMER	TEMPORARY ENTITY		4	
DEPARTURE	EVENT NOTICE		2	
IDLE	DEFINE TO MEAN		9	
MAT	ROUTINE		13	
MST	ROUTINE		14	
MWT	ROUTINE		15	
N.QUEUE	PERMANENT ATTRIBUTE	INTEGER	11	
NCUST	GLOBAL VARIABLE	INTEGER	8	
QUEUE	SET		5	6
STATUS	GLOBAL VARIABLE	INTEGER	8	12
STOP.SIM	EVENT NOTICE		2	
SVC	GLOBAL VARIABLE	DOUBLE	7	14
TIME.OF.ARRIVA	TEMPORARY ATTRIBUTE	DOUBLE	4	
TIMES	GLOBAL VARIABLE	INTEGER	8	
WAIT.TIM	GLOBAL VARIABLE	DOUBLE	7	15
XBUSY	ROUTINE		12	

FIGURE 2-10   Single-Queue Single-Server System—PREAMBLE

```
LINE   CACI SIMSCRIPT II.5   RELEASE 8H

  1    MAIN
  2      LET ARR = EXPONENTIAL.F(0.2,1)
  3      SCHEDULE AN ARRIVAL IN ARR MINUTES
  4      SCHEDULE A STOP.SIM IN 5 HOURS
  5      START SIMULATION
  6    END
```

C R O S S - R E F E R E N C E

NAME	TYPE	MODE	LINE NUMBERS OF REFERENCES	
ARR	GLOBAL VARIABLE	DOUBLE	2	3
ARRIVAL	EVENT NOTICE		3	
	+ GLOBAL VARIABLE	INTEGER	3*	
EXPONENTIAL.F	ROUTINE		2	
STOP.SIM	EVENT NOTICE		4	
	+ GLOBAL VARIABLE	INTEGER	4*	

FIGURE 2-10   Single-Queue Single-Server System—MAIN Routine

```
LINE   CACI SIMSCRIPT II.5   RELEASE 8H

  1    EVENT ARRIVAL
  2       LET ARR = EXPONENTIAL.F(0.2,1)
  3       SCHEDULE AN ARRIVAL IN ARR MINUTES
  4       ADD 1 TO NCUST
  5       IF STATUS = BUSY
  6          CREATE A CUSTOMER
  7          LET TIME.OF.ARRIVAL(CUSTOMER) = TIME.V
  8          FILE CUSTOMER IN QUEUE
  9          RETURN
 10       ELSE
 11          LET WAIT.TIM = 0.0
 12          LET SVC = EXPONENTIAL.F(0.1,1)
 13          SCHEDULE A DEPARTURE IN SVC MINUTES
 14          LET STATUS = BUSY
 15          RETURN
 16    END
```

C R O S S - R E F E R E N C E

NAME	TYPE	MODE	LINE NUMBERS OF REFERENCES		
ARR	GLOBAL VARIABLE	DOUBLE	2	3	
ARRIVAL	EVENT NOTICE		1	3	
+	GLOBAL VARIABLE	INTEGER	1	3*	
BUSY	DEFINE TO MEAN		5	14	
CUSTOMER	TEMPORARY ENTITY		6		
+	GLOBAL VARIABLE	INTEGER	6	7	8
DEPARTURE	EVENT NOTICE		13		
+	GLOBAL VARIABLE	INTEGER	13*		
EXPONENTIAL.F	ROUTINE		2	12	
NCUST	GLOBAL VARIABLE	INTEGER	4*		
QUEUE	SET		8		
STATUS	GLOBAL VARIABLE	INTEGER	5	14	
SVC	GLOBAL VARIABLE	DOUBLE	12	13	
TIME.OF.ARRIVA	TEMPORARY ATTRIBUTE	DOUBLE	7		
TIME.V	PERMANENT ATTRIBUTE	DOUBLE	7		
WAIT.TIM	GLOBAL VARIABLE	DOUBLE	11		

FIGURE 2-10   Single-Queue Single-Server System—ARRIVAL Routine

```
LINE   CACI SIMSCRIPT II.5   RELEASE 8H

  1    EVENT DEPARTURE
  2       IF QUEUE IS EMPTY
  3          LET STATUS = IDLE
  4          RETURN
  5       ELSE
  6          REMOVE FIRST CUSTOMER FROM QUEUE
  7          LET WAIT.TIM = TIME.V - TIME.OF.ARRIVAL(CUSTOMER)
  8          DESTROY CUSTOMER
  9          LET SVC = EXPONENTIAL.F(0.1,1)
 10          SCHEDULE A DEPARTURE IN SVC MINUTES
 11          RETURN
 12    END
```

C R O S S - R E F E R E N C E

NAME	TYPE	MODE	LINE NUMBERS OF REFERENCES		
CUSTOMER	TEMPORARY ENTITY		8		
+	GLOBAL VARIABLE	INTEGER	6	7	8
DEPARTURE	EVENT NOTICE		1	10	
+	GLOBAL VARIABLE	INTEGER	1	10*	
EXPONENTIAL.F	ROUTINE		9		
IDLE	DEFINE TO MEAN		3		
QUEUE	SET		2	6	
STATUS	GLOBAL VARIABLE	INTEGER	3		
SVC	GLOBAL VARIABLE	DOUBLE	9	10	
TIME.OF.ARRIVA	TEMPORARY ATTRIBUTE	DOUBLE	7		
TIME.V	PERMANENT ATTRIBUTE	DOUBLE	7		
WAIT.TIM	GLOBAL VARIABLE	DOUBLE	7		

FIGURE 2-10   Single-Queue Single-Server System—DEPARTURE Routine

```
LINE   CACI SIMSCRIPT II.5  RELEASE 8H

   1    EVENT STOP.SIM
   2       PRINT 12 LINES WITH
   3            ANIQ,
   4            XBUSY,
   5            MAT,
   6            MST,
   7            MWT*HOURS.V*MINUTES.V,
   8            AND NCUST THUS
        SIMSCRIPT II.5 TEST CASE
        SINGLE QUEUE - SINGLE SERVER
        EXPONENTIAL - PICTURE EVERY 5 HOURS FOR 50 HOURS
            AVERAGE QUEUE LENGTH        **.***
            UTILIZATION OF SERVER        *.***
            MEAN ARRIVAL TIME           **.***   MINUTES
            MEAN SERVICE TIME           **.***   MINUTES
            AVERAGE WAITING TIME        **.***   MINUTES
            TOTAL CUSTOMERS SERVED     ****
            (SIMULATION INTERRUPTED EVERY 5 HOURS


   9    ADD 1 TO TIMES
  10    IF TIMES = 10
  11        STOP
  12    ELSE
  13        SCHEDULE A STOP.SIM IN 5 HOURS
  14    RETURN
  15    END
```

CROSS - REFERENCE

NAME	TYPE	MODE	LINE NUMBERS OF REFERENCES
ANIQ	ROUTINE		2
HOURS.V	PERMANENT ATTRIBUTE	DOUBLE	2
MAT	ROUTINE		2
MINUTES.V	PERMANENT ATTRIBUTE	DOUBLE	2
MST	ROUTINE		2
MWT	ROUTINE		2
NCUST	GLOBAL VARIABLE	INTEGER	2
STOP.SIM	EVENT NOTICE		1 13
	+ GLOBAL VARIABLE	INTEGER	1 13*
TIMES	GLOBAL VARIABLE	INTEGER	9* 10
XBUSY	ROUTINE		2

FIGURE 2-10 Single-Queue Single-Server System—STOP.SIM Routine

of the server (XBUSY), the average arrival time (MAT), average service time (MST), average waiting time (MWT), and the total number of customers served (NCUST).

The output (Figure 2-10) is printed every 5 hours for 50 hours. The statistics for the last time period show that the utilization of the server is .501 after 14,982 customers have been served.

Example 2

The purpose of this SIMSCRIPT II.5 program (Figure 2-13) is to develop a model for a single-server feedback queue with exponential arrival and departure time. Figure 2-11 illustrates the simple model. New arrivals enter the system (to the queue) with mean rate L. If the service facility is not presently in use, the transaction enters the service facility; otherwise, it must wait in the queue. When the transaction leaves the server (after a

39

```
SIMSCRIPT II.5 TEST CASE
SINGLE QUEUE - SINGLE SERVER
EXPONENTIAL - PICTURE EVERY 5 HOURS FOR 50 HOURS
     AVERAGE QUEUE LENGTH          .383
     UTILIZATION OF SERVER         .485
     MEAN ARRIVAL TIME             .207   MINUTES
     MEAN SERVICE TIME             .100   MINUTES
     AVERAGE WAITING TIME          .079   MINUTES
     TOTAL CUSTOMERS SERVED    1451
     (SIMULATION INTERRUPTED EVERY 5 HOURS


SIMSCRIPT II.5 TEST CASE
SINGLE QUEUE - SINGLE SERVER
EXPONENTIAL - PICTURE EVERY 5 HOURS FOR 50 HOURS
     AVERAGE QUEUE LENGTH          .439
     UTILIZATION OF SERVER         .487
     MEAN ARRIVAL TIME             .204   MINUTES
     MEAN SERVICE TIME             .099   MINUTES
     AVERAGE WAITING TIME          .090   MINUTES
     TOTAL CUSTOMERS SERVED    2943
     (SIMULATION INTERRUPTED EVERY 5 HOURS


SIMSCRIPT II.5 TEST CASE
SINGLE QUEUE - SINGLE SERVER
EXPONENTIAL - PICTURE EVERY 5 HOURS FOR 50 HOURS
     AVERAGE QUEUE LENGTH          .418
     UTILIZATION OF SERVER         .486
     MEAN ARRIVAL TIME             .205   MINUTES
     MEAN SERVICE TIME             .100   MINUTES
     AVERAGE WAITING TIME          .086   MINUTES
     TOTAL CUSTOMERS SERVED     4379
     (SIMULATION INTERRUPTED EVERY 5 HOURS


SIMSCRIPT II.5 TEST CASE
SINGLE QUEUE - SINGLE SERVER
EXPONENTIAL - PICTURE EVERY 5 HOURS FOR 50 HOURS
     AVERAGE QUEUE LENGTH          .427
     UTILIZATION OF SERVER         .484
     MEAN ARRIVAL TIME             .204   MINUTES
     MEAN SERVICE TIME             .099   MINUTES
     AVERAGE WAITING TIME          .087   MINUTES
     TOTAL CUSTOMERS SERVED     5892
     (SIMULATION INTERRUPTED EVERY 5 HOURS


SIMSCRIPT II.5 TEST CASE
SINGLE QUEUE - SINGLE SERVER
EXPONENTIAL - PICTURE EVERY 5 HOURS FOR 50 HOURS
     AVERAGE QUEUE LENGTH          .444
     UTILIZATION OF SERVER         .488
     MEAN ARRIVAL TIME             .204   MINUTES
     MEAN SERVICE TIME             .099   MINUTES
     AVERAGE WAITING TIME          .090   MINUTES
     TOTAL CUSTOMERS SERVED     7361
     (SIMULATION INTERRUPTED EVERY 5 HOURS


SIMSCRIPT II.5 TEST CASE
SINGLE QUEUE - SINGLE SERVER
EXPONENTIAL - PICTURE EVERY 5 HOURS FOR 50 HOURS
     AVERAGE QUEUE LENGTH          .458        ¼
     UTILIZATION OF SERVER         .493
     MEAN ARRIVAL TIME             .202   MINUTES
     MEAN SERVICE TIME             .100   MINUTES
     AVERAGE WAITING TIME          .093   MINUTES
     TOTAL CUSTOMERS SERVED     8905
     (SIMULATION INTERRUPTED EVERY 5 HOURS
```

FIGURE 2-10   Single-Queue Single-Server-Output Report

```
SIMSCRIPT II.5 TEST CASE
SINGLE QUEUE - SINGLE SERVER
EXPONENTIAL - PICTURE EVERY 5 HOURS FOR 50 HOURS
     AVERAGE QUEUE LENGTH          .468
     UTILIZATION OF SERVER         .495
     MEAN ARRIVAL TIME             .202   MINUTES
     MEAN SERVICE TIME             .100   MINUTES
     AVERAGE WAITING TIME          .094   MINUTES
     TOTAL CUSTOMERS SERVED   10413
     (SIMULATION INTERRUPTED EVERY 5 HOURS


SIMSCRIPT II.5 TEST CASE
SINGLE QUEUE - SINGLE SERVER
EXPONENTIAL - PICTURE EVERY 5 HOURS FOR 50 HOURS
     AVERAGE QUEUE LENGTH          .483
     UTILIZATION OF SERVER         .499
     MEAN ARRIVAL TIME             .201   MINUTES
     MEAN SERVICE TIME             .100   MINUTES
     AVERAGE WAITING TIME          .097   MINUTES
     TOTAL CUSTOMERS SERVED   11950
     (SIMULATION INTERRUPTED EVERY 5 HOURS


SIMSCRIPT II.5 TEST CASE
SINGLE QUEUE - SINGLE SERVER
EXPONENTIAL - PICTURE EVERY 5 HOURS FOR 50 HOURS
     AVERAGE QUEUE LENGTH          .493
     UTILIZATION OF SERVER         .499
     MEAN ARRIVAL TIME             .201   MINUTES
     MEAN SERVICE TIME             .100   MINUTES
     AVERAGE WAITING TIME          .099   MINUTES
     TOTAL CUSTOMERS SERVED   13458
     (SIMULATION INTERRUPTED EVERY 5 HOURS


SIMSCRIPT II.5 TEST CASE
SINGLE QUEUE - SINGLE SERVER


EXPONENTIAL - PICTURE EVERY 5 HOURS FOR 50 HOURS
     AVERAGE QUEUE LENGTH          .494
     UTILIZATION OF SERVER         .501
     MEAN ARRIVAL TIME             .200   MINUTES
     MEAN SERVICE TIME             .100   MINUTES
     AVERAGE WAITING TIME          .099   MINUTES
     TOTAL CUSTOMERS SERVED   14982
     (SIMULATION INTERRUPTED EVERY 5 HOURS
```

FIGURE 2-10   Output Report (*continued*)

random time with mean T), it either leaves the system or returns to the queue. In this example, $(1 - p)$ 100% of the transactions leave the system, whereas p 100% of the transactions reenter the system. In the SIMSCRIPT II.5 program (Figure 2-13), $L = 0.2$, $T = 0.1$, and $p = 0.3$.

Figure 2-12 gives the flow charts describing events ARRIVAL and DEPARTURE.

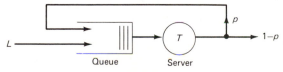

FIGURE 2-11

41

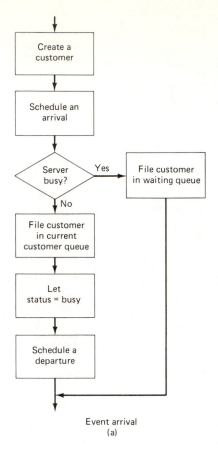

Event arrival
(a)

FIGURE 2-12   (a) Event Arrival

In this example, the *non-zero* waiting time of a customer, denoted by WAIT.TIME (CUSTOMER), is collected in 50 batches of size 100. The value of the mean printed at the end of the simulation is .236059. The reason for batches is that the method of batch means is utilized. This method will be described more fully in Chapter 5.

As will be seen in Chapter 5, this output can be checked against analytically known results, since the arrival rate and service rate are both exponential. In this case, one can check whether the program is running correctly.

The following describe the variables used in the SIMSCRIPT II.5 program:

ST.TIME: time when customer enters system.

WAIT.TIME: amount of time spent in the queue.

TOT.TIME: total time spent in system.

ARR.TIME: arrival rate.

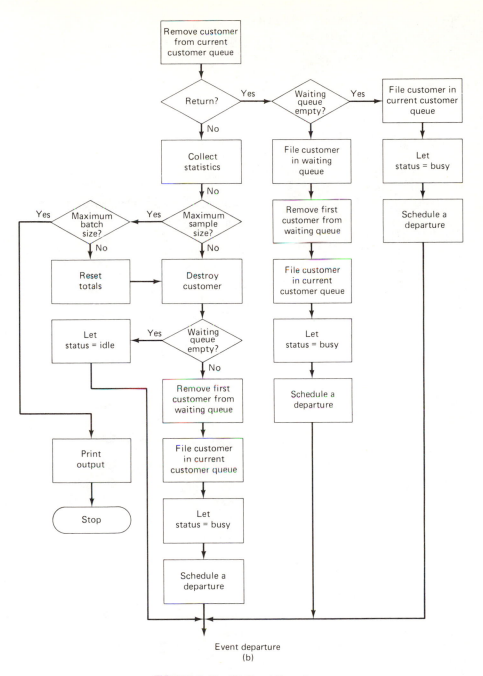

Event departure
(b)

FIGURE 2-12   (b) Event Departure

43

```
LINE  CACI SIMSCRIPT II.5  RELEASE 8H

   1    PREAMBLE
   2        EVENT NOTICES INCLUDE ARRIVAL, DEPARTURE
   3        TEMPORARY ENTITIES
   4           EVERY CUSTOMER HAS A ST.TIME, A WAIT.TIME,
   5           AND MAY BELONG TO THE QUEUE, AND THE CUR.CUS
   6        THE SYSTEM OWNS THE QUEUE
   7        THE SYSTEM OWNS THE CUR.CUS
   8        DEFINE IDLE TO MEAN 0
   9        DEFINE BUSY TO MEAN 1
  10        DEFINE ARR, DEP, RET AS VARIABLES
  11        DEFINE PER,COUNT, KOUNT, STATUS AS INTEGER VARIABLES
  12        NORMALLY MODE IS REAL
  13        DEFINE T, XT.1 AS VARIABLES
  14        TALLY TT AS THE MEAN OF T
  15        TALLY M20 AS THE MEAN, SD20 AS THE STD.DEV OF XT.1
  16    END
```

C R O S S - R E F E R E N C E

NAME	TYPE	MODE	LINE NUMBERS OF REFERENCES
ARR	GLOBAL VARIABLE	DOUBLE	10
ARRIVAL	EVENT NOTICE		2
BUSY	DEFINE TO MEAN		9
COUNT	GLOBAL VARIABLE	INTEGER	11
CUR.CUS	SET		5 7
CUSTOMER	TEMPORARY ENTITY		4
DEP	GLOBAL VARIABLE	DOUBLE	10
DEPARTURE	EVENT NOTICE		2
IDLE	DEFINE TO MEAN		8
KOUNT	GLOBAL VARIABLE	INTEGER	11
M20	ROUTINE		15
PER	GLOBAL VARIABLE	INTEGER	11
QUEUE	SET		5 6
RET	GLOBAL VARIABLE	DOUBLE	10
SD20	ROUTINE		15
ST.TIME	TEMPORARY ATTRIBUTE	DOUBLE	4
STATUS	GLOBAL VARIABLE	INTEGER	11
T	GLOBAL VARIABLE	REAL	13 14
TT	ROUTINE		14
WAIT.TIME	TEMPORARY ATTRIBUTE	DOUBLE	4
XT.1	GLOBAL VARIABLE	REAL	13 15

FIGURE 2-13 Single Server Feedback Queue—PREAMBLE

```
LINE  CACI SIMSCRIPT II.5  RELEASE 8H

   1    MAIN
   2        LET COUNT = 0
   3        LET KOUNT = 0
   4        LET PER = 1
   5        LET ARR = EXPONENTIAL.F(0.2,4)
   6        SCHEDULE AN ARRIVAL IN ARR DAYS
   7        START SIMULATION
   8    END
```

C R O S S - R E F E R E N C E

NAME	TYPE	MODE	LINE NUMBERS OF REFERENCES
ARR	GLOBAL VARIABLE	DOUBLE	5 6
ARRIVAL	EVENT NOTICE		6
	+ GLOBAL VARIABLE	INTEGER	6*
COUNT	GLOBAL VARIABLE	INTEGER	2
EXPONENTIAL.F	ROUTINE		5
KOUNT	GLOBAL VARIABLE	INTEGER	3
PER	GLOBAL VARIABLE	INTEGER	4

FIGURE 2-13 Single Server Feedback Queue—MAIN Routine

44

```
LINE   CACI SIMSCRIPT II.5   RELEASE 8H

  1     EVENT ARRIVAL
  2        LET ARR = EXPONENTIAL.F(0.2,4)
  3        SCHEDULE AN ARRIVAL IN ARR DAYS
  4        CREATE A CUSTOMER
  5        IF STATUS = BUSY
  6            LET ST.TIME(CUSTOMER) = TIME.V
  7            FILE CUSTOMER IN QUEUE
  8            RETURN
  9        ELSE
 10            LET WAIT.TIME(CUSTOMER) = 0.0
 11            LET DEP = EXPONENTIAL.F(0.1,7)
 12            SCHEDULE A DEPARTURE IN DEP DAYS
 13            FILE CUSTOMER IN CUR.CUS
 14            LET STATUS = BUSY
 15            RETURN
 16     END
```

                    C R O S S - R E F E R E N C E

NAME	TYPE	MODE	LINE NUMBERS OF REFERENCES			
ARR	GLOBAL VARIABLE	DOUBLE	2	3		
ARRIVAL	EVENT NOTICE		1	3		
+	GLOBAL VARIABLE	INTEGER	1	3*		
BUSY	DEFINE TO MEAN		5	14		
CUR.CUS	SET		13			
CUSTOMER	TEMPORARY ENTITY		4			
+	GLOBAL VARIABLE	INTEGER	4	6	7	10 13
DEP	GLOBAL VARIABLE	DOUBLE	11	12		
DEPARTURE	EVENT NOTICE		12			
+	GLOBAL VARIABLE	INTEGER	12*			
EXPONENTIAL.F	ROUTINE		2	11		
QUEUE	SET		7			
ST.TIME	TEMPORARY ATTRIBUTE	DOUBLE	6			
STATUS	GLOBAL VARIABLE	INTEGER	5	14		
TIME.V	PERMANENT ATTRIBUTE	DOUBLE	6			
WAIT.TIME	TEMPORARY ATTRIBUTE	DOUBLE	10			

FIGURE 2-13   Single Server Feedback Queue—ARRIVAL Routine

```
LINE   CACI SIMSCRIPT II.5   RELEASE 8H

  1     EVENT DEPARTURE
  2        REMOVE FIRST CUSTOMER FROM CUR.CUS
  3        LET RET = UNIFORM.F(1.0,2.0,5)
  4        IF RET < 1.3
  5            IF QUEUE IS NOT EMPTY
  6                LET ST.TIME(CUSTOMER) = TIME.V
  7                FILE CUSTOMER IN QUEUE
  8                REMOVE FIRST CUSTOMER FROM THE QUEUE
  9                LET WAIT.TIME(CUSTOMER) = TIME.V - ST.TIME
 10                FILE CUSTOMER IN CUR.CUS
 11                LET DEP = EXPONENTIAL.F(0.1,7)
 12                SCHEDULE A DEPARTURE IN DEP DAYS
 13                LET STATUS = BUSY
 14                RETURN
 15            ELSE
 16                LET WAIT.TIME(CUSTOMER) = WAIT.TIME(CUSTOMER) + 0.0
 17                FILE CUSTOMER IN CUR.CUS
 18                LET DEP = EXPONENTIAL.F(0.1,7)
 19                SCHEDULE A DEPARTURE IN DEP DAYS
 20                LET STATUS = BUSY
 21                RETURN
 22        ELSE
 23            LET COUNT = COUNT + 1
 24            LET KOUNT = KOUNT + 1
 25                IF KOUNT <= 100 LET T = WAIT.TIME(CUSTOMER)
 26            ALWAYS
```

FIGURE 2-13   Single Server Feedback Queue—DEPARTURE Routine

```
27          DESTROY CUSTOMER
28          IF KOUNT = 100
29              CALL COLLECT
30          ALWAYS
31          IF QUEUE IS EMPTY
32              LET STATUS = IDLE
33              RETURN
34          ELSE
35              REMOVE FIRST CUSTOMER FROM QUEUE
36              LET WAIT.TIME(CUSTOMER) = TIME.V - ST.TIME
37              FILE CUSTOMER IN CUR.CUS
38              LET DEP = EXPONENTIAL.F(0.1,7)
39              SCHEDULE A DEPARTURE IN DEP DAYS
40              LET STATUS = BUSY
41              RETURN
42      END
```

C R O S S - R E F E R E N C E

NAME	TYPE	MODE	LINE NUMBERS OF REFERENCES				
BUSY	DEFINE TO MEAN		13	20	40		
COLLECT	ROUTINE		29				
COUNT	GLOBAL VARIABLE	INTEGER	23*				
CUR.CUS	SET		2	10	17	37	
CUSTOMER	TEMPORARY ENTITY		27				
+	GLOBAL VARIABLE	INTEGER	2	6	7	8	9	10
			16*	17	25	27	3
+	IMPLIED SUBSCRIPT	INTEGER	9	36			
DEP	GLOBAL VARIABLE	DOUBLE	11	12	18	19	38	39
DEPARTURE	EVENT NOTICE		1	12	19	39	
+	GLOBAL VARIABLE	INTEGER	1	12*	19*	39*	
EXPONENTIAL.F	ROUTINE		11	18	38		
IDLE	DEFINE TO MEAN		32				
KOUNT	GLOBAL VARIABLE	INTEGER	24*	25	28		
QUEUE	SET		5	7	8	31	35
RET	GLOBAL VARIABLE	DOUBLE	3	4			
ST.TIME	TEMPORARY ATTRIBUTE	DOUBLE	6	9	36		
STATUS	GLOBAL VARIABLE	INTEGER	13	20	32	40	
T	GLOBAL VARIABLE	REAL	25				
TIME.V	PERMANENT ATTRIBUTE	DOUBLE	6	9	36		
UNIFORM.F	ROUTINE		3				
WAIT.TIME	TEMPORARY ATTRIBUTE	DOUBLE	9	16*	25	36	

FIGURE 2-13   —DEPARTURE Routine (*continued*)

```
LINE   CACI SIMSCRIPT II.5   RELEASE 8H

 1      ROUTINE COLLECT
 2          LET KOUNT = 0
 3          LET PER = PER + 1
 4          LET XT.1 = TT
 5          IF PER = 51
 6              CALL PICTURE
 7              STOP
 8          ELSE RESET TOTALS OF T
 9          RETURN
10      END
```

C R O S S - R E F E R E N C E

NAME	TYPE	MODE	LINE NUMBERS OF REFERENCES	
COLLECT	ROUTINE		1	
KOUNT	GLOBAL VARIABLE	INTEGER	2	
PER	GLOBAL VARIABLE	INTEGER	3*	5
PICTURE	ROUTINE		6	
T	GLOBAL VARIABLE	REAL	8	
TT	ROUTINE		4	
XT.1	GLOBAL VARIABLE	REAL	4	

FIGURE 2-13   Single Server Feedback Queue—COLLECT Routine

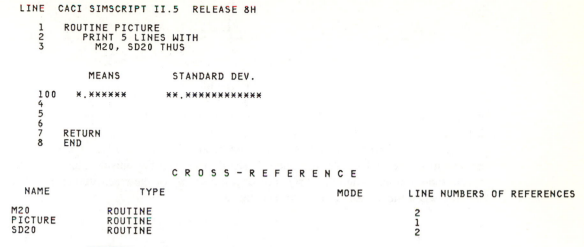

```
LINE  CACI SIMSCRIPT II.5  RELEASE 8H

  1    ROUTINE PICTURE
  2       PRINT 5 LINES WITH
  3         M20, SD20 THUS

            MEANS          STANDARD DEV.

100    *.******     **.************
  4
  5
  6
  7    RETURN
  8    END

          C R O S S - R E F E R E N C E

   NAME            TYPE              MODE        LINE NUMBERS OF REFERENCES

  M20          ROUTINE                            2
  PICTURE      ROUTINE                            1
  SD20         ROUTINE                            2
```

FIGURE 2-13 Single Server Feedback Queue—PICTURE Routine

```
          MEANS          STANDARD DEV.

100      .236059         .138279194391
```

FIGURE 2-13 Single Server Feedback Queue—Output Report

SER.TIME: time spent being served.

QUEUE: waiting queue.

CUR.CUS: current customer in queue.

PER: number of batches completed.

COUNT: total number of customers processed.

KOUNT: total number of customers processed in current batch.

STATUS: status of the server.

Example 3

The purpose of this SIMSCRIPT II.5 program (Figure 2-16) is to develop a model of traffic merging. Figure 2-14 illustrates the model. Transactions enter the system (queue 1) with a mean rate L_1. Transactions enter the systems (queue 2) with a mean rate L_2. These two ways of entering the system are independent of each other. If the first service facility (server 1) is not presently in use, the transaction enters the service facility; otherwise, it must wait in queue 1. When the transaction leaves server 1 (after a random exponential time with mean T_1), it enters queue 2. Since this is traffic merging, transactions enter queue 2 from two different sources. In either case, after the transaction departs from

47

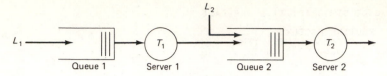

FIGURE 2-14

the second server (server 2), it leaves the system. In the SIMSCRIPT II.5 program (Figure 2-16) $L_1 = 0.4$, $L_2 = 0.4$, $T_1 = 0.2$, and $T_2 = 0.1$.

Since the servers can be considered independently, care must be taken that the arrivals to the second server from the first server and from the outside can be handled by the same routine. The only difference is in the setting of the rescheduling flag. It is set only when the arrival comes from the outside.

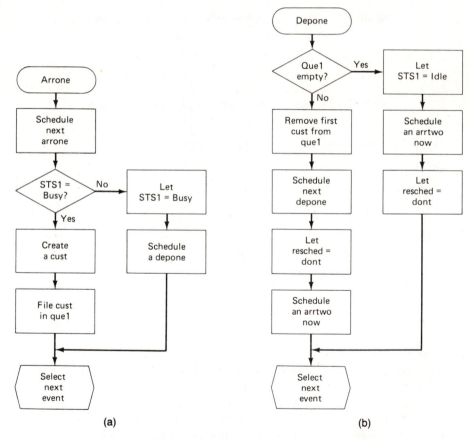

(a) (b)

FIGURE 2-15   (a) Flow Chart for the Event ARRONE, (b) Flow Chart for Event DEPONE

48

The program has six main parts:

1. The program is initiated in the routine MAIN. The parameters are initialized, and the first arrival to both the first and second servers is scheduled.
2. ARRONE creates customers and files them in queue 1. It schedules the departure of some of the jobs from server 1. It also reschedules more ARRONEs.
3. DEPONE schedules an immediate arrival at ARRTWO and sets the rescheduling flag so that another ARRTWO will not be scheduled. Also, if its queue is not empty, it schedules the next departure (DEPONE).
4. ARRTWO reschedules itself if the flag is set and also creates customers and files them in the queue of server 2. It also schedules their departure from server 2.

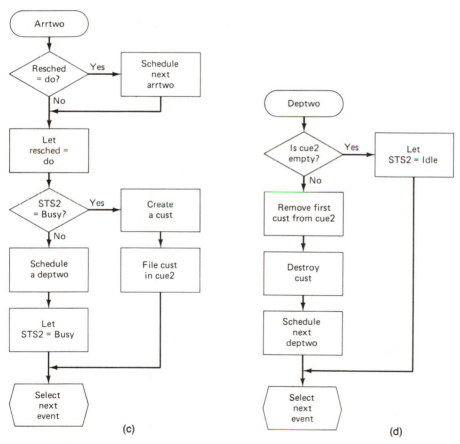

(c)   (d)

FIGURE 2-15   (c) Flow Chart for Event ARRTWO, (d) Flow Chart for Event DEP-TWO

5. DEPTWO destroys customers as they depart and reschedules itself if its queue is not empty.

6. Statistics are gathered by a large number of routines and by coding in some of the events, which causes the routines to be called when a certain statistic needs to be collected.

Figure 2-15 gives the flowcharts that describe the preceding events.

The SIMSCRIPT II.5 program (Figure 2-16 on the following 7 pages) collects waiting time (WT1 for queue 1 and WT2 for queue 2) in batches of size 10, 20, 30, 40, . . . , 100. This is done so that initial bias is removed on this statistic. This will be described more fully in Chapter 5.

As can be seen from the output, the mean waiting time for a batch size of 100 is .102839. The utilization for server #1 is .504954 and for server #2 is .491615. This output can be checked against analytically known results, since arrival rates and service rates are both exponential.

The purpose of this text is not to be a manual, but to give the novice the feel of

```
LINE  CACI SIMSCRIPT II.5  RELEASE 8H

  1    PREAMBLE
  2      EVENT NOTICES INCLUDE ARRONE, ARRTWO, DEPONE, DEPTWO AND STOPSIM
  3      TEMPORARY ENTITIES
  4         EVERY CUST HAS A TIMEARR AND MAY BELONG TO A QUE1 AND A QUE2
  5      THE SYSTEM OWNS A QUE1 AND A QUE2
  6      DEFINE DEP, LEFT AS VARIABLES
  7      DEFINE WT1, WT2 AS VARIABLES
  8      DEFINE ARR1, ARR2, SVC1, SVC2 AS VARIABLES
  9      DEFINE STS1, STS2 AS INTEGER VARIABLES
 10      DEFINE IDLE TO MEAN 0
 11      DEFINE BUSY TO MEAN 1
 12      DEFINE RESCHED AS AN INTEGER VARIABLE
 13      DEFINE DO TO MEAN 0
 14      DEFINE DONT TO MEAN 1
 15      DEFINE X1, X2, X3, X4, X5, X6, X7, X8, X9, X10
 16              AS VARIABLES
 17      TALLY DT AS THE MEAN OF DEP
 18      TALLY MWT1 AS THE MEAN OF WT1
 19      TALLY MWT2 AS THE MEAN OF WT2
 20      TALLY NO1 AS THE NUMBER AND ST1 AS THE MEAN OF SVC1
 21      TALLY NO2 AS THE NUMBER AND ST2 AS THE MEAN OF SVC2
 22      TALLY M1 AS THE MEAN AND S1 AS THE STD OF X1
 23      TALLY M2 AS THE MEAN AND S2 AS THE STD OF X2
 24      TALLY M3 AS THE MEAN AND S3 AS THE STD OF X3
 25      TALLY M4 AS THE MEAN AND S4 AS THE STD OF X4
 26      TALLY M5 AS THE MEAN AND S5 AS THE STD OF X5
 27      TALLY M6 AS THE MEAN AND S6 AS THE STD OF X6
 28      TALLY M7 AS THE MEAN AND S7 AS THE STD OF X7
 29      TALLY M8 AS THE MEAN AND S8 AS THE STD OF X8
 30      TALLY M9 AS THE MEAN AND S9 AS THE STD OF X9
 31      TALLY M10 AS THE MEAN AND S10 AS THE STD OF X10
 32      ACCUMULATE UT1 AS THE MEAN OF STS1
 33      ACCUMULATE UT2 AS THE MEAN OF STS2
 34      TALLY AT1 AS THE MEAN OF ARR1
 35      TALLY AT2 AS THE MEAN OF ARR2
 36      ACCUMULATE NQ1 AS THE AVERAGE OF N.QUE1
 37      ACCUMULATE NQ2 AS THE AVERAGE OF N.QUE2
 38    END
```

FIGURE 2-16 Traffic Merging System—PREAMBLE

C R O S S - R E F E R E N C E

NAME	TYPE	MODE	LINE NUMBERS OF REFERENCES	
ARRONE	EVENT NOTICE		2	
ARRTWO	EVENT NOTICE		2	
ARR1	GLOBAL VARIABLE	DOUBLE	8	34
ARR2	GLOBAL VARIABLE	DOUBLE	8	35
AT1	ROUTINE		34	
AT2	ROUTINE		35	
BUSY	DEFINE TO MEAN		11	
CUST	TEMPORARY ENTITY		4	
DEP	GLOBAL VARIABLE	DOUBLE	6	17
DEPONE	EVENT NOTICE		2	
DEPTWO	EVENT NOTICE		2	
DO	DEFINE TO MEAN		13	
DONT	DEFINE TO MEAN		14	
DT	ROUTINE		17	
IDLE	DEFINE TO MEAN		10	
LEFT	GLOBAL VARIABLE	DOUBLE	6	
MWT1	ROUTINE		18	
MWT2	ROUTINE		19	
M1	ROUTINE		22	
M10	ROUTINE		31	
M2	ROUTINE		23	
M3	ROUTINE		24	
M4	ROUTINE		25	
M5	ROUTINE		26	
M6	ROUTINE		27	
M7	ROUTINE		28	
M8	ROUTINE		29	
M9	ROUTINE		30	
N.QUE1	PERMANENT ATTRIBUTE	INTEGER	36	
N.QUE2	PERMANENT ATTRIBUTE	INTEGER	37	
NO1	GLOBAL VARIABLE	DOUBLE	20	
NO2	GLOBAL VARIABLE	DOUBLE	21	
NQ1	ROUTINE		36	
NQ2	ROUTINE		37	
QUE1	SET		4	5
QUE2	SET		4	5
RESCHED	GLOBAL VARIABLE	INTEGER	12	
STOPSIM	EVENT NOTICE		2	
STS1	GLOBAL VARIABLE	INTEGER	9	32
STS2	GLOBAL VARIABLE	INTEGER	9	33
ST1	ROUTINE		20	
ST2	ROUTINE		21	
SVC1	GLOBAL VARIABLE	DOUBLE	8	20
SVC2	GLOBAL VARIABLE	DOUBLE	8	21
S1	ROUTINE		22	
S10	ROUTINE		31	
S2	ROUTINE		23	
S3	ROUTINE		24	
S4	ROUTINE		25	
S5	ROUTINE		26	
S6	ROUTINE		27	
S7	ROUTINE		28	
S8	ROUTINE		29	
S9	ROUTINE		30	
TIMEARR	TEMPORARY ATTRIBUTE	DOUBLE	4	
UT1	ROUTINE		32	
UT2	ROUTINE		33	
WT1	GLOBAL VARIABLE	DOUBLE	7	18
WT2	GLOBAL VARIABLE	DOUBLE	7	19
X1	GLOBAL VARIABLE	DOUBLE	15	22
X10	GLOBAL VARIABLE	DOUBLE	15	31
X2	GLOBAL VARIABLE	DOUBLE	15	23
X3	GLOBAL VARIABLE	DOUBLE	15	24
X4	GLOBAL VARIABLE	DOUBLE	15	25
X5	GLOBAL VARIABLE	DOUBLE	15	26
X6	GLOBAL VARIABLE	DOUBLE	15	27
X7	GLOBAL VARIABLE	DOUBLE	15	28
X8	GLOBAL VARIABLE	DOUBLE	15	29
X9	GLOBAL VARIABLE	DOUBLE	15	30

FIGURE 2-16   PREAMBLE (*continued*)

```
LINE   CACI SIMSCRIPT II.5  RELEASE 8H

   1     MAIN
   2        LET ARR1 = EXPONENTIAL.F(0.4,2)
   3        SCHEDULE AN ARRONE IN ARR1 MINUTES
   4        LET ARR2 = EXPONENTIAL.F(0.4,4)
   5        SCHEDULE AN ARRTWO IN ARR2 MINUTES
   6        LET STS1 = IDLE
   7        LET STS2 = IDLE
   8        LET RESCHED = DO
   9        START SIMULATION
  10     END
```

C R O S S - R E F E R E N C E

NAME	TYPE	MODE	LINE NUMBERS OF REFERENCES
ARRONE	EVENT NOTICE		3
+	GLOBAL VARIABLE	INTEGER	3*
ARRTWO	EVENT NOTICE		5
+	GLOBAL VARIABLE	INTEGER	5*
ARR1	GLOBAL VARIABLE	DOUBLE	2 3
ARR2	GLOBAL VARIABLE	DOUBLE	4 5
DO	DEFINE TO MEAN		8
EXPONENTIAL.F	ROUTINE		2 4
IDLE	DEFINE TO MEAN		6 7
RESCHED	GLOBAL VARIABLE	INTEGER	8
STS1	GLOBAL VARIABLE	INTEGER	6
STS2	GLOBAL VARIABLE	INTEGER	7

FIGURE 2-16 Traffic Merging System—MAIN Routine

```
LINE   CACI SIMSCRIPT II.5  RELEASE 8H

   1     EVENT ARRONE
   2        LET ARR1 = EXPONENTIAL.F(0.4,2)
   3        SCHEDULE AN ARRONE IN ARR1 MINUTES
   4        IF STS1 = BUSY
   5            CREATE A CUST
   6            LET TIMEARR(CUST) = TIME.V
   7            FILE CUST IN QUE1
   8            RETURN
   9        ELSE
  10            LET WT1 = 0.0
  11            LET SVC1 = EXPONENTIAL.F(0.2,2)
  12            SCHEDULE A DEPONE IN SVC1 MINUTES
  13            LET STS1 = BUSY
  14            RETURN
  15     END
```

C R O S S - R E F E R E N C E

NAME	TYPE	MODE	LINE NUMBERS OF REFERENCES
ARRONE	EVENT NOTICE		1 3
+	GLOBAL VARIABLE	INTEGER	1 3*
ARR1	GLOBAL VARIABLE	DOUBLE	2 3
BUSY	DEFINE TO MEAN		4 13
CUST	TEMPORARY ENTITY		5
+	GLOBAL VARIABLE	INTEGER	5 6 7
DEPONE	EVENT NOTICE		12
+	GLOBAL VARIABLE	INTEGER	12*
EXPONENTIAL.F	ROUTINE		2 11
QUE1	SET		7
STS1	GLOBAL VARIABLE	INTEGER	4 13
SVC1	GLOBAL VARIABLE	DOUBLE	11 12
TIME.V	PERMANENT ATTRIBUTE	DOUBLE	6
TIMEARR	TEMPORARY ATTRIBUTE	DOUBLE	6
WT1	GLOBAL VARIABLE	DOUBLE	10

FIGURE 2-16 Traffic Merging System—ARRONE Routine

52

```
LINE   CACI SIMSCRIPT II.5  RELEASE 8H

   1    EVENT ARRTWO
   2      IF RESCHED = DO
   3            LET ARR2 = EXPONENTIAL.F(0.4,4)
   4            SCHEDULE AN ARRTWO IN ARR2 MINUTES
   5      ALWAYS
   6      LET RESCHED = DO
   7      IF STS2 = BUSY
   8            CREATE A CUST
   9            LET TIMEARR(CUST) = TIME.V
  10            FILE CUST IN QUE2
  11            RETURN
  12      ELSE
  13            LET WT2 = 0.0
  14            LET SVC2 = EXPONENTIAL.F(0.1,4)
  15            SCHEDULE A DEPTWO IN SVC2 MINUTES
  16            IF MOD.F(NO2,10) = 0
  17                CALL STATS
  18            ALWAYS
  19            LET STS2 = BUSY
  20            RETURN
  21    END
```

C R O S S - R E F E R E N C E

NAME	TYPE	MODE	LINE NUMBERS OF REFERENCES
ARRTWO	EVENT NOTICE		1 4
+	GLOBAL VARIABLE	INTEGER	1 4*
ARR2	GLOBAL VARIABLE	DOUBLE	3 4
BUSY	DEFINE TO MEAN		7 19
CUST	TEMPORARY ENTITY		8
+	GLOBAL VARIABLE	INTEGER	8 9 10
DEPTWO	EVENT NOTICE		15
+	GLOBAL VARIABLE	INTEGER	15*
DO	DEFINE TO MEAN		2 6
EXPONENTIAL.F	ROUTINE		3 14
MOD.F	ROUTINE		16
NO2	GLOBAL VARIABLE	DOUBLE	16
QUE2	SET		10
RESCHED	GLOBAL VARIABLE	INTEGER	2 6
STATS	ROUTINE		17
STS2	GLOBAL VARIABLE	INTEGER	7 19
SVC2	GLOBAL VARIABLE	DOUBLE	14 15
TIME.V	PERMANENT ATTRIBUTE	DOUBLE	9
TIMEARR	TEMPORARY ATTRIBUTE	DOUBLE	9
WT2	GLOBAL VARIABLE	DOUBLE	13

FIGURE 2-16 Traffic Merging System—ARRTWO Routine

```
LINE   CACI SIMSCRIPT II.5  RELEASE 8H

   1    EVENT DEPTWO
   2      IF QUE2 IS EMPTY
   3            LET STS2 = IDLE
   4            RETURN
   5      ELSE
   6            REMOVE FIRST CUST FROM QUE2
   7            LET WT2 = TIME.V - TIMEARR(CUST)
   8            DESTROY CUST
   9            LET SVC2 = EXPONENTIAL.F(0.1,4)
  10            SCHEDULE A DEPTWO IN SVC2 MINUTES
  11            IF MOD.F(NO2,10) = 0
  12                CALL STATS
  13            ALWAYS
  14            RETURN
  15    END
```

FIGURE 2-16 Traffic Merging System—DEPTWO Routine

NAME	TYPE	MODE	LINE NUMBERS OF REFERENCES		
CUST	TEMPORARY ENTITY		8		
+	GLOBAL VARIABLE	INTEGER	6	7	8
DEPTWO	EVENT NOTICE		1	10	
+	GLOBAL VARIABLE	INTEGER	1	10*	
EXPONENTIAL.F	ROUTINE		9		
IDLE	DEFINE TO MEAN		3		
MOD.F	ROUTINE		11		
NO2	GLOBAL VARIABLE	DOUBLE	11		
QUE2	SET		2	6	
STATS	ROUTINE		12		
STS2	GLOBAL VARIABLE	INTEGER	3		
SVC2	GLOBAL VARIABLE	DOUBLE	9	10	
TIME.V	PERMANENT ATTRIBUTE	DOUBLE	7		
TIMEARR	TEMPORARY ATTRIBUTE	DOUBLE	7		
WT2	GLOBAL VARIABLE	DOUBLE	7		

FIGURE 2-16 DEPTWO Routine (*continued*)

```
LINE  CACI SIMSCRIPT II.5  RELEASE 8H

   1   ROUTINE STATS
   2     IF NO2 GE 9000
   3         SCHEDULE A STOPSIM NOW
   4     ALWAYS
   5     GO TO A(MOD.F(NO2/10,10)+1)
   6   'A(1)'   LET X10 = MWT2
   7           RESET TOTALS OF WT2
   8           RETURN
   9   'A(2)'   LET X1 = MWT2
  10           RETURN
  11   'A(3)'   LET X2 = MWT2
  12           RETURN
  13   'A(4)'   LET X3 = MWT2
  14           RETURN
  15   'A(5)'   LET X4 = MWT2
  16           RETURN
  17   'A(6)'   LET X5 = MWT2
  18           RETURN
  19   'A(7)'   LET X6 = MWT2
  20           RETURN
  21   'A(8)'   LET X7 = MWT2
  22           RETURN
  23   'A(9)'   LET X8 = MWT2
  24           RETURN
  25   'A(10)'  LET X9 = MWT2
  26           RETURN
  27   END
```

NAME	TYPE	MODE	LINE NUMBERS OF REFERENCES					
A	SUBSCRIPTED LABEL		5	6	9	11	13	15
			17	19	21	23	2	
MOD.F	ROUTINE		5					
MWT2	ROUTINE		6	9	11	13	15	17
			19	21	23	25		
NO2	GLOBAL VARIABLE	DOUBLE	2	5				
STATS	ROUTINE		1					
STOPSIM	EVENT NOTICE		3					
+	GLOBAL VARIABLE	INTEGER	3*					
WT2	GLOBAL VARIABLE	DOUBLE	7					
X1	GLOBAL VARIABLE	DOUBLE	9					
X10	GLOBAL VARIABLE	DOUBLE	6					
X2	GLOBAL VARIABLE	DOUBLE	11					
X3	GLOBAL VARIABLE	DOUBLE	13					
X4	GLOBAL VARIABLE	DOUBLE	15					
X5	GLOBAL VARIABLE	DOUBLE	17					
X6	GLOBAL VARIABLE	DOUBLE	19					
X7	GLOBAL VARIABLE	DOUBLE	21					
X8	GLOBAL VARIABLE	DOUBLE	23					
X9	GLOBAL VARIABLE	DOUBLE	25					

FIGURE 2-16 Traffic Merging System—STATS Routine

```
LINE   CACI SIMSCRIPT II.5   RELEASE 8H

  1     EVENT DEPONE
  2       LET  DEP = TIME.V - LEFT
  3       LET LEFT = TIME.V
  4       IF QUE1 IS EMPTY
  5               LET STS1 = IDLE
  6               SCHEDULE AN ARRTWO NOW
  7               LET RESCHED = DONT
  8               RETURN
  9       ELSE
 10               REMOVE FIRST CUST FROM QUE1
 11               LET WT1 = TIME.V - TIMEARR(CUST)
 12               DESTROY CUST
 13               LET SVC1 = EXPONENTIAL.F(0.2,2)
 14               SCHEDULE A DEPONE IN SVC1 MINUTES
 15               SCHEDULE AN ARRTWO NOW
 16               LET RESCHED = DONT
 17               RETURN
 18     END
```

                    C R O S S - R E F E R E N C E

NAME	TYPE	MODE	LINE NUMBERS OF REFERENCES		
ARRTWO	EVENT NOTICE		6	15	
+	GLOBAL VARIABLE	INTEGER	6*	15*	
CUST	TEMPORARY ENTITY		12		
+	GLOBAL VARIABLE	INTEGER	10	11	12
DEP	GLOBAL VARIABLE	DOUBLE	2		
DEPONE	EVENT NOTICE		1	14	
+	GLOBAL VARIABLE	INTEGER	1	14*	
DONT	DEFINE TO MEAN		7	16	
EXPONENTIAL.F	ROUTINE		13		
IDLE	DEFINE TO MEAN		5		
LEFT	GLOBAL VARIABLE	DOUBLE	2	3	
QUE1	SET		4	10	
RESCHED	GLOBAL VARIABLE	INTEGER	7	16	
STS1	GLOBAL VARIABLE	INTEGER	5		
SVC1	GLOBAL VARIABLE	DOUBLE	13	14	
TIME.V	PERMANENT ATTRIBUTE	DOUBLE	2	3	11
TIMEARR	TEMPORARY ATTRIBUTE	DOUBLE	11		
WT1	GLOBAL VARIABLE	DOUBLE	11		

FIGURE 2-16 Traffic Merging System—DEPONE Routine

SIMSCRIPT II.5. Therefore, only those instructions that would be of greatest help to a beginning SIMSCRIPT II.5 programmer are discussed in great depth. Other instructions may not be mentioned or mentioned only in passing. There are outstanding texts written on the subject of SIMSCRIPT II.5. The novice is encouraged to consult these texts and the appropriate user's manual to gain the knowledge to be an experienced SIMSCRIPT II.5. programmer.

EXERCISES

2-1. Modify the single-queue, single-server SIMSCRIPT program described in this chapter to include a feedback. Figure 2-17 illustrates the new model. New arrivals enter the system (to the queue) with a mean rate L. If the service facility is not presently in use, the job (entity) enters the service facility; otherwise, it must wait (in the queue). When the job leaves the server (after a random time with mean T), it either

```
LINE  CACI SIMSCRIPT II.5  RELEASE 8H

  1    EVENT STOPSIM
  2       PRINT 23 LINES WITH
  3          M1*1440,S1*1440,M2*1440,S2*1440,M3*1440,S3*1440,
  4          M4*1440,S4*1440,M5*1440,S5*1440,
  5          M6*1440,S6*1440,M7*1440,S7*1440,M8*1440,S8*1440,
  6          M9*1440,S9*1440,M10*1440,S10*1440,
  7          MWT1*1440,NO1,NO2,AT1,AT2,ST1,ST2,UT1,UT2,NQ1,NQ2,DT*1440
  8       THUS
       BATCH SIZE                    M(N)              S(N,P)
          10                       **.******          **.******
          20                       **.******          **.******
          30                       **.******          **.******
          40                       **.******          **.******
          50                       **.******          **.******
          60                       **.******          **.******
          70                       **.******          **.******
          80                       **.******          **.******
          90                       **.******          **.******
         100                       **.******          **.******
       MEAN WAITING TIME QUEUE1             .******
       NO. OF CUSTOMERS AT SER #1        ******
       NO. OF CUSTOMERS AT SER #2        ******
       MEAN ARRIVAL RATE FOR SERVER #1      .******
       MEAN ARRIVAL RATE FOR SERVER #2      .******
       MEAN SERVICE RATE FOR SERVER #1 .******
       MEAN SERVICE RATE FOR SERVER #2 .******
       UTILIZATION FOR SERVER #1       .******
       UTILIZATION FOR SERVER #2       .******
       MEAN QUEUE LENGTH FOR SERVER #1 .******
       MEAN QUEUE LENGTH FOR SERVER #2 .******
     MEAN DEPARTURE INTERVAL FROM SER #1  .******
  9    STOP
 10    END


                    C R O S S - R E F E R E N C E

   NAME              TYPE              MODE      LINE NUMBERS OF REFERENCES

 AT1            ROUTINE                           2
 AT2            ROUTINE                           2
 DT             ROUTINE                           2
 MWT1           ROUTINE                           2
 M1             ROUTINE                           2
 M10            ROUTINE                           2
 M2             ROUTINE                           2
 M3             ROUTINE                           2
 M4             ROUTINE                           2
 M5             ROUTINE                           2
 M6             ROUTINE                           2
 M7             ROUTINE                           2
 M8             ROUTINE                           2
 M9             ROUTINE                           2
 NO1            GLOBAL VARIABLE        DOUBLE      2
 NO2            GLOBAL VARIABLE        DOUBLE      2
 NQ1            ROUTINE                            2
 NQ2            ROUTINE                            2
 STOPSIM        EVENT NOTICE                       1
              + GLOBAL VARIABLE        INTEGER     1
 ST1            ROUTINE                            2
 ST2            ROUTINE                            2
 S1             ROUTINE                            2
 S10            ROUTINE                            2
 S2             ROUTINE                            2
 S3             ROUTINE                            2
 S4             ROUTINE                            2
 S5             ROUTINE                            2
 S6             ROUTINE                            2
 S7             ROUTINE                            2
 S8             ROUTINE                            2
 S9             ROUTINE                            2
 UT1            ROUTINE                            2
 UT2            ROUTINE                            2
```

FIGURE 2-16 Traffic Merging System—STOP.SIM Routine

```
BATCH SIZE                                    M(N)                    S(N,P)
      10                                     .104305                 .132021
      20                                     .105415                 .109081
      30                                     .100186                 .078943
      40                                     .104739                 .062315
      50                                     .104121                 .057108
      60                                     .103567                 .061429
      70                                     .102619                 .058131
      80                                     .101511                 .053839
      90                                     .101574                 .054514
     100                                     .102837                 .054013
   MEAN WAITING TIME QUEUE1                          .214259
   NO. OF CUSTOMERS AT SER #1                        4534
   NO. OF CUSTOMERS AT SER #2                        9000
   MEAN ARRIVAL RATE FOR SERVER #1               .403881
   MEAN ARRIVAL RATE FOR SERVER #2               .409975
   MEAN SERVICE RATE FOR SERVER #1    .203884
   MEAN SERVICE RATE FOR SERVER #2    .100001
   UTILIZATION FOR SERVER #1                     .504954
   UTILIZATION FOR SERVER #2                     .491615
   MEAN QUEUE LENGTH FOR SERVER #1    .530649
   MEAN QUEUE LENGTH FOR SERVER #2   .505564
MEAN DEPARTURE INTERVAL FROM SER #1    .403649
```

FIGURE 2-16   Traffic Merging System—Output Report

leaves the system or returns to the queue. $(1 - p)100\%$ of the jobs leave the system, whereas $p100\%$ of the jobs reenter the system.

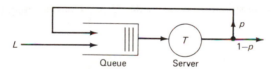

FIGURE 2-17

2-2. Modify the single-queue, single-server SIMSCRIPT program described in this chapter to include two queues in tandem. Figure 2-18 illustrates the new model. New arrivals enter the system (to queue 1) with a mean rate L. If the first service facility (server 1) is not presently in use, the arrival enters the facility; otherwise, it must wait (in the queue). When the job leaves the server (after a random time with mean T_1), it enters the next queue in line, and so on. After the transaction departs from the last service facility (server 2), it leaves the system.

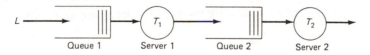

FIGURE 2-18

2-3. Consider a system consisting of n service facilities operating in parallel. Arrivals enter the system and are admitted to the first vacant service station on a first-come, first-served basis. The time interval between arrivals is a stochastic variate with a known probability distribution. The service time for each of the n service stations is a stochastic variate, with each station having its own given probability distribution for service time. When an input arrives at the system, the n service stations are checked to determine whether any one of them is vacant at the moment. If all n are occupied, waiting time occurs until one station becomes vacant. When a service station becomes vacant before another unit arrives at the system, idle time occurs until a unit arrives and enters the vacant service station. Draw a flow chart for the events (endogenous and exogenous) that occur in the simulation of this system. Explain what each event accomplishes and explain the interaction of the events of this system. Explain which stochastic variates would be appropriate for this system and why. Use the concepts of SIMSCRIPT.

2-4. Consider the following example of a telephone booth system. During any given time interval, customers may arrive at the booth and wish to make telephone calls. If the booth is occupied at the time of arrival, the prospective caller must join the waiting line. When the phone is available, the first person in line will enter the booth and use the phone for a certain amount of time. He then leaves, making the booth available for the next user. Draw the flow chart of a SIMSCRIPT simulation of the telephone booth system. In drawing your flow chart, be sure to distinguish event routines, entities, and sets.

2-5. What does the user really need in simulation languages? List at least five points about which a comparison may be made. (*Hint:* Consider major language components.)

REFERENCES

1. The SIMSCRIPT II.5 Reference Handbook, CACI, Inc., Los Angeles, CA, 1971.

2. RUSSELL, E. C., and ANNINO, J. S., *A Quick Look at SIMSCRIPT II.5*, CACI, Inc., Los Angeles, CA, 1971.

3. KIVIAT, P. J., VILLANUEVA, R., and MARKOWITZ, H. M., *SIMSCRIPT II.5 Programming Language* (edited by E. C. Russell), CACI, Inc., Los Angeles, CA, 1973.

4. MARKOWITZ, H. M., HAUSNER, B., and KARR, H. W., *SIMSCRIPT: A Simulation Programming Language,* Prentice-Hall, Inc., Englewood Cliffs, N.J., 1963.

5. *SIMSCRIPT II.5 User's Manual Honeywell 600/6000 Version,* CACI, Inc., Los Angeles, CA, 1973.

6. *SIMSCRIPT II.5 User's Manual S/360-370 Version,* CACI, Inc., Los Angeles, CA, 1974.

3

INTRODUCTION TO GPSS

GPSS is a language used in discrete-system simulations. Since it was written for simulation, it provides automatic support for the programmer in the form of an automatic clock, automatic data collection, highly descriptive language statements, and automatic printout of simulation results.

The following briefly summarizes the main language components in a GPSS simulation:

1. *Transactions:* represent traffic in the system.
2. *Blocks:* cause some basic action to occur.
3. *Facilities:* can be seized by one or more transactions at a time.
4. *Storages:* can be entered by one or more transactions.
5. *Logic switches:* determine flow of transactions through the model.
6. *Arithmetic variables:* used for mathematical relationships.
7. *Boolean variables:* represent multiple logical conditions.
8. *Functions:* compute relationships.
9. *Queues:* used to accumulate information about delayed transactions.
10. *Tables:* used to provide more specific information than automatically provided by the system.
11. *Savevalues:* global storage locations.
12. *Matrix savevalues:* used to store selected values arrayed in matrix.
13. *User chains:* represent queues and status of inactive transactions.
14. *Groups:* represent transactions with common attributes.

The basic flow through a model is of a transaction created at a GENERATE block to move through a model until it is terminated at a TERMINATE block. Along the way it could SEIZE and then RELEASE a facility, ENTER a storage and then LEAVE it, be placed in a QUEUE and DEPART the queue, cause a VARIABLE to be evaluated, use a FUNCTION, and cause logic switches to be set and reset.

GPSS provides a process for each transaction in a system. Each transaction moves through the system and hence through time. As seen by the QUEUE block, it is possible for a transaction to encounter a delay in progress and wait. It is because of this time flow within GPSS that it is called a process interaction language.

Each block type is given a unique name, which represents a descriptive action of the system. Table 3-1 describes some of the 48 block types. Table 3-1 also lists the required field information, referred to as field A, B, C, and so forth.

Each of the 14 entity types is characterized by externally addressable attributes called *standard numerical attributes* (SNA), and *standard logical attributes* (SLA). Some of these attributes are system manipulated (such as the "relative clock"). Others are used strictly by the user, for example, Parameters (Pk) associated with each transaction. The SNAs and SLAs are addressable and can be used to store information in and/or monitor system progress. The use to which these attributes is put is dependent on the entity to

TABLE 3-1

GPSS Block Types (Geoffrey Gordon, *System Simulation, 2nd ed.*, © 1978, page 200. Reprinted by permission of Prentice-Hall, Inc., Englewood Cliffs, N.J.)

Operation	A	B	C	D	E	F
ADVANCE	Mean	Modifier				
ASSIGN	Param. No. (±)	Source	(Funct. No.)	Param. type		
DEPART	Queue No.	(Units)				
ENTER	Storage No.	(Units)				
GATE	Item No.	(Next block *B*)				
GENERATE	Mean	Modifier	(Offset)	(Count)	(Priority)	(Params.)
LEAVE	Storage No.	(Units)				
LINK	Chain No.	Order	(Next block *B*)			
LOGIC { R S I }	Switch No.					
MARK	(Param. No.)					
PRIORITY	Priority					
QUEUE	Queue No.	(Units)				
RELEASE	Facility No.					
SAVEVALUE	S.V. No. (±)	SNA				
SEIZE	Facility No.					
TABULATE	Table No.	(Units)				
TERMINATE	(Units)					
TEST	Arg. 1	Arg. 2	(Next block *B*)			
TRANSFER	Select. Factor	Next block *A*	Next block *B*			
UNLINK	Chain No.	Next block *A*	Count	(Param. No.)	(Arg.)	(Next block *B*)

(±) indicates optional field.

which it is attached. Some are "read only" while others are programmer modifiable. The SNAs and SLAs will be discussed more fully when the entity to which they are attached is discussed.

Table 3-2 describes a partial list of the program SNAs. The letter *n* in Table 3-2 represents the number of a specific entity. GPSS also allows for an entity to be described

TABLE 3-2

GPSS Standard Numerical Attributes (Geoffrey Gordon, *System Simulation, 2nd ed.,* © 1978, Page 225. Reprinted by permission of Prentice-Hall, Inc., Englewood Cliffs, N.J.)

C1	The current value of clock time.
CHn	The number of transactions on chain *n*.
Fn	The current status of facility number *n*. This variable is 1 if the facility is busy and 0 if not.
FNn	The value of function *n*. (The function value may be computed to have a fractional part but the SNA gives only the integral part, unrounded.)
Kn	The integer *n* (the notation n may also be used).
M1	The transit time of a transaction.
Nn	The total number of transactions that have entered block *n*.
Pxn	Parameter number *n* of a transaction, of type *x*.
Qn	The length of queue *n*.
Rn	The space remaining in storage *n*.
RNn	A computed random number having one of the values 1 through 999 with equal probability. (When the reference is made to provide the input for a function, the value is automatically scaled to the range 0 to 1.) Eight different generators can be referenced by n = 1, 2, . . . , 8.
Sn	The current occupancy of storage *n*.
Vn	The value of variable statement number *n*.
Wn	The number of transactions currently at block *n*.
Xxn	The value of savevalue location *n* of type *x*.

by a symbolic name. If a symbolic name is used, it must be preceded by a $ sign. For example, see Figure 3-1.

GPSS automatically accumulates statistics concerning conditions within the model. Furthermore, the programmer has the ability to cause the system to accumulate other information that she or he believes important. All statistics accumulated are output automatically at the end of the simulation run, and they can be output during the run under the control of the programmer.

The flexibility of GPSS allows the programmer to redefine portions of the model or redefine specific characteristics of system entities. Some entities, as found in Table 3-3, can be redefined merely by labeling the required statements in the model, and then placing the redefined input statement between the START statement, which initiated the simulation, and the next START statement. Other entities can be redefined by using an

CARD NUMBER: 1 2 3 4 5 6 7 8 9 10 11 12 13 14 15 16 17 18 19 20 21 22 23

```
BLOCK
NUMBER   *LOC   OPERATION   A,B,C,D,E,F,G          COMMENTS

                SIMULATE
         *      SIMPLE QUEUE EXAMPLE
         EXP    FUNCTION    RN1,C24
         0,0/.1,.104/.2,.222/.3,.355/.4,.509/.5,.69/.6,.915/.7,1.2/.75,1.38
         .8,1.6/.84,1.83/.88,2.12/.9,2.3/.92,2.52/.94,2.81/.95,2.99/.96,3.2
         .97,3.5/.98,3.9/.99,4.6/.995,5.3/.998,6.2/.999,7/.9998,8
         *      BLOCK DEFINITION CARDS
    1           GENERATE    10,FN$EXP
    2           QUEUE       LINE
    3           SEIZE       SERV
    4           DEPART      LINE
    5           ADVANCE     8,FN$EXP
    6           RELEASE     SERV
    7           TABULATE    TAB
    8           TERMINATE   1
         *      DEFINITION CARDS
         TAB    TABLE       M1,10,10,100
         QTAB   QTABLE      LINE,10,10,100
         *      CONTROL CARDS
                START       100,NP
                RESET
                START       1000
                END
```

FIGURE 3-1   One-Queue One-Server GPSS Program

63

TABLE 3-3

Entity to be Defined	Input Statement
Storage	Storage statement
Arithmetic variable	Variable statement
Floating arithmetic variable	F variable statement
Boolean variable	B variable statement
Function	Function and function follower statement
Table	Table or Q table statement
Savevalue	Initial statement
Matrix savevalue	Matrix and initial statement
Logic switch	Initial statement

ORG statement to cause the compiler to set the location counter to a value in field A. This advanced knowledge of the block numbers will allow the programmer to overlay the information found there and thus change the specifications of his model.

BASIC CONCEPTS

To gain a basic understanding of GPSS, four entities need to be elaborated: (1) dynamic entity, (2) equipment entity, (3) statistical entity, and (4) operational entity.

Dynamic entities are called transactions. These are similar to temporary entities in SIMSCRIPT. These transactions are created and destroyed during a simulation. An example of a transaction would be a customer in a service-station model. Basically, a transaction is the unit of traffic. As with all entities, transactions have attributes. Transaction attributes are defined by assigning values to sets of parameters associated with each transaction.

Equipment entities are available in GPSS to simulate items of equipment that are used by transactions. They are divided into two types, *facilities* and *storages. Facilities* are used to simulate equipment that processes only one transaction at a time, for example, a single pump in a service station. A *storage* is an equipment entity that can service more than one transaction at a time. For example, a service station of 12 pumps could be simulated as a single unit by using a storage entity. GPSS automatically maintains *statistics* on utilization, average contents, and so forth, of such equipment entities. These values are printed automatically at the end of the simulation. Reference can be made at any time to the value of these accumulated statistics.

Statistical entities are available to analyze the simulation. A *queue* represents one type of statistical entity. The *queue* or *chain* entity is used to simulate and measure the contention arising from competition among transactions for the use of equipment entities. The queue possesses several SNAs, which are as follows (the mnemonic reference used in GPSS is shown in parentheses):

1. Current contents or length (Qn).
2. Maximum contents (QMn).
3. Average contents (QAn).
4. Total number of entries (QCn).
5. The number of times the queue is empty (QZn).
6. Average time transactions spend in queue (QTn).
7. Average time transactions spend in nonempty queue (excluding zero entries) (QXn).

The other statistical entity is called a TABLE. A table is used to collect the different frequency distributions that arise naturally during the modeling process.

Operational entities are called *blocks* and are the GPSS equivalent of statements. Blocks determine the logic of the system by controlling the flow and interaction of transactions. Some blocks control the ways in which transactions can use equipment entities; others affect transaction parameters. Other types control output, control the direction of transaction flow, and two types control transaction creation and destruction.

GPSS automatically controls the flow of transactions from block to block. Also, GPSS keeps track of which block each transaction is to enter next and how long it will remain there. A system-wide clock is maintained to schedule these operations.

LANGUAGE ELEMENTS

Four types of statements are needed in GPSS to specify the *program structure:*

1. BLOCK definition statements (Table 3-1).
2. ENTITY definition statements (Table 3-3).
3. GPSS control statements (Table 3-4).
4. GPSS system (e.g., IBM) control cards.

Table 3-4 describes the GPSS control statements. The first blocks to be discussed control the birth and death of transactions. These actions are specified by GENERATE and TERMINATE in GPSS. As an example, TERMINATE 1 results in a 1 being subtracted from a preset counter, and when the counter is zero, simulation ends. The block GENERATE 22, 12 will create transactions with interarrival time uniformly distributed in the closed interval [10, 34]; that is, mean = 22 and spread = 12.

Simulation of the usage of an equipment entity *usually* requires three blocks. Two

TABLE 3-4

GPSS Control Statements (Geoffrey Gordon, *System Simulation, 2nd ed.,* © 1978, page 201.
Reprinted by permission of Prentice-Hall, Inc., Englewood Cliffs, N.J.)

Location	Operation	A	B	C	D
	CLEAR				
	END				
Function no.	FUNCTION	Argument	$\left\{\begin{matrix} C \\ D \\ L \end{matrix}\right\}$ No. of points		
	INITIAL	Entity	Value		
	JOB				
	RESET				
	SIMULATE				
	START	Run count	(NP)		
Storage no.	STORAGE	Capacity			
Table no.	TABLE	Argument	Lower limit	Interval	No. of intervals

blocks are used to identify the entity that is to be used and freed; the third is used to indicate how long the entity is to be used. The third block (which is used to indicate the service or delay time) is the ADVANCE block. For example, ADVANCE 15, 5 indicates that the entity will be used according to a uniform distribution with mean 15 and spread 5. If no ADVANCE block is indicated in the system, each transaction will flow through all blocks in zero time. The other two blocks used to simulate equipment usage vary with the type of equipment. For facilities, SEIZE and RELEASE are used. For example, let PUMP be a facility. Consider

```
SEIZE PUMP
ADVANCE 15, 5
RELEASE PUMP
```

When the transaction enters the SEIZE block, PUMP is recorded as busy. The ADVANCE block specifies that the PUMP will remain busy for 15 ± 5 time units. The RELEASE block records the PUMP as free. For storages, ENTER and LEAVE are required instead of SEIZE and RELEASE.

A certain amount of congestion results when transactions are halted because a facility is in use or because a storage is full. Because such congestion is often a major objective of the simulation, several blocks are available to simulate queues. The blocks QUEUE and DEPART are used to simulate first-in, first-out (FIFO) and to measure

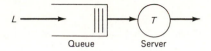

Queue   Server

FIGURE 3-2

congestion; that is, they force transactions into and out of a queue. In general, these blocks immediately surround the block(s) that can cause congestion. For example,

    QUEUE LINE
    SEIZE PUMP
    DEPART LINE

Transactions that find the PUMP in use will remain in a waiting LINE until the PUMP is RELEASED. At that time, the transaction at the head of the line is allowed to enter the SEIZE block and immediately pass through the DEPART block to leave the LINE. The system automatically accumulates and prints out at the end of the simulation the average queue contents, the number of elements in the queue, and the average time per transaction on the queue.

Example 1

Figure 3-1 consists of a simple one-queue, one-server GPSS program. Figure 3-2 illustrates the model. New arrivals enter the system (to the queue) with a mean rate L. If the service facility is not presently in use, the transaction enters the facility; otherwise, it must wait (in the queue). When the transaction leaves the server (after a random time with mean T), it leaves the system. In Figure 3-1, $L = 10$ and $T = 8$. Figure 3-3 is a flow chart of the transaction flow for a single-queue, single-server system.

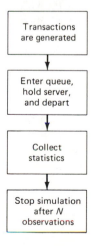

FIGURE 3-3 Transaction Flow for a Single-Queue, Single-Server System

The block TABULATE TAB causes an entry to be made into the TABLE named TAB whenever a transaction enters the block. The exact definition of each TABLE is made in a definition card. In this example, TABLE M1, 10, 10, 100 has the following meaning. M1 is the numerical attribute to be tabulated and denotes the transit time of a transaction. The next three values (10, 10, 100) denote the upper limit of the first interval, the tabulation interval size, and the number of intervals, respectively. Figure 3-4 illustrates the output from this table, where 37.278. represents the average transit time in the system. QTAB is a special entity called a queue table entity. QTABLE records the distribution of waiting times in the queue, LINE. The next three fields (10, 10, 100) have the same meaning as in TABLE. Figure 3-4 illustrates the output from this table, where 29.983 represents the mean time a transaction spends in the queue. The control statement START denotes the end of the problem deck and contains in the first field the value the terminating counter (TERMINATE) is to reach to cause the simulation run to end. With the first START statement, the simulation is set to stop at 100 transactions. The reset statement clears out (zeros) the statistics gathered in that run. In this example, the second START statement has restarted the simulation from the point at which the 100th transaction finished and has continued for a further 1000 transactions.

As will be seen in Chapter 4, an analytical solution of the queue probability distribution at steady state is derivable when the service-time distribution is exponential with mean T. To guarantee steady state, the simulation run is reset after 100 transactions. This point will be elaborated on in Chapter 5.

To define a function, at least two cards are needed. The first is called a FUNCTION statement, and it is immediately followed by one or more function *data* statements. In the first statement, the first field contains the SNA to be used as input, and the second field tells the system that the value represented in the function data cards contains n pairs of numbers. Cn instructs the program that linear interpolation between the defined n points will be performed by the system. As a convenience for the GPSS user, two commonly used continuous functions are defined in the GPSS system. These are the exponential distribution with mean 1.0 and the standard normal distribution. In each case, it is the cumulative distribution function that is supplied. In this example, the exponential function is named EXP. The SNA RN1 instructs the system to use random number generator 1: GPSS has eight pseudo-random number generators, which are specified RN1 through RN8. Hence, the block GENERATE 10, FN$EXP will generate transaction with inter-arrival time distribution with mean 10 and modified (multiplied) by a value from function EXP (a value in the interval 0 to 8). This will be elaborated on in Chapter 8.

The other statistics in Figure 3-4 are generated automatically by the simulation. For example, 3.152 denotes the average number of transactions in the queue named LINE. The value 0.766 denotes the average utilization of the service facility named SERV.

Example 2

The program in Figure 3-5 consists of a simple one-queue, one-server with feedback model. Figure 3-6 illustrates the simple model. New arrivals enter the system (to the

FACILITY	AVERAGE UTILIZATION	NUMBER ENTRIES	AVERAGE TIME/TRAN	SEIZING TRANS. NO.	PREEMPTING TRANS. NO.
SERV	.766	1000	7.294		

FIGURE 3-4 One-Queue One-Server Output Report

RELATIVE CLOCK   9522   ABSOLUTE CLOCK   10404
BLOCK COUNTS

BLOCK CURRENT	TOTAL	BLOCK CURRENT	TOTAL	BLOCK CURRENT	TOTAL	BLOCK CURRENT
1 0	1001					
2 7	1001					
3 0	1000					
4 0	1000					
5 0	1000					
6 0	1000					
7 0	1000					
8 0	1000					

FIGURE 3-4 *(continued)*

QUEUE	MAXIMUM CONTENTS	AVERAGE CONTENTS	TOTAL ENTRIES	ZERO ENTRIES	PERCENT ZEROS	AVERAGE TIME/TRANS	$AVERAGE TIME/TRANS	TABLE NUMBER	CURRENT CONTENTS
LINE	25	3.152	1007	210	20.8	29.809	37.663	2	7

$AVERAGE TIME/TRANS = AVERAGE TIME/TRANS EXCLUDING ZERO ENTRIES

FIGURE 3-4 *(continued)*

69

TABLE TAB
ENTRIES IN TABLE 1000   MEAN ARGUMENT 37.278   STANDARD DEVIATION 39.312   SUM OF ARGUMENTS 37279.000   NON-WEIGHTED

UPPER LIMIT	OBSERVED FREQUENCY	PER CENT OF TOTAL	CUMULATIVE PERCENTAGE	CUMULATIVE REMAINDER	MULTIPLE OF MEAN	DEVIATION FROM MEAN
10	255	25.49	25.4	74.5	.268	-.693
20	149	14.89	40.3	59.6	.536	-.439
30	153	15.29	55.6	44.3	.804	-.185
40	129	12.89	68.5	31.4	1.072	.069
50	80	7.99	76.5	23.4	1.341	.323
60	31	3.09	79.6	20.3	1.609	.577
70	60	5.99	85.6	14.3	1.877	.832
80	45	4.49	90.1	9.8	2.145	1.086
90	23	2.29	92.4	7.5	2.414	1.341
100	20	1.99	94.4	5.5	2.682	1.595
110	7	.69	95.1	4.8	2.950	1.849
120	5	.49	95.6	4.3	3.218	2.104
130	8	.79	96.4	3.5	3.487	2.358
140	5	.49	96.9	3.0	3.755	2.612
150	2	.19	97.1	2.8	4.023	2.867
160	2	.19	97.3	2.6	4.291	3.121
170	1	.09	97.4	2.5	4.560	3.376
180	0	.00	97.4	2.5	4.828	3.630
190	1	.09	97.5	2.4	5.096	3.884
200	0	.00	97.5	2.4	5.364	4.139
210	10	.99	98.5	1.4	5.633	4.393
220	8	.79	99.3	.6	5.901	4.647
230	4	.39	99.7	.2	6.169	4.902
	2	.19	100.0	.0		

REMAINING FREQUENCIES ARE ALL ZERO

FIGURE 3-4 (continued)

70

TABLE QTAB MEAN ARGUMENT 29.983 STANDARD DEVIATION 38.500 SUM OF ARGUMENTS 29984.000 NON-WEIGHTED
ENTRIES IN TABLE 1000

UPPER LIMIT	OBSERVED FREQUENCY	PER CENT OF TOTAL	CUMULATIVE PERCENTAGE	CUMULATIVE REMAINDER	MULTIPLE OF MEAN	DEVIATION FROM MEAN
10	398	39.79	39.7	60.2	.333	-.519
20	127	12.69	52.4	47.5	.667	-.259
30	137	13.69	66.1	33.8	1.000	.000
40	95	9.49	75.6	24.3	1.334	.260
50	47	4.69	80.3	19.6	1.667	.519
60	30	2.99	83.3	16.6	2.001	.779
70	59	5.89	89.2	10.7	2.334	1.039
80	28	2.79	92.0	7.9	2.668	1.299
90	24	2.39	94.4	5.5	3.001	1.558
100	8	.79	95.2	4.7	3.335	1.818
110	4	.39	95.6	4.3	3.668	2.078
120	5	.49	96.1	3.8	4.002	2.338
130	8	.79	96.9	3.0	4.335	2.597
140	2	.19	97.1	2.8	4.669	2.857
150	4	.39	97.5	2.4	5.002	3.117
160	1	.09	97.6	2.3	5.336	3.377
170	0	.00	97.6	2.3	5.669	3.636
180	0	.00	97.6	2.3	6.003	3.896
190	3	.29	97.9	2.0	6.336	4.156
200	12	1.19	99.1	.8	6.670	4.415
210	4	.39	99.5	.4	7.003	4.675
220	4	.39	100.0	.0	7.337	4.935

REMAINING FREQUENCIES ARE ALL ZERO

FIGURE 3-4 (continued)

```
BLOCK                                                               CARD
NUMBER  *LOC    OPERATION  A,B,C,D,E,F,G                 COMMENTS    NUMBER

                SIMULATE                                              1
                SIMPLE FEEDBACK EXAMPLE                               2
        *EXP    FUNCTION   RN1,C24                                    3
        0,0/.1,.104/.2,.222/.3,.355/.4,.509/.5,.69/.6,.915/.7,1.2/.75,1.38    4
        .8,1.6/.84,1.83/.88,.2.12/.9,2.3/.92,2.52/.94,2.81/.95,2.99/.96,3.2   5
        .97,3.5/.98,3.9/.99,4.6/.995,5.3/.998,6.2/.999,7/.9998,8      6
        *       BLOCK DEFINITION CARDS                                7
 1              GENERATE   10,FN$EXP                                  8
 2              QUEUE      LINE                                       9
 3              SEIZE      SERV                                      10
 4       RET    DEPART     LINE                                      11
 5              ADVANCE    8,FN$EXP                                  12
 6              RELEASE    SERV                                      13
 7              TABULATE   TAB                                       14
 8              TRANSFER   .9,RET,LEV                                15
 9       LEV    TERMINATE  1                                         16
        *       DEFINITION CARDS                                     17
         TAB    TABLE      M1,10,10,100                              18
         QTAB   QTABLE     LINE,10,10,100                            19
        *       CONTROL CARDS                                        20
                START      100,NP                                    21
                RESET                                                22
                START      5000                                      23
                END                                                  24
```

FIGURE 3-5   Simple Feedback GPSS Program

72

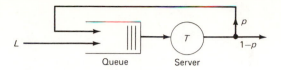

FIGURE 3-6

queue) with a mean rate L. If the service facility is not presently in use, the transaction enters the service facility; otherwise, it must wait (in the queue). When the transaction leaves the server (after a random time with mean T), it either leaves the system or returns to the queue. In this example, $(1 - p)$ 100% of the transactions leave the system, whereas p 100% of the transactions reenter the system. Figure 3-7 is the flow chart of the transaction flow for the single-queue, single-server with feedback system.

The TRANSFER block allows a location other than the next block to be selected. There are nine possible uses of the TRANSFER block. One use of the TRANSFER block is made by setting the selector factor, p, to a decimal fraction (three-digit maximum). The probability of going to the block labeled LEV is p and to the block labeled RET is $1 - p$. In Figure 3-5, $p = 0.9$.

Another possible use of the TRANSFER block is an unconditional transfer. In this case, the selection factor is left blank and the unconditional transfer is made to the block labeled by the name following the comma, for example, TRANSFER, A. Figure 3-8 illustrates the output from the program contained in Figure 3-5. For example, 7.868

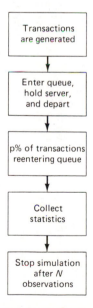

FIGURE 3-7 Transaction Flow for Single-Queue, Single-Server with Feedback

RELATIVE CLOCK   44994   ABSOLUTE CLOCK   45898

BLOCK COUNTS

BLOCK	CURRENT	TOTAL	BLOCK	CURRENT	TOTAL	BLOCK	CURRENT	TOTAL	BLOCK	CURRENT
1	0	5004								
2	7	5564								
3	0	5560								
4	0	5560								
5	0	5560								
6	0	5560								
7	0	5560								
8	0	5560								
9	0	5000								

FIGURE 3-8 Simple Feedback Output Report

FACILITY	AVERAGE UTILIZATION	NUMBER ENTRIES	AVERAGE TIME/TRAN	SEIZING TRANS. NO.	PREEMPTING TRANS. NO.
SERV	.891	5560	7.213		

FIGURE 3-8 *(continued)*

QUEUE	MAXIMUM CONTENTS	AVERAGE CONTENTS	TOTAL ENTRIES	ZERO ENTRIES	PERCENT ZEROS	AVERAGE TIME/TRANS	$AVERAGE TIME/TRANS	TABLE NUMBER	CURRENT CONTENTS
LINE	41	7.868	5567	1069	19.2	63.597	78.712	2	7

$AVERAGE TIME/TRANS = AVERAGE TIME/TRANS EXCLUDING ZERO ENTRIES

FIGURE 3-8 *(continued)*

TABLE TAB ENTRIES IN TABLE 5560 MEAN ARGUMENT 79.116 STANDARD DEVIATION 67.375 SUM OF ARGUMENTS 439889.000 NON-WEIGHTED

UPPER LIMIT	OBSERVED FREQUENCY	PER CENT OF TOTAL	CUMULATIVE PERCENTAGE	CUMULATIVE REMAINDER	MULTIPLE OF MEAN	DEVIATION FROM MEAN
10	668	12.01	12.0	87.9	.126	-1.025
20	480	8.63	20.6	79.3	.252	-.877
30	511	9.19	29.8	70.1	.379	-.729
40	426	7.66	37.4	62.5	.505	-.580
50	375	6.74	44.2	55.7	.631	-.432
60	304	5.46	49.7	50.2	.758	-.283
70	287	5.16	54.8	45.1	.884	-.135
80	255	4.58	59.4	40.5	1.011	.013
90	254	4.56	64.0	35.9	1.137	.161
100	246	4.42	68.4	31.5	1.263	.309
110	232	4.17	72.6	27.3	1.390	.458
120	203	3.65	76.2	23.7	1.516	.606
130	168	3.02	79.2	20.7	1.643	.755
140	174	3.12	82.4	17.5	1.769	.903
150	158	2.84	85.2	14.7	1.895	1.052
160	118	2.12	87.3	12.6	2.022	1.200
170	102	1.83	89.2	10.7	2.148	1.348
180	78	1.40	90.6	9.3	2.275	1.497
190	73	1.31	91.9	8.0	2.401	1.645
200	80	1.43	93.3	6.6	2.527	1.794
210	44	.79	94.1	5.8	2.654	1.942
220	51	.91	95.0	4.9	2.780	2.091
230	45	.80	95.8	4.1	2.907	2.239
240	47	.84	96.7	3.2	3.033	2.387
250	40	.71	97.4	2.5	3.159	2.536
260	33	.59	98.0	1.9	3.286	2.684
270	33	.59	98.6	1.3	3.412	2.833
280	25	.44	99.1	.8	3.539	2.981
290	18	.32	99.4	.5	3.665	3.129
300	11	.19	99.6	.3	3.791	3.278
310	4	.07	99.6	.3	3.918	3.426
320	10	.17	99.8	.1	4.044	3.575
330	1	.01	99.9	.0	4.171	3.723
340	1	.01	99.9	.0	4.297	3.872
350	2	.03	100.0	.0	4.423	4.020

REMAINING FREQUENCIES ARE ALL ZERO

FIGURE 3-8 *(continued)*

TABLE QTAB
ENTRIES IN TABLE 5560
MEAN ARGUMENT 63.638
STANDARD DEVIATION 67.062
SUM OF ARGUMENTS 353828.000
NON-WEIGHTED

UPPER LIMIT	OBSERVED FREQUENCY	PER CENT OF TOTAL	CUMULATIVE PERCENTAGE	CUMULATIVE REMAINDER	MULTIPLE OF MEAN	DEVIATION FROM MEAN
10	1558	28.02	28.0	71.9	.157	-.799
20	429	7.71	35.7	64.5	.314	-.650
30	430	7.73	43.4	56.5	.471	-.501
40	308	5.53	49.0	50.9	.628	-.352
50	313	5.62	54.6	45.3	.785	-.203
60	235	4.22	58.8	41.1	.942	-.054
70	253	4.55	63.4	36.5	1.099	.094
80	212	3.81	67.2	32.7	1.257	.243
90	202	3.63	70.8	29.1	1.414	.393
100	229	4.11	74.9	25.0	1.571	.542
110	170	3.05	78.0	21.9	1.728	.691
120	164	2.94	80.9	19.0	1.885	.840
130	150	2.69	83.6	16.3	2.042	.989
140	155	2.78	86.4	13.5	2.199	1.138
150	119	2.14	88.6	11.3	2.357	1.287
160	87	1.56	90.1	9.8	2.514	1.436
170	76	1.36	91.5	8.4	2.671	1.586
180	62	1.11	92.6	7.3	2.828	1.735
190	60	1.07	93.7	6.2	2.985	1.884
200	54	.97	94.7	5.2	3.142	2.033
210	42	.75	95.4	4.5	3.299	2.182
220	42	.79	96.2	3.7	3.457	2.331
230	44	.79	97.0	2.9	3.614	2.480
240	38	.68	97.6	2.3	3.771	2.629
250	26	.46	98.1	1.8	3.928	2.778
260	29	.52	98.6	1.3	4.085	2.928
270	29	.52	99.2	.7	4.242	3.077
280	11	.19	99.4	.5	4.399	3.226
290	13	.23	99.6	.3	4.557	3.375
300	6	.10	99.7	.2	4.714	3.524
310	6	.07	99.8	.1	4.871	3.673
320	6	.10	99.9	.1	5.028	3.822
330	4	.07	100.0	.0	5.185	3.971

REMAINING FREQUENCIES ARE ALL ZERO

FIGURE 3-8 *(continued)*

```
BLOCK
NUMBER   *LOC   OPERATION   A,B,C,D,E,F,G              COMMENTS

**              SIMULATE
                TWO QUEUES IN TANDEM

         EXP    FUNCTION    RN1,C24
0,0/.1,.104/.2,.222/.3,.355/.4,.509/.5,.69/.6,.915/.7,1.2/.75,1.38
.8,1.6/.84,1.83/.88,2.12/.9,2.3/.92,2.52/.94,2.81/.95,2.99/.96,3.2
.97,3.5/.98,3.9/.99,4.6/.995,5.3/.998,6.2/.999,7/.9998,8

**              BLOCK DEFINITION CARDS
**

 1              GENERATE    14,FN$EXP
 2              QUEUE       LINE1
 3              SEIZE       SERV1
 4              DEPART      LINE1
 5              ADVANCE     12,FN$EXP
 6              RELEASE     SERV1
 7              TABULATE    TAB1
 8              QUEUE       LINE2
 9              SEIZE       SERV2
10              DEPART      LINE2
11              ADVANCE     10,FN$EXP
12              RELEASE     SERV2
13              TABULATE    TAB2
14              TERMINATE   1

***             DEFINITION CARDS
**

         TAB1   TABLE       M1,10,10,100
         TAB2   TABLE       M1,10,10,100
         QUE1   QTABLE      LINE1,10,10,100
         QUE2   QTABLE      LINE2,10,10,10

***             CONTROL CARDS
**

                START       100,NP
                RESET
                START       1000
                END
```

CARD NUMBER: 1 2 3 4 5 6 7 8 9 10 11 12 13 14 15 16 17 18 19 20 21 22 23 24 25 26 27 28 29 30 31 32 33 34 35 36 37 38

FIGURE 3-9 Two Queues in Tandem GPSS Program

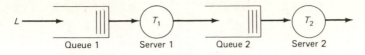

FIGURE 3-10

denotes the average number of transactions in the queue, named LINE. The value 0.891 denotes the average utilization of the service facility, SERV. QTAB records the various statistics associated with the waiting times in the queue, LINE. TAB records the various statistics associated with the total transit time in the system (i.e., wait time plus service time).

Example 3

The program in Figure 3-9 consists of a simple tandem queue model. Figure 3-10 illustrates the model. Transactions enter the system (to queue 1) with a mean rate L. If the first service facility (server 1) is not presently in use, the transaction enters the facility; otherwise, it must wait (in the queue). When the transaction leaves the server (after a random time with mean T_1), it enters the next queue in line, and so on. After the transaction departs from the last service facility (server 2), it leaves the system. Figure 3-11 is the flow chart of the transaction flow for two queues in a tandem system.

Figure 3-12 illustrates the output from the program contained in Figure 3-9. (It is

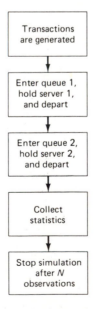

FIGURE 3-11 Transaction Flow for Two Queues in Tandem System

78

RELATIVE CLOCK 12270   ABSOLUTE CLOCK   13482
BLOCK COUNTS

BLOCK	CURRENT	TOTAL	BLOCK	CURRENT	TOTAL	BLOCK	CURRENT	TOTAL	BLOCK	CURRENT
1	0	997	11	0	1000					
2	3	997	12	0	1000					
3	0	995	13	0	1000					
4	0	995	14	0	1000					
5	1	995								
6	0	995								
7	0	995								
8	2	995								
9	0	1000								
10	0	1000								

FIGURE 3-12 Two Queues in Tandem Output Report

FACILITY	AVERAGE UTILIZATION	NUMBER ENTRIES	AVERAGE TIME/TRAN	SEIZING TRANS. NO.	PREEMPTING TRANS. NO.
SERV1	.911	996	11.225	34	
SERV2	.731	1000	8.970		

FIGURE 3-12 (continued)

QUEUE	MAXIMUM CONTENTS	AVERAGE CONTENTS	TOTAL ENTRIES	ZERO ENTRIES	PERCENT ZEROS	AVERAGE TIME/TRANS	$AVERAGE TIME/TRANS	TABLE NUMBER	CURRENT CONTENTS
LINE1	28	8.646	998	69	6.9	106.305	114.201	3	3
LINE2	21	2.349	1002	265	26.4	28.765	39.108	4	2

$AVERAGE TIME/TRANS = AVERAGE TIME/TRANS EXCLUDING ZERO ENTRIES

FIGURE 3-12 (continued)

TABLE ENTRIES IN TABLE 995 TABL TABL MEAN ARGUMENT 117.840 STANDARD DEVIATION 78.875 SUM OF ARGUMENTS 117251.000 NON-WEIGHTED

UPPER LIMIT	OBSERVED FREQUENCY	PER CENT OF TOTAL	CUMULATIVE PERCENTAGE	CUMULATIVE REMAINDER	MULTIPLE OF MEAN	DEVIATION FROM MEAN
10	60	6.03	6.0	93.9	.084	-1.367
20	69	6.93	12.9	87.0	.169	-1.240
30	45	4.52	17.4	82.5	.254	-1.113
40	37	3.71	21.2	78.7	.339	-.986
50	61	6.13	27.3	72.6	.424	-.860
60	34	3.41	30.7	69.2	.509	-.733
70	35	3.51	34.2	65.8	.594	-.606
80	39	3.91	38.1	61.8	.678	-.479
90	35	3.51	41.7	58.2	.763	-.352
100	34	3.41	45.1	54.8	.848	-.226
110	48	4.82	49.9	50.0	.933	-.099
120	29	2.91	52.8	47.1	1.018	.027
130	33	3.31	56.1	43.8	1.103	.154
140	38	3.81	59.9	40.0	1.188	.280
150	28	2.81	62.8	37.1	1.272	.407
160	39	3.91	66.7	33.2	1.357	.534
170	52	5.22	71.9	28.0	1.442	.661
180	37	3.71	75.6	24.3	1.527	.788
190	31	3.11	78.7	21.2	1.612	.914
200	43	4.32	82.7	17.2	1.697	1.041
210	26	2.61	87.0	12.9	1.782	1.168
220	18	1.80	89.6	10.3	1.866	1.295
230	13	1.30	91.7	8.5	1.951	1.421
240	19	1.90	94.6	5.3	2.036	1.548
250	12	1.20	95.8	4.1	2.121	1.675
260	10	1.00	96.8	3.1	2.206	1.802
270	12	1.20	98.0	1.9	2.291	1.929
280	5	.50	98.5	1.4	2.376	2.055
290	7	.70	99.2	.7	2.460	2.182
300	1	.10	99.3	.6	2.545	2.309
310	1	.10	99.4	.5	2.630	2.436
320	2	.20	99.6	.3	2.715	2.563
330	2	.20	99.8	.1	2.800	2.689
340	1	.10	100.0	.0	2.885	2.816
350					2.970	2.943

REMAINING FREQUENCIES ARE ALL ZERO

FIGURE 3-12 (continued)

TABLE   TAB2   MEAN ARGUMENT   STANDARD DEVIATION   SUM OF ARGUMENTS   NON-WEIGHTED
ENTRIES IN TABLE   155.308   83.625   155309.000
    1000

UPPER LIMIT	OBSERVED FREQUENCY	PER CENT OF TOTAL	CUMULATIVE PERCENTAGE	CUMULATIVE REMAINDER	MULTIPLE OF MEAN	DEVIATION FROM MEAN
10	8	.79	.7	99.1	.064	-1.737
20	28	2.79	3.5	96.3	.128	-1.618
30	29	2.89	6.4	93.5	.193	-1.498
40	18	1.79	8.2	91.6	.257	-1.378
50	18	1.79	10.0	89.8	.321	-1.259
60	38	3.79	13.8	86.0	.386	-1.139
70	45	4.49	18.3	81.6	.450	-1.020
80	52	5.19	23.5	76.4	.515	-.900
90	29	2.89	26.4	73.5	.579	-.780
100	28	2.79	29.2	70.7	.643	-.661
110	41	4.09	33.3	66.6	.708	-.541
120	37	3.69	37.0	62.9	.772	-.422
130	31	3.09	40.1	59.8	.837	-.302
140	41	4.09	44.2	55.7	.901	-.183
150	53	5.29	49.5	50.4	.965	-.063
160	36	3.59	53.1	46.8	1.030	.056
170	38	3.79	56.9	43.0	1.094	.175
180	45	4.49	61.4	38.5	1.158	.295
190	44	4.39	65.8	34.1	1.223	.414
200	39	3.89	69.7	30.2	1.287	.534
210	54	5.39	75.1	24.8	1.352	.654
220	47	4.69	79.8	20.1	1.416	.773
230	22	2.19	82.0	17.9	1.480	.893
240	21	2.09	84.1	15.8	1.545	1.012
250	24	2.39	86.5	13.4	1.609	1.132
260	19	1.89	88.4	11.5	1.674	1.251
270	17	1.69	90.1	9.8	1.738	1.371
280	12	1.19	91.3	8.6	1.802	1.491
290	14	1.39	92.7	7.2	1.867	1.610
300	16	1.59	94.3	5.6	1.931	1.730
310	22	2.19	96.5	3.4	1.996	1.849
320	8	.79	97.3	2.6	2.060	1.969
330	9	.89	98.2	1.7	2.124	2.088
340	0	.00	98.4	1.5	2.189	2.208
350	2	.19	98.6	1.3	2.253	2.328
360	2	.19	98.8	1.1	2.317	2.447
370	2	.19	99.0	.9	2.382	2.567
380	3	.29	99.3	.6	2.446	2.686
390	4	.39	99.7	.2	2.511	2.806
400	2	.19	100.0	.0	2.575	2.926
410					2.639	3.045

REMAINING FREQUENCIES ARE ALL ZERO

FIGURE 3-12 *(continued)*

81

TABLE QUE1
ENTRIES IN TABLE 995   MEAN ARGUMENT 106.607   STANDARD DEVIATION 78.375   SUM OF ARGUMENTS 106074.000   NON-WEIGHTED

UPPER LIMIT	OBSERVED FREQUENCY	PER CENT OF TOTAL	CUMULATIVE PERCENTAGE	CUMULATIVE REMAINDER	MULTIPLE OF MEAN	DEVIATION FROM MEAN
10	129	12.96	12.9	87.0	.093	-1.232
20	49	4.92	17.8	82.1	.187	-1.105
30	43	4.32	22.2	77.7	.281	-.977
40	54	5.42	27.6	72.3	.375	-.849
50	46	4.62	32.2	67.7	.469	-.722
60	31	3.11	35.3	64.6	.562	-.594
70	34	3.41	38.7	61.2	.656	-.467
80	41	4.12	42.9	57.0	.750	-.339
90	32	3.21	46.1	53.8	.844	-.211
100	40	4.02	50.1	49.8	.938	-.084
110	33	3.31	53.4	46.5	1.031	.043
120	31	3.11	56.5	43.4	1.125	.170
130	41	4.12	60.7	39.2	1.219	.298
140	32	3.21	63.9	36.0	1.313	.426
150	38	3.81	67.7	32.2	1.407	.553
160	49	4.92	72.6	27.3	1.500	.681
170	35	3.51	76.1	23.8	1.594	.808
180	32	3.21	79.3	20.6	1.688	.936
190	39	3.91	83.3	16.6	1.782	1.064
200	44	4.42	87.7	12.2	1.876	1.191
210	22	2.21	89.9	10.0	1.969	1.319
220	20	2.01	91.9	8.0	2.063	1.446
230	12	1.20	93.1	6.8	2.157	1.574
240	14	1.40	94.5	5.4	2.251	1.701
250	15	1.50	96.0	3.9	2.345	1.829
260	10	1.00	97.0	2.9	2.438	1.957
270	11	1.10	98.1	1.8	2.532	2.084
280	5	.50	98.6	1.3	2.626	2.212
290	4	.40	99.0	.9	2.720	2.339
300	3	.30	99.3	.6	2.814	2.467
310	2	.20	99.5	.4	2.907	2.595
320	0	.00	99.5	.4	3.001	2.722
330	3	.30	99.8	.1	3.095	2.850
340	1	.10	100.0	.0	3.189	2.977

REMAINING FREQUENCIES ARE ALL ZERO

FIGURE 3-12 (continued)

82

```
TABLE  QUE2           MEAN ARGUMENT        STANDARD DEVIATION      SUM OF ARGUMENTS
ENTRIES IN TABLE         29.028                   33.500              29029.000          NON-WEIGHTED
   1000

UPPER      OBSERVED    PER CENT     CUMULATIVE    CUMULATIVE     MULTIPLE      DEVIATION
LIMIT      FREQUENCY   OF TOTAL     PERCENTAGE    REMAINDER      OF MEAN       FROM MEAN
   10         424        42.39         42.3          57.6           .344        -.568
   20         116        11.59         53.9          46.0           .688        -.269
   30         103        10.29         64.2          35.7          1.033         .028
   40          73         7.29         71.5          28.4          1.377         .327
   50          54         5.39         76.9          23.0          1.722         .626
   60          41         4.09         81.0          18.9          2.066         .924
   70          48         4.79         85.8          14.1          2.411        1.223
   80          35         3.49         89.3          10.6          2.755        1.521
   90          35         3.49         92.8           7.1          3.100        1.820
  100          23         2.29         95.1           4.8          3.444        2.118
  110          16         1.59         96.7           3.2          3.789        2.417
  120          13         1.29         98.0           1.9          4.133        2.715
  130          14         1.39         99.4            .5          4.478        3.014
  140           4          .39         99.8            .1          4.822        3.312
  150           1          .09        100.0            .0          5.167        3.611

REMAINING FREQUENCIES ARE ALL ZERO
```

FIGURE 3-12 (continued)

BLOCK
NUMBER   *LOC   OPERATION A,B,C,D,E,F,G   COMMENTS   CARD
                                                               NUMBER

```
         *LOC   OPERATION  A,B,C,D,E,F,G        COMMENTS
                SIMULATE
**              MULTI-SERVER EXAMPLE
**
         EXP    FUNCTION   RN1,C24
0,0/.1,.104/.2,.222/.3,.355/.4,.509/.5,.69/.6,.915/.7,1.2/.75,1.38
.8,1.6/.84,1.83/.88,2.12/.9,2.3/.92,2.52/.94,2.81/.95,2.99/.96,3.2
.97,3.5/.98,3.9/.99,4.6/.995,5.3/.998,6.2/.999,7/.9998,8
***             BLOCK DEFINITION CARDS
***
1        GENERATE   10,FN$EXP
2        ASSIGN     1,FN$CNT
3        QUEUE      LINE
4        ENTER      SERV
5        DEPART     LINE
6        ADVANCE    V1
7        LEAVE      SERV
8        TABULATE   INT
9        TABULATE   ICNT
10       TERMINATE  1
***             DEFINITION CARDS
***
         INT    TABLE      M1,10,10,100
         ICNT   TABLE      P1,1,1,5
         SERV   STORAGE    3
         CNT    FUNCTION   RN2,D4
.6,1/.9,2/.95,3/1.0,4
1        VARIABLE   P1*3+5
         START      100,NP
         RESET
         START      1000
         END
```

FIGURE 3-13 Multiserver GPSS Program

84

obvious that this example is just a simple extension of Example 1.) In Figure 3-12, the statistics labeled QUEUE and FACILITY are automatically generated by the system. For example, .9110 denotes the average utilization of the first server, SERV1, and .7310 denotes the average utilization of the second server, SERV2. The average content of the first queue, LINE1, is 8.646, and the average content of the second queue, LINE2, is 2.349. QUE1 and QUE2 record the various statistics associated with the waiting time in the queues, LINE1 and LINE2, respectively. TAB1 records the various statistics associated with the transit time in the system through SERV1. TAB2 records the various statistics associated with the total transit time in the system.

Example 4

The program in Figure 3-13 consists of a single-queue, multiple-server model. Figure 3-14 illustrates the model. Transactions enter the system (to queue) with mean rate L. If a service facility is not presently in use, the transaction enters the facility; otherwise, it must wait (in the queue). An entering transaction only waits when all n servers are occupied. When the transaction leaves a server (after a random time with mean T), it leaves the system. Figure 3-15 is a flow chart for the transaction flow of a single-queue, multiple-server system.

This example introduces a few new GPSS blocks. First, the ASSIGN block can either add to, subtract from, or replace the value of a parameter. In this example, replacement is accomplished. As is seen in Table 3-2, Pxn is a SNA, which denotes a parameter number n of a transaction of type x. The symbol x takes the F, H, B, or L for full word, half-word, byte size, or floating point, respectively. On many compliers, only Pn is recognized. Hence, the ASSIGN block assigns P1 the value 1, 2, 3, or 4 to parameter number 1, depending on the discrete probability function defined by CNT.

Simulation of the usage of a storage requires three blocks. Two blocks identify the entity that is to be used and freed; the third indicates how long the entity is to be used. For storages, ENTER and LEAVE are used. The number of service facilities contained in the storage is defined in the STORAGE control statement. In this example, this value is 3. As in the previous examples, the blocks QUEUE and DEPART are used to simulate first-in, first-out (FIFO).

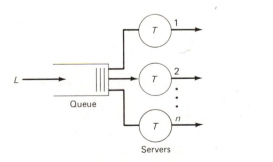

FIGURE 3-14

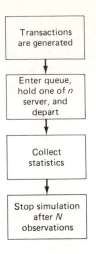

FIGURE 3-15 Transaction Flow for Single-Queue, Multiple-Server System

The ADVANCE block representing the service time is set to V1. As each transaction enters the block, the program computes the service time from VARIABLE statement number 1, which is assumed to require 3 seconds times the number of items to be attended to (for example, checking the oil or checking the tires) plus 5 seconds. Figure 3-16 illustrates the output from the program contained in Figure 3-13.

In Figure 3-16 the statistics labeled QUEUE and STORAGE are automatically generated by the system. For example, 0.351 denotes the average utilization of the storage, SERV, which consists of three servers. The TABLE ICNT records the various statistics associated with the parameter P1. The TABLE INT records the various statistics associated with the total transit time in the system (10.126 = 9.636 + 0.479 or average total time in system = average service time + average time in queue).

Example 5

The program in Figure 3-17 consists of a closed tandem queue model. Figure 3-18 illustrates the model. In this model, there exists a fixed number of transactions in the system, and these transactions cycle the two servers in a first-come, first-served manner. As in the previous example, an analytical solution of the queue probability distribution at steady state is derivable when the server-time distribution of both servers is exponential with means $T1$ and $T2$.

Figure 3-19 is a flow chart of the transaction flow for the closed queueing system. The unique aspect of this transaction flow is that the collection of statistics is independent of the main transaction flow. In Figure 3-19 a fixed number of transactions is generated at the beginning of the simulation, and only this fixed number cycle through the system. In block 4 of Figure 3-19 the simulation is stopped when N (of the preassigned number)

RELATIVE CLOCK 9154   ABSOLUTE CLOCK 10017

BLOCK COUNTS

BLOCK CURRENT	TOTAL	BLOCK CURRENT	TOTAL	BLOCK CURRENT	TOTAL	BLOCK CURRENT	TOTAL	BLOCK CURRENT
1	0	1002						
2	0	1002						
3	0	1002						
4	0	1002						
5	0	1002						
6	2	1002						
7	0	1000						
8	0	1000						
9	0	1000						
10	0	1000						

FIGURE 3-16 Multiserver Output Report

STORAGE	CAPACITY	AVERAGE CONTENTS	AVERAGE UTILIZATION	ENTRIES	AVERAGE TIME/TRAN	CURRENT CONTENTS	MAXIMUM CONTENTS
SERV	3	1.054	.351	1002	9.636	2	3

FIGURE 3-16 (continued)

QUEUE	MAXIMUM CONTENTS	AVERAGE CONTENTS	TOTAL ENTRIES	ZERO ENTRIES	PERCENT ZEROS	AVERAGE TIME/TRANS	$AVERAGE TIME/TRANS	TABLE NUMBER	CURRENT CONTENTS
LINE	4	.052	1002	885	88.3	.479	4.102		

$AVERAGE TIME/TRANS = AVERAGE TIME/TRANS EXCLUDING ZERO ENTRIES

FIGURE 3-16 (continued)

TABLE INT
ENTRIES IN TABLE 1000   MEAN ARGUMENT 10.126   STANDARD DEVIATION 2.847   SUM OF ARGUMENTS 10127.000   NON-WEIGHTED

UPPER LIMIT	OBSERVED FREQUENCY	PER CENT OF TOTAL	CUMULATIVE PERCENTAGE	CUMULATIVE REMAINDER	MULTIPLE OF MEAN	DEVIATION FROM MEAN
10	538	53.79	53.7	46.2	.987	-.044
20	457	45.69	99.4	.5	1.974	3.467
30	5	.49	100.0	.0	2.962	6.978

REMAINING FREQUENCIES ARE ALL ZERO

FIGURE 3-16 (continued)

TABLE ICNT
ENTRIES IN TABLE 1000   MEAN ARGUMENT 1.548   STANDARD DEVIATION .790   SUM OF ARGUMENTS 1549.000   NON-WEIGHTED

UPPER LIMIT	OBSERVED FREQUENCY	PER CENT OF TOTAL	CUMULATIVE PERCENTAGE	CUMULATIVE REMAINDER	MULTIPLE OF MEAN	DEVIATION FROM MEAN
1	593	59.29	59.2	40.7	.645	-.694
2	311	31.09	90.3	9.6	1.291	.570
3	50	4.99	95.3	4.6	1.936	1.836
4	46	4.59	100.0	.0	2.582	3.102

REMAINING FREQUENCIES ARE ALL ZERO

FIGURE 3-16 (continued)

```
        *LOC    OPERATION  A,B,C,D,E,F,G                              COMMENTS

                SIMULATE
        **      TWO STATION CLOSED MODEL
        **
        EXP     FUNCTION   RN1,C24
0,0/.1,.104/.2,.222/.3,.355/.4,.509/.5,.69/.6,.915/.7,1.2/.75,1.38
.8,1.6/.84,1.83/.88,2.12/.9,2.3/.92,2.52/.94,2.81/.95,2.99/.96,3.2
.97,3.5/.98,3.9/.99,4.6/.995,5.3/.998,6.2/.999,7/.9998,8
        **      TRANSACTION GENERATION
        **
        LOOP    GENERATE   ,,16
                QUEUE      LINE1
                SEIZE      SERV1
                DEPART     LINE1
                ADVANCE    12,FN$EXP
                RELEASE    SERV1
                QUEUE      LINE2
                SEIZE      SERV2
                DEPART     LINE2
                ADVANCE    10,FN$EXP
        CNT     RELEASE    SERV2
                TEST E     N$CNT,X$NUMB,LOOP
        ***     TERMINATION STATISTICS COLLECTION
        ***
                GENERATE   100
                TABULATE   TAB1
                TABULATE   TAB2
                TERMINATE  0
                INITIAL    X$NUMB,5000
        TAB1    TABLE      Q$LINE1,0,1,17
        TAB2    TABLE      Q$LINE2,0,1,17
                START      1
                END
```

Block Numbers: 1 2 3 4 5 6 7 8 9 10 11 12 13 14 15 16

Card Numbers: 1 2 3 4 5 6 7 8 9 10 11 12 13 14 15 16 17 18 19 20 21 22 23 24 25 26 27 28 29 30 31 32 33 34 35

FIGURE 3-17 Two Station Closed System GPSS Program

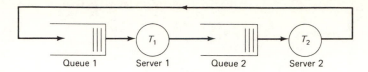

FIGURE 3-18

pass this point. In the actual simulation (Figure 3-17), the preassigned number of generated transactions is 16 and the value of N is 5000.

The language features introduced in this example are the new use of GENERATE, TEST, and an independent data-collection capability. The statement GENERATE ,,,16 creates 16 transactions simultaneously. Thus, 16 transactions begin on LINE1. To test the simulation run length, the TEST E statement is used. Each time a transaction enters the TEST E block, the total number of transactions that have entered the RELEASE block (named COUNT) is compared with the save value NUMB. NUMB is initiated to 5000 by the INITIAL statement. If they are not equal, the transaction is directed to the block labeled LOOP. When they are equal, the transaction is directed to the TERMINATE block, which is the statement directly following the TEST E statement, and the simulation ends.

The data collection is done independently by the GENERATE 100, TABULATE, and TERMINATE 0 statements. The GENERATE 100 statement generates a transaction every 100 time units. Whenever a transaction enters the TABULATE blocks, an entry is made in the tables named TAB1 and TAB2. The TERMINATE 0 block absorbs the transaction generated by the GENERATE 100 block. Since a zero (0) follows the TER-MINATE block, this TERMINATE does not affect the START statement. Thus we

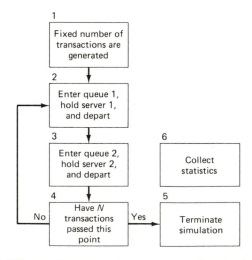

FIGURE 3-19 Transaction Flow for Closed Queuing System

90

FACILITY	AVERAGE UTILIZATION	NUMBER ENTRIES	AVERAGE TIME/TRAN	SEIZING TRANS. NO.	PREEMPTING TRANS. NO.
SERV1	.992	5007	11.073	12	
SERV2	.807	5000	9.020		

FIGURE 3-20 Two Station Closed System Output Report

CONTENTS OF FULLWORD SAVEVALUES (NON-ZERO)

SAVEVALUE NR,	VALUE	NR,	VALUE	NR,	VALUE	NR,	VALUE
NUMB	5000						

FIGURE 3-20 (continued)

QUEUE	MAXIMUM CONTENTS	AVERAGE CONTENTS	TOTAL ENTRIES	ZERO ENTRIES	PERCENT ZEROS	AVERAGE TIME/TRANS	$AVERAGE TIME/TRANS	TABLE NUMBER	CURRENT CONTENTS
LINE1	16	10.981	5015	133	2.6	122.261	125.591		8
LINE2	16	3.217	5006	951	18.9	35.891	44.308		6

$AVERAGE TIME/TRANS = AVERAGE TIME/TRANS EXCLUDING ZERO ENTRIES

FIGURE 3-20 (continued)

91

TABLE TAB1   MEAN ARGUMENT 10.964   STANDARD DEVIATION 3.808   SUM OF ARGUMENTS 6118.000   NON-WEIGHTED
ENTRIES IN TABLE 558

UPPER LIMIT	OBSERVED FREQUENCY	PER CENT OF TOTAL	CUMULATIVE PERCENTAGE	CUMULATIVE REMAINDER	MULTIPLE OF MEAN	DEVIATION FROM MEAN
0	11	1.97	1.9	98.0	-.000	-2.878
1	4	.71	2.6	97.3	.091	-2.616
2	6	1.07	3.7	96.2	.182	-2.353
3	9	1.61	5.3	94.6	.273	-2.091
4	17	3.04	8.4	91.5	.364	-1.828
5	12	2.15	10.5	89.4	.456	-1.565
6	18	3.22	13.7	86.2	.547	-1.303
7	21	3.76	17.5	82.4	.638	-1.040
8	41	7.34	24.9	75.0	.729	-.778
9	23	4.12	29.0	70.9	.820	-.515
10	47	8.42	37.4	62.5	.912	-.253
11	43	7.70	45.1	54.8	1.003	.009
12	60	10.75	55.9	44.0	1.094	.271
13	57	10.21	66.1	33.8	1.185	.534
14	82	14.69	80.8	19.1	1.276	.797
15	107	19.17	100.0	.0	1.368	1.059

REMAINING FREQUENCIES ARE ALL ZERO

FIGURE 3-20 (continued)

TABLE TAB2   MEAN ARGUMENT 3.238   STANDARD DEVIATION 3.656   SUM OF ARGUMENTS 1807.000   NON-WEIGHTED

ENTRIES IN TABLE 558

UPPER LIMIT	OBSERVED FREQUENCY	PER CENT OF TOTAL	CUMULATIVE PERCENTAGE	CUMULATIVE REMAINDER	MULTIPLE OF MEAN	DEVIATION FROM MEAN
0	189	33.87	33.8	66.1	-.000	-.885
1	57	10.21	44.0	55.9	.308	-.612
2	60	10.75	54.8	45.1	.617	-.338
3	43	7.70	62.5	37.4	.926	-.065
4	47	8.42	70.9	29.0	1.235	.208
5	23	4.12	75.0	24.9	1.543	.481
6	41	7.34	82.4	17.5	1.852	.755
7	21	3.76	86.2	13.7	2.161	1.028
8	18	3.22	89.4	10.5	2.470	1.302
9	12	2.15	91.5	8.4	2.779	1.575
10	17	3.04	94.6	5.3	3.087	1.849
11	9	1.61	96.2	3.7	3.396	2.122
12	6	1.07	97.3	2.6	3.705	2.396
13	4	.71	98.0	1.9	4.014	2.669
14	5	.89	98.9	1.0	4.323	2.943
15	6	1.07	100.0	.0	4.631	3.216

REMAINING FREQUENCIES ARE ALL ZERO

FIGURE 3-20 (continued)

93

GENERATE 100 and TERMINATE 0 just to obtain periodic statistics on the concurrent (closed) systems.

The statistics labeled QUEUE and FACILITY are automatically generated by the system (Figure 3-20, page 91). For example, the average content of the first queue, LINE1, is 10.981, and the average content of the second queue, LINE2, is 3.217. The TABLE TAB1 records the statistics associated with the periodic collection (every 100 time units) of the content of the queue, LINE 1. This periodic collection will give a better estimate of the average content of LINE1. The TABLE TAB2 records the statistics associated with the periodic collection (every 100 time units) of the content of the queue, LINE2.

The purpose of these notes is not to be a manual, but to give the novice the feel of GPSS. Therefore, only those instructions which would be of greatest help to a beginning GPSS programmer are discussed in great depth. Other instructions may not be mentioned or mentioned only in passing. There are some outstanding texts written on the subject of GPSS. The novice is encouraged to consult these texts and the appropriate user's manual to gain the knowledge to be an experienced GPSS programmer.

EXERCISES

3-1. Write a GPSS program that modifies Example 3 in the following way: Transactions enter the system in two ways. First, transactions enter the system (to queue 1) with a mean rate L_1. Second, transactions enter the system (to queue 2) with a mean rate L_2. Transactions also enter queue 2 after being served by server 1 (see Figure 3-21). Collect statistics on the average time in both queues as well as the average number in both queues. Do they appear to be related?

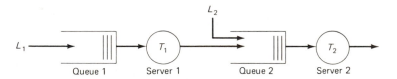

FIGURE 3-21

3-2. Do Exercise 2-3 with respect to GPSS.

3-3. Do Exercise 2-4 with respect to GPSS.

3-4. Modify Example 3-1 with a different service distribution and/or arrival distribution (an example is to change the mean of the exponential distribution) and compare queue length statistics.

3-5. Modify Example 3-2 with a different service distribution and/or arrival distribution (an example is to change the mean of the exponential distribution) and compare queue length statistics.

3-6. Modify Example 3-3 with a different service distribution and/or arrival distribution (an example is to change the mean of the exponential distribution) and compare queue length statistics.

3-7. Modify Example 3-4 with a different service distribution and/or arrival distribution (an example is to change the mean of the exponential distribution) and compare queue length statistics.

REFERENCES

1. GORDON, GEOFFREY, *System Simulation,* 2nd Edition, Prentice Hall, 1978.

2. GREENBERG, STANLEY, *GPSS Primer,* Wiley-Interscience, New York, 1972.

3. *Honeywell Users Manual,* Series 60 (Level 66) General Purpose Simulator System/66 (GPSS/66) Reference Manual.

4. SHRIBER, THOMAS J., *Simulation Using GPSS,* John Wiley Sons, Inc., New York, 1974.

4

ANALYSIS
OF SOME
QUEUING
MODELS

INTRODUCTION

Two major reasons motivate the inclusion of this chapter. First, queuing analysis gives an excellent insight into the basics of model building and points out the constraints and assumptions that make analytical solutions possible. Second, analytical solutions are excellent limited checks of pruned versions of complex simulations. Hence, the queuing systems presented in this chapter are useful in validating (proving correct) a simulation model of a queuing situation.

Queuing analysis is a recent branch of probability theory that studies the characteristics and effects of congestion in *systems* subject to random flows. Examples of systems are banks, airports, or a real-time computer system. Ideally, the behavior of each of these systems could be represented in mathematical terms, the common elements identical, and the appropriate analysis applied to determine the effects of various modes of input. Practically, however, no such extensive analysis can be carried out. This is due to the following: (1) the lack of complete knowledge of the system specifications at the time the analysis is required and (2) the present limitation of the mathematics itself. We will study a few idealized systems that can be solved, and show later how they are useful in estimating the traffic delays and indicating points of congestion within a nonidealized queuing situation. Also, the few idealized queuing systems presented in this chapter will be useful in validating (proving correct) a simulation model of a queuing situation.

POISSON PROCESS

Experiments with systems such as a busy airport, a supermarket, or a message processor indicate that the Poisson probability function may be used with excellent results. For example, let X denote the number of aircraft arrivals at a busy airport during a prescribed interval of time. With a suitable value of m, the mean of the Poisson distribution, X may be assumed to have a Poisson distribution. In all the examples where the random variable X is said to have a Poisson distribution, they are each thought of as a process that generates a number of changes (accidents, arrivals, services, errors, etc.) in a fixed interval (of time or space and so on). If a process leads to a Poisson distribution, the process is called a *Poisson process* (Theorem P). Some of the assumptions that ensure a Poisson process will now be discussed.

Let $p(x, h)$ denote the probability of x changes in an interval of length h. Furthermore, let the symbol $0(h)$ denote any function such that $\text{Lim } h \to 0 \ [0(h)/h] = 0$; for example,

$$h^3 = 0(h), \quad h^2 = 0(h), \quad \text{and} \quad 0(h) + 0(h) = 0(h)$$

The Poisson postulates are the following:

1. $p(1, h) = \lambda h + 0(h)$, where $\lambda > 0$ and $h > 0$.
2. $p(i, h) = 0(h)$, where $i > 1$.
3. The number of changes in nonoverlapping intervals are independent.

Postulates 1 and 3 state that the probability of one change in a short interval h is independent of changes in other nonoverlapping intervals and is approximately proportional to the length of the interval. Postulate 2 states that the probability of two or more changes in the same short interval h is essentially equal to zero. If $x = 0$, then $p(0, 0) = 1$. By postulates 1 and 2, the probability of at least one change in an interval of length h is $\lambda h + 0(h)$. Hence, the probability of zero changes in this interval of length h is $1 - \lambda h - 0(h)$.

Theorem P

$$p(x, \tau) = \frac{(\lambda \tau)^x e^{-\lambda \tau}}{x!}, \qquad x = 0, 1, 2, 3, \ldots$$

where $p(x, \tau) = P[x$ changes in an interval of length $\tau]$

Proof: By property 3, the probability $p(o, w + h) = p(o, w)p(o, h)$ and hence

$$p(o, w + h) = p(o, w) [1 - \lambda h - 0(h)].$$

Then

$$\frac{p(o, w + h) - p(o, w)}{h} = -\lambda p(o, w) - p(o, w)\frac{0(h)}{h}.$$

If we take the limit as $h \to o$, we have

$$\frac{dp(o, w)}{dw} = -\lambda p(o, w).$$

The solution of this differential equation is

$$p(o, w) = ce^{-\lambda w} = e^{-\lambda w}, \qquad w > 0$$

since $p(o, o) = 1$ implies $c = 1$. If x is a positive integer and we take $p(x, 0) = 0$, the postulates imply that

$$p(x, w + h) = P[x \text{ changes in } w, o \text{ changes in } h \text{ or}$$

$$x - 1 \text{ changes in } w, 1 \text{ changes in } h \text{ or}$$

$$x - 2 \text{ changes in } w, 2 \text{ changes in } h \text{ or}$$

$$\text{etc.}]$$

$$= P(x, w) p(o, h) + p(x - 1, w)p(1, h) + 0(h).$$

Accordingly,

$$\frac{p(x, w + h) - p(x, w)}{h} = -\lambda p(x, w) + \lambda p(x - 1, w) + \frac{0(h)}{h}$$

and

$$\frac{dp(x, w)}{dw} = -\lambda p(x, w) + \lambda p(x - 1, w)$$

The solution to this differential equation is

$$p(x, w) = \frac{(\lambda w)^x e^{-\lambda w}}{x!}, \qquad x = 0, 1, \ldots$$

It can be proved by mathematical induction that the preceding solution to these differential equations is unique.

Hence, the number of changes X in an interval of length τ has a Poisson distribution with mean $m = \lambda \tau$. *Random change* is the term used for changes that follow a Poisson distribution. Arrivals and services are examples of random change.

The interarrival time distribution for random arrivals may be easily derived from the Poisson process. Pick an interval of time T starting at an arrival point. Denote the distance to the arrival point by W. Then the interarrival distribution will be expressed as

$$p[W < T] = \text{Prob[interarrival time for a job} < T].$$

If W is less than the interval T, it is implied that there are one or more arrivals during time T. The probability of one or more arrivals during time T is found to be

$$\sum_{k = 1}^{\infty} p(k, T) = 1 - p(0, T) = 1 - e^{-\lambda T}.$$

Since the interval T is arbitrary, the

$$p[W < \tau] = 1 - e^{\lambda \tau}, \qquad \tau > 0.$$

This is commonly referred to as the exponential distribution.

SINGLE-SERVER QUEUE

The first system to be studied will be the classical single-server queue with exponential (random) arrivals and exponential (random) services. This model is very useful in providing a basic understanding of queues. A diagram of a single-server queue is shown in Figure 4-1, where T_s denotes the mean service time and $T_a = 1/\lambda$ denotes the mean interarrival time. Customers (jobs) arrive from an infinite source, so arrivals do not cause a depletion in the source. The server is always busy as long as there is a customer in the queue. Queuing discipline is assumed to be first in, first out (FIFO).

Arrivals are described by the Poisson distribution. If the mean input *rate* is λ jobs per second, then

$$\text{Prob}(k \text{ arrivals in } T \text{ sec}) = p(k, T) = \frac{e^{-\lambda T}(\lambda T)^k}{k!}, \qquad k = 0, 1, 2, \ldots$$

The parameter λ is often referred to as the *throughput* of the system, since it is also the

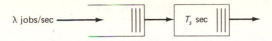

FIGURE 4-1 Single-Server Queue

rate of departure from the server. As in the equation found in the previous section,

$$\text{Prob(interarrival time for a job} < \tau) = 1 - e^{-\lambda \tau}.$$

Hence, interarrival time follows an exponential distribution.

The term random service implies that the length of time required to service a job follows the exponential distribution

$$\text{Prob(service time} < \tau) = 1 - e^{-\tau/T_s},$$

where T_s denotes the mean service time.

With the previous assumptions, the following theorems may be proved concerning the single-server queuing model. The theorems are presented since mathematical models that can be analyzed are excellent limited checks of pruned versions of complex simulations.

Theorem 1: Let $P_N(\tau)$ denote the probability of there being N units in the system at time τ. Assume $P_N(\tau)$ does not depend upon τ and $\rho = \lambda T_s < 1$; then

$$P_N(\tau) = P_N = (1 - \rho)\rho^N, N = 0, 1, 2, \ldots.$$

Proof: The proof is contained in Appendix A.

The parameter ρ is sometimes referred to as the traffic intensity. If $\rho < 1$, then, on the average, the server is able to deal with more than one job requirement (on the average) before the next job arrives. Therefore, we expect the server to cope with his task. Note that, in general, ρ is the expected fraction of the system's capacity (servers) that is in use. In Theorem 1, we were interested when $P_N(\tau) = P_n$. This is called the stationary (equilibrium) distribution.

Theorem 2: Given that the steady-state probability $P_N = (1 - \rho)\rho^N$ has been reached, the expected number of units in the system is $E(N) = \rho/(1 - \rho)$.

The rest of the theorems in this section assume that the steady state probability $P_N = (1 - \rho)\rho^N$ has been reached.

Theorem 3: Let Q_M denote the probability of exactly M units in the queue (waiting line); then

$$Q_M = (1 - \rho)(1 + \rho), \quad \text{if } M = 0,$$

$$= (1 - \rho)\rho^{M + 1}, \quad \text{if } M \geq 1.$$

Theorem 4: The expected queue length, $E(M) = \rho^2/(1 - \rho)$.

101

Theorem 5: Let Q_M ($M > 0$) denote the probability of exactly M units in the queue relative to the hypothesis (given) that the queue is nonempty; then

$$Q_M (M > 0) = (1 - \rho)\rho^{M-1}, \qquad M = 1, 2, 3, \ldots .$$

Theorem 6: The expected length of a nonempty queue is $1/(1 - \rho)$.

Theorem 7: Let W denote the time a unit has to wait before being taken into service. Then

$$P[W < \tau] = F_w(\tau) = 1 - \rho \exp\left[\frac{-1}{T_s}(1 - \rho)\tau\right], \qquad \text{if } \tau > 0$$

$$= 1 - \rho, \qquad \text{if } \tau = 0$$

$$= 0, \qquad \text{if } \tau < 0.$$

Note that $P(W \leq 0) = 1 - \rho$, and so we have a positive probability of no waiting time. In fact, $P(W \leq 0) = 1 - \rho = P_0 = $ probability of no units being in the system. This is sometimes called a mixed distribution function (continuous and discrete parts).

Theorem 8: The expected waiting time of a unit is $\rho T_s/(1 - \rho)$.

Theorem 9: The probability density function of waiting times, given that waiting time is greater than zero, is

$$\frac{1 - \rho}{T_s} \exp\left[\frac{-1}{T_s}(1 - \rho)\tau\right]$$

for $\tau > 0$ and zero elsewhere.

Theorem 10: The expected waiting time of a unit, given that waiting time is greater than zero, is $T_s/(1 - \rho)$.

Theorem 11: Let T denote the total time spent in the system. The probability density function of T is given by

$$\frac{1 - \rho}{T_s} \exp\left[\frac{-1}{T_s}(1 - \rho)\tau\right]$$

for $\tau > 0$ and zero elsewhere.

Theorem 12: The expected total time spent in the system is $T_s/(1 - \rho)$.

GENERAL SINGLE-STATION QUEUING PROBLEM

To generalize the results just stated, we will restate and expand the postulates used for the Poisson process. Let X_τ denote the number of units in the queuing system at time τ.

The new postulates are the following:

(a) $P[X_{\tau + h} = n + 1 \mid X_\tau = n] = \lambda_n h + 0_1(h),$

(b) $P[X_{\tau + h} = n - 1 \mid X_\tau = n] = \mu_n h + 0_2(h),$

(c) $P[X_{\tau + h} = n \pm i \mid X_\tau = n] = 0_3(h), \qquad i > 1.$

Postulate (a) states that the probability of one arrival (change) in a short interval h is a function of the number of units in the system at time τ and the interval h. Postulate (b) states that the probability of one service (change) in a short interval h is a function of the number of units in the system at time τ and the interval h. The parameter λ_n denotes the mean arrival rate as a function of n; for example, $\lambda_n = n\lambda$. The parameter μ_n denotes the mean service rate as a function of n; for example, $\mu_n = n\mu$. Postulate (c) states that the probability of more than one change in a short interval h is essentially equal to zero.

With these postulates, the following theorems may be proved. Let $P_N(\tau)$ denote the probability of exactly N units in the system at time τ. In the following, assume $P_N(\tau)$ does *not* depend upon τ; that is, $P_N(\tau) = P_N$. Recall we are still under the assumptions of random arrivals and random servers.

Theorem 13: If $\lambda_n = \lambda$ and $\mu_n = \mu$, then

$$P_n = (1 - \rho)\rho^n,$$

where $\rho = \lambda/\mu < 1$.

Note that this is just a restatement of Theorem 1.

Theorem 14: If $\lambda_n = \lambda/(n + 1)$ and $\mu_n = \mu$, then

$$P_n = \frac{(\lambda/\mu)^n e^{-\lambda/\mu}}{n!}, \qquad n = 0, 1, 2, \ldots ,$$

where $e^{\lambda/\mu} < \infty$.

Theorem 14 is called a *queue with discouragement;* that is, the sight of a long queue discourages fresh customers.

Theorem 15: If $\lambda_n = \lambda$ and $\mu_n = n\mu$, then

$$P_n = \frac{(\lambda/\mu)^n e^{-\lambda/\mu}}{n!}, n = 0, 1, 2, \ldots ,$$

where $e^{\lambda/\mu} < \infty$.

Theorem 15 is called a *queue with ample servers,* since the service rate increases linearly as the number of units in the system increase. Note also that a waiting line cannot exist.

Theorem 16:   If

$$\lambda_n = \lambda \text{ and } \mu_n = n\mu,\ 0 < n < s$$

$$= s\mu,\ n \geqslant s,$$

Then

$$P_n = P_0 \frac{(\lambda/\mu)^n}{n!}, \qquad n < s$$

$$= P_0 \frac{(\lambda/\mu)^n}{s!\ s^{n-s}},\ n \geqslant s,$$

where $\lambda/\mu < S$ and

$$P_0 = \left[\sum_{k=0}^{s-1} \frac{(\lambda/\mu)^k}{k!} + \frac{(\lambda/\mu)^s}{s!(1 - \frac{\lambda}{\mu s})} \right]^{-1}$$

Theorem 16 is an example of a queue with $S = s$ servers. It can also be used like Theorem 15, except we are imposing an upper limit S on the number of servers that can be made available. A waiting line can exist only when $n > S$ and there are $n - S$ units in the waiting line. A diagram of a multiserver queue is shown in Figure 4-2, where $T_s = 1/\mu$ denotes mean service times.

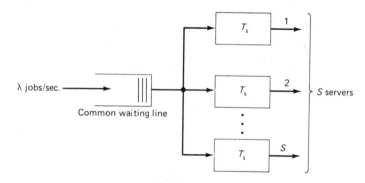

FIGURE 4-2

Theorem 17:   If

$$\lambda_n = \lambda, \qquad n < R$$

$$= 0, \qquad n \geqslant R$$

$$\mu_n = \mu, \qquad n = 1, 2, \ldots,$$

then

$$P_n = \frac{(\lambda/\mu)^n \, [1 \, - \, (\lambda/\mu)]}{[1 \, - \, (\lambda/\mu)^{R \, + \, 1}]}, \qquad n \leqslant R$$

Theorem 17 is an example of a *queue with limited waiting room*. This implies that customers who arrive and find no waiting room leave without service and do not return later. The maximum capacity of the waiting line is $R \, - \, 1$ units.

Theorem 18: If

$$\lambda_n = \lambda, \qquad n < k$$

$$= 0, \qquad n \geqslant k$$

$$\mu_n = n\mu, \qquad n \leqslant k,$$

then

$$P_n = \frac{(1/n!) \, (\lambda/\mu)^n}{\displaystyle\sum_{j \, = \, 0}^{k} \frac{(\lambda/\mu)^j}{j!}} \qquad n \leqslant k$$

Theorem 18 is an example of a *call on a telephone exchange with k lines*. We have only k servers and waiting room for only k customers. P_k is the proportion of time for which the system is fully occupied (called Erlang's loss formula).

Theorem 19: If

$$\lambda_n = (k \, - \, n)\lambda, \qquad n \leqslant k$$

$$= 0, \qquad n > k$$

$$\mu_n = \mu, \qquad n = 1, 2, \ldots,$$

then

$$P_n = P_0 k(k \, - \, 1) \ldots (k \, - \, n \, + \, 1)(\lambda/\mu)^n, \qquad n = 1, 2, \ldots, k,$$

where

$$P_0 = [1 \, + \, k(\lambda/\mu) \, + \, k(k \, - \, 1)(\lambda/\mu)^2 \, + \, \cdots \, + \, k!(\lambda/\mu)^k]^{-1}.$$

Theorem 19 is an example of *machine minding*. We have the situation of k machines under the core of a single operator. Now no time is lost in the single operator's moving from the location of one machine to that of another, and the worker keeps working whenever there is a machine stopped. This setup can be thought of as a queue in which stopped machines represent customers awaiting service. Furthermore, the longer the "queue," the slower the arrival of fresh "customers." A diagram of machine minding is shown in Figure 4-3, where $T_a \, = \, 1/\lambda$ and $T_s \, = \, 1/\mu$.

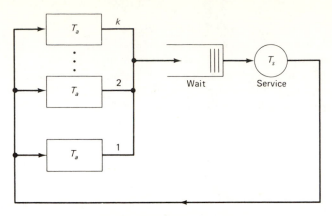

FIGURE 4-3 Machine Minding

In Theorems 13 through 19, we have determined P_n, the probability of exactly n units in the system at time t (steady-state probability). From P_n we could determine the expected number in the system L_q by the formula

$$L_q = \sum_{n=0}^{\infty} nP_n.$$

Now the mean values for number of customers and delays in the system are related by the following simple relations:

$$\alpha T_q = L_q$$

$$\alpha T_w = L_w$$

$$\alpha T_s = L_s$$

where α denotes the average rate of arrival, T_q denotes the expected time in the system, T_w denotes the expected time in the queue, T_w denotes the expected number in the queue, T_s denotes average service time, and L_s denotes the expected number in the service facility and may be dependent on the state of the system. This result is known as Little's theorem. Note that it is always true that

$$L_q = L_w + L_s \quad \text{and} \quad T_q = T_w + T_s.$$

The term "traffic intensity" of a queueing discipline is generally taken to describe the ratio of the steady-state average of service demanded by the job stream to the steady-state average capacity of the system and is denoted by the symbol ρ. This ratio is also often termed the *utilization coefficient* of the system.

As noted previously, α represents the arrival rate when the system is in equilibrium. Since the system is in equilibrium, the average rate of arrival is equal to average rate of departure (throughput). Mathematically, this is represented as

$$\alpha = \sum_{n=0}^{\infty} \lambda_n P_n = \sum_{n=1}^{\infty} \mu_n P_n.$$

Thus with L_q, α, and Little's theorem, one can derive the remaining expected values. In the single-server case (Theorem 13), $L_s = \rho$, since $\alpha = \lambda$ and $T_s = 1/\mu$. In the multiple-server case (Theorem 16), $L_s = m\rho_2 = \lambda/\mu$, since $\alpha = \lambda$ and $T_s = 1/\mu$.

The traffic intensity is related to the probability P_0 that the server is idle. In the case when demand for service by each customer depends on the number of customers in service, it can be shown that $\rho = 1 - P_0 =$ probability that the server is busy and $\rho = L_s$. If we know α, then by Little's formula the average time statistics (T) can be derived.

In the single-server system, this parameter was expressed (Theorem 13) as

$$\rho_1 = \lambda T_s = \frac{\lambda}{\mu}.$$

Since the capacity of the system is one unit time of processing per unit of elapsed time, and since on the average λ jobs arrive per unit time, demanding T_s units of service per job, this quantity is seen to indeed represent the previously defined *traffic intensity*.

In the case of multiple servers (m servers), the capacity of the system is m units of processing per unit of elapsed time, so the formula becomes

$$\rho_1 = \frac{\lambda T_s}{m} = \frac{\lambda}{m\mu}.$$

In the case of an infinite number of servers, the capacity is infinite, and the concept of traffic intensity ceases to bear a valid meaning. Nevertheless, tradition often confusingly provides a formula $\lambda T_s = \lambda/\mu$ in this case also. The significance of this parameter is not the traffic intensity, but rather simply the average service demand per unit time, and it is therefore a formula for the mean number of servers utilized.

In other queueing situations (Theorems 14 and 17 through 19), the demand for service by each customer depends on the number of customers in service. The traffic intensity is generally more difficult to evaluate. Since it is a ratio of steady-state expectation, it is nevertheless always well defined.

The traffic intensity is naturally related to the mean number in the service facility (L_s) by Little's formula,

$$L_s = \alpha T_s.$$

Example:

From Theorem 4, we determined that

$$L_w = \frac{\rho^2}{1 - \rho},$$

where $\rho = \lambda/\mu = \lambda T_s$. Now $L_s = \rho$, and hence

$$L_q = \frac{\rho^2}{1 - \rho} + \rho = \frac{\rho}{1 - \rho}.$$

Thus, using Little's theorem, we have proved Theorem 2. Also from Little's theorem

$$T_q = \frac{L_q}{\lambda} = \frac{T_s}{1 - \rho} \qquad \text{(Theorem 12)},$$

$$T_w = \frac{L_w}{\lambda} = \frac{\rho T_s}{1 - \rho} \qquad \text{(Theorem 8)}.$$

Example:

From Theorem 14, we can determine that $L_q = \lambda/\mu$ (the mean of a Poisson distribution). Since the maximum service rate is dependent on the state of the system, $\rho = 1 - P_0 = 1 - e^{-\lambda/\mu} = L_s$. Therefore,

$$L_w = L_q - \rho = \frac{\lambda}{\mu} - (1 - e^{-\lambda/\mu}), \qquad \alpha = \mu\rho.$$

Also from Little's theorem,

$$T_q = \frac{L_q}{\alpha}, \qquad T_s = \frac{L_s}{\alpha}, \quad \text{and} \quad T_w = \frac{L_w}{\alpha}.$$

Example:

From Theorem 19, we can prove $\alpha = (k - L_q)\lambda$. Hence from Little's theorem and the probability distribution, P_n, we can determine L_q, L_w, T_q, and T_w.

Two other statistics of interest are the expected length of a nonempty queue and the expected waiting time of a unit given that waiting time is greater than zero.

The expected waiting time of a unit given that waiting time is greater than zero, denoted by $T_w(>0)$, is given by

$$T_w(>0) = \frac{T_w}{P[w > 0]}.$$

The proof of this result is from the definition of conditional probability. $P[w > 0]$ denotes the probability that waiting time is greater than zero.

The expected length of a nonempty queue, denoted by $L_w(>0)$ is given by

$$L_w(>0) = \frac{L_w}{1 - Q_0},$$

where Q_0 is the probability of exactly zero units in the queue (waiting line). Note that $Q_0 = (P_0 + P_1 + \ldots + P_s)$, where s is the maximum number of servers available.

Example:

From Theorem 4, we determined that $L_w = \rho^2/(1 - \rho)$, where $\rho = \lambda T_s = \lambda/\mu$. From Theorem 8, $T_w = \dfrac{\rho T_s}{1 - \rho}$.

Hence,

$$T_w\,(>0) = \frac{\dfrac{\rho T_s}{1 - \rho}}{1 - (1 - \rho)} = \frac{T_s}{1 - \rho}$$

and

$$L_w\,(>0) = \frac{L_w}{1 - [P_0 + P_1]} = \frac{\dfrac{\rho^2}{1 - \rho}}{1 - [(1 - \rho) + (1 - \rho)\rho]}$$

$$= \frac{1}{1 - \rho}$$

MORE ABOUT SINGLE-SERVER QUEUES

Again, let us concern ourselves with $P_n(\tau)$, the probability of exactly n units in the system at time τ. In the following discussion, we concern ourselves with the time τ. If we assume the postulates (a), (b), and (c) and add the following four mutually exclusive events,

1. n units in the system at time τ, no units arrive during h, no units are served during h,
2. $n - 1$ units in the system at time τ, one unit arrives during h, no units are serviced during h,
3. $n + 1$ units in the system at time τ, no units arrive during h, 1 unit is serviced during h,
4. during h, two or more actions occur,

then we obtain an expression for the $P_n(\tau + h)$. That is, $P_n(\tau + h)$ is the probability of 1 plus the probability of 2, plus the probability of 3, plus the probability of 4. By evaluating

$$\lim_{h \to 0} \frac{P_n(\tau + h) - P(\tau)}{h} = \frac{dP_n(\tau)}{d\tau} = P'_n(\tau),$$

109

we obtain

$$P_n'(\tau) = -(\lambda_n + \mu_n)P_n(\tau) + \lambda_{n-1}P_{n-1}(\tau) + \mu_{n+1}P_{n+1}(\tau)$$

$$P_0'(\tau) = -\lambda_0 P_0(\tau) + \mu_1 P_1(\tau),$$

where

$$P_0(0) = 1 \quad \text{and} \quad P_i(0) = 0, \qquad i \geqslant 1.$$

As an example, consider the situation where $\lambda_n = \lambda$ and $\mu_n = n\mu$, that is, a queue with ample servers [Theorem 15 except $P_n(\tau)$ depends on τ]. After substituting $\lambda_n = \lambda$ and $\mu_n = n\mu$,

$$\frac{dP_n(\tau)}{d\tau} = (\lambda + n\mu)\,P_n(\tau) + \lambda P_{n-1}(\tau) + (n+1)\mu P_{n+1}(\tau), \qquad n > 0 \ (4-1)$$

$$\frac{dP_0(\tau)}{d\tau} = -\lambda P_0(\tau) + \mu P_i(\tau),$$

where

$$P_0(0) = 1 \quad \text{and} \quad P_i(0) = 0, \qquad i \geqslant 1.$$

The solution to this differential equation is

$$P_n(\tau) = \frac{\exp[-\lambda/\mu(1 - e^{-\mu r})]\left[(\lambda/\mu)\,(1 - e^{-\mu r})\right]^n}{n!}, \; n \geqslant 0,$$

when

$$P_0(0) = 1 \quad \text{and} \quad P_i(0) = 0, \qquad i \geqslant 1.$$

Given the preceding equation for $P_n(\tau)$, one can obtain P_n by the following theorem [2]:

> **Theorem 20:** The limits $\underset{\tau \to \infty}{\text{Lim}} P_n(\tau) = P_n$ exist and are independent of the initial conditions $P_0(0) = 1$ and $P_i(0) = 0$, $i \geqslant 1$; they satisfy the system of linear equations obtained from equation (4-1) on putting $P_n'(\tau) = 0$.

As an example of Theorem 20, one can derive Theorem 15 by solving the following equations with $P_n(\tau) = P_n$:

$$0 = \frac{dP_n(\tau)}{d\tau} = -(\lambda + n\mu)\,P_n + \lambda P_{n-1} + (n+1)\mu P_{n+1}$$

$$0 = \frac{dP_0(\tau)}{d\tau} = -\lambda P_0 + \mu P_1$$

and obtain by induction

$$P_n = \frac{(\lambda/\mu)^n e^{-\lambda/\mu}}{n!}$$

In this particular example, this could have been shown directly by

$$\lim_{\tau \to \infty} P_n(\tau) = \frac{\exp[-(\lambda/\mu)] \, (\lambda/\mu)^n}{n!} = P_n$$

Therefore, for a sufficiently long period, the probability of exactly n customers is Poisson distributed with mean λ/μ.

NETWORK OF QUEUES

Often a system designer is faced with the problem of analyzing several interconnected queues. If we denote these queues by nodes connected by lines indicating traffic flow, a typical system may be represented by a network as in Figure 4-4. The first is the partioning and merging of traffic; the second is the use of tandem (in series) queues. In the special case of Poisson traffic flow and exponential service, an exact solution is available for the general solution of the queuing problem containing these elements. This special solution is useful in estimating the traffic delays and indicating points of congestion within a non-Poisson, nonexponential queuing network. It is also useful in validating (proving correct) a simulation model of a queuing situation.

We shall refer to an *exponential service node* containing two descriptive numbers: N, the number of servers, and T_s, the mean service time for each server. Also, this exponential service node satisfies Theorem 16. The following theorem is credited to J. R. Jackson [6].

JACKSON'S THEOREM

If:

a. The queuing network contains m exponential service nodes. The kth node ($k = 1, 2, \ldots, m$) consists of N_k servers, each with a mean service time T_{sk}.

b. Customers from outside the system arrive at node k in a Poisson stream at mean rate λ_k (customers also arrive at node k from other nodes inside the network).

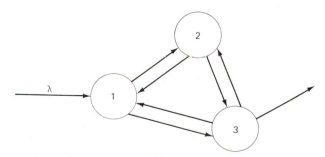

FIGURE 4-4   Network of Three Queues

c. Once served at node k, a customer goes (instantaneously) either to node j ($j = 1, 2, \ldots, m$) with probability P_{kj} or out of the system, completing his service with probability $1 - \sum\limits_{j=1}^{m} P_{kj}$.

Let Λ_k be the total arriving traffic rate to node k, both from inside and outside the system. Adding up the sources, we must have in the steady state

$$\Lambda_k = \lambda_k + \sum_{j=1}^{m} P_{jk}\Lambda_j$$

where $k = 1, 2, \ldots, m$.

To appreciate Jackson's Theorem, consider the following example.

Example:

Consider a feedback queue where a fraction p of the traffic from a single exponential server ($N_1 = 1$) is fed back into the input (see Figure 4-5). New traffic arrives at the queue with mean rate λ. The system throughput Λ is given by

$$\Lambda_1 = \lambda + p\Lambda_1.$$

Therefore,
$$\Lambda_1 = \frac{\lambda}{1 - p}.$$

Let
$$T_a = 1/\Lambda, \text{ and}$$

$$\rho = \frac{T_s}{T_a} = \Lambda_1, \qquad T_s = \frac{\lambda T_s}{1 - p}.$$

where ρ denotes the server utilization. From Theorem 12, the expected total time spent in the system for one pass is

$$\frac{T_s}{1 - \rho} = \frac{(1 - p)T_s}{1 - p - \lambda T_s}$$

Now a single server may cycle several times before leaving the system. The expected (mean) number of passes through the server is

$$N = 1 \cdot (1 - p) + 2 \cdot (1 - p) \cdot p + 3(1 - p)p^2 + \cdots$$

$$= (1 - p) \sum_{n=1}^{\infty} n\, p^{n-1} = \frac{1}{1 - p}.$$

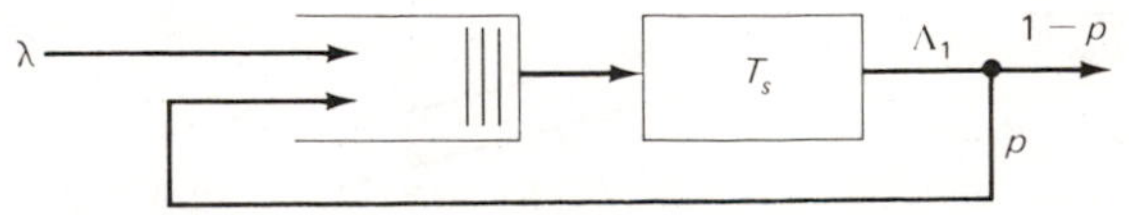

FIGURE 4-5

Now the number of cycles is independent of the time in the system; the total expected time in the system is

$$N \cdot \frac{T_s}{1 - \rho} = \frac{T_s}{1 - p - \lambda T_s}.$$

To determine the total expected time in the system for a more complex network, we will introduce the concept of a routing-generation process [6]. The routing-generating process is specified by a set of parameters

$$R = \{p_{j,k} \mid j \in [o, m]; k \in [1, m + 1]\}.$$

The probability is $p_{0,k}$ that node k will be first on a routing and $p_{j, m + 1}$ that, if node j is on a routing, then this node is the last one. The probability is $p_{0, m + 1}$ that the routing will be empty. The product

$$p_{o,n_1} p_{n_1,n_2} \cdots p_{n_{i-1},n_i} \, p_{n_i,m+1}$$

is the probability of the routing $(n_1, n_2, \ldots, n_i)$. For each $j \in [o, m]$, the set $\{p_{jk} \mid k \in [1, m + 1]\}$ is a probability distribution; that is,

$$\sum_{k=1}^{m+1} p_{jk} = 1 \quad \text{and} \quad p_{jk} \geqslant 0.$$

Let $e(n)$ denote the expected (mean) number of passes through the nth server. By the law of total probability,

$$e(j) = p_{o, j} + \sum_{k=1}^{m} e(k) p_{k,j}.$$

We assume that the preceding set of equations has a unique solution, $\{e(j) \mid j \in [1, m]\}$ and $e(j) \geqslant 0$. This is the same as the assumption that every routing is of finite length (with probability 1). Now the number of cycles is independent of the time in the system; hence the expected total time in the system is

$$\sum_{n=1}^{m} e(n) T_{qn}$$

where T_{qn} is expected total time in the nth node.

Similarly, the expected total number in the system is

$$\sum_{n=1}^{m} e(n) L_{qn}$$

where L_{qn} is the expected total number in the nth node.

Example:

Figure 4-6 is a double feedback queue where a fraction p_1 of the traffic from a single exponential server ($N_1 = 1$) is fed back into the input, and a fraction p_2 of the traffic is

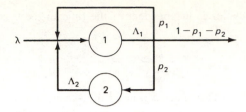

FIGURE 4-6

fed into a second node with a single exponential server ($N_2 = 1$). The output of node 2 is fed back into the input of node 1.

The system throughout (Λ_k, $k = 1, 2$) is given by

$$\Lambda_1 = \lambda + p_1\Lambda_1 + \Lambda_2,$$

$$\Lambda_2 = p_2\Lambda_1.$$

Therefore,

$$\Lambda_1 = \frac{\lambda}{(1 - p_1 - p_2)},$$

$$\Lambda_2 = \frac{p_2\lambda}{(1 - p_1 - p_2)}.$$

Recall that

$$T_{ai} = \frac{1}{\Lambda_i} \quad \text{and} \quad \rho_i = \frac{T_{s_i}}{T_{a_i}} = \Lambda_i T_{s_i}.$$

From Theorem 12, the expected total time spent in the ith node ($i = 1, 2$) for one pass is

$$T_{q1} = \frac{T_{s_1}}{1 - \rho_1} = \frac{T_{s_1}}{1 - \Lambda_1 T_{s_1}} = \frac{(1 - p_1 - p_2)T_{s_1}}{(1 - p_1 - p_2) - \lambda T_{s_1}}$$

$$T_{q2} = \frac{T_{s_2}}{1 - \rho_2} = \frac{T_{s_2}}{1 - \Lambda_2 T_{s_2}} = \frac{(1 - p_1 - p_2)T_{s_2}}{(1 - p_1 - p_2) - \lambda p_2 T_{s_2}},$$

where T_{s_i} denotes the expected service time for node i. The expected number of passes through each node is

$$e(1) = 1 + e(1)p_1 + e(2) \cdot 1,$$

$$e(2) = 0 + e(1)p_2 + e(2) \cdot 0.$$

Therefore,

$$e(1) = \frac{1}{(1 - p_1 - p_2)},$$

114

$$e(2) = \frac{p_2}{(1 - p_1 - p_2)}.$$

Now the number of cycles is independent of the time in the system; the total expected time in the system, T_s, is

$$T_s = e(1)T_{q1} + e(2)T_{q2}$$

$$= \frac{T_{s_1}}{(1 - p_1 - p_2) - \lambda T_{s_i}} + \frac{p_2 T_{s_2}}{(1 - p_1 - p_2) - \lambda T_{s_2}}$$

EXERCISES

4-1. Given Theorem 1, determine the probability of exactly m units in the queue and the expected queue length.

4-2. Given Theorem 17, determine the expected number of units in the system, the expected number of units in the queue, and the expected number of units in a nonempty queue.

4-3. Given Theorem 14, prove that the expected queue length is $\lambda/\mu - (1 - P_0)$.

4-4. Prove Theorem 17. (*Hint:* Use the definition of conditional probability.)

4-5. Given Theorem 7, prove that $T_w = \rho T_s/(1 - \rho)$ and the variance of waiting time $= (2 - \rho)T_s^2/(1 - \rho)^2$.

4-6. Given Theorem 16, determine L_w and, hence, L_q.

4-7. Prove Theorem 18.

4-8. Given Theorem 19, prove that $P(W > 0) = 1 - (P_0 + P_k)$, where W denotes waiting time.

4-9. Consider the network of queues in Figure 4-7. Assume that the queuing network contains exponential service nodes. The kth node ($k = 1, 3$) consists of N_k servers, each with a mean service time of $T_{sk} = 1/\mu_k$. Mean arrival rate, λ, is exponential. Assume that the mean queuing time for one pass through each node is known and

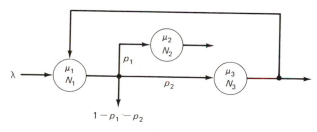

FIGURE 4-7

is equal to T_{qk} ($k = 1, 3$). Determine the average total time spent in the system by a customer.

4-10. Consider the network of queues in Figure 4-8.

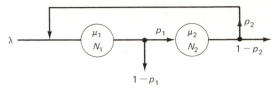

FIGURE 4-8

(a) Assume that the queuing network contains exponential service nodes. The kth node ($k = 1, 2$) consists of N_k servers, each with a mean service time of $T_{sk} = 1/\mu_k$. Mean arrival rate, λ, is exponential. Determine the average time spent in the system by a customer.
(b) If in one system $N_1 = 1$ and in the other system $N_1 = 10$, what is the effect on the average total time spent in the two systems? Discuss in what situations the average total time spent in the two systems would be equal.
(c) Discuss why this is probably not a good model of a "real" system. (Detail each reason given.)
(d) Discuss the preceding system and solution if each queue has a maximum queue length and rejects arrivals when that maximum number are present in the queue.

4-11. The queuing system of Figure 4-9 with four stations (each has one queue and one server) in series operates with the following characteristics: (a) Poisson arrivals, $\lambda = 0.04$; (b) $\mu_1 = 0.05$, $\mu_2 = 0.06$, $\mu_3 = 0.05$, $\mu_4 = 0.07$ (all distributions are exponential); (c) only 50% of the units enter facility 2. The other units go either to facility 3 or 4 with equal probability. Solve the system analytically. What would happen if only 20% of the units enter facility 2 and the others go with equal probability to facilities 3 and 4? Discuss the solution to this problem if each queue has a maximum queue length and rejects arrivals when that maximum number are present in the queue.

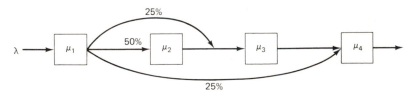

FIGURE 4-9

REFERENCES

1. COX, D. R., and SMITH, W. L., *Queues,* John Wiley & Sons, Inc., New York, 1961.

2. FELLER, W., *An Introduction to Probability Theory and Its Application,* 2nd ed., John Wiley & Sons, Inc., New York, 1961.

3. IBM Corp., *Analysis of Some Queueing in Real-Time Systems,* No. GF20-0007-1, IBM Corp., Data Processing Division, White Plains, N.Y.

4. KLEINROCK, L., *Queueing Systems, Vol. II: Computer Applications,* John Wiley & Sons, Inc., New York, 1976.

5. TAKACS, L., *Introduction to the Theory of Queues,* Oxford University Press, New York, 1962.

6. JACKSON, J. R., "Networks of Waiting Line," *Operations Research,* Vol. 5, 1957.

5

SIMULATION EXPERIMENTATION AND VERIFICATION

Chapter 1 outlined briefly the task of deriving a model of a system. The first task is that of establishing the model structure and the second is that of supplying the data. To present this subject in a unified manner, an example will be presented. The example is intended to illustrate how to design a simple simulation study. The model of interest will be of a simple feedback queue involving one queue, one server, and one feedback path into the queue (Figures 5-1 and 5-2). The remainder of the chapter deals with simulation and model verification. After the model is introduced, the important topic of model verification and validation is introduced. The last section is a statistical analysis of the simple feedback model.

Simulation will replace a system to be studied by some other representation called a model. Since digital computers are used for simulation, the model (simulation model) will take the form of a set of numbers that essentially count the entities and indicate their status.

Example

A simulation of the simple feedback queue is driven primarily by the execution of two classes of events: arrivals and departures. The primary entity of concern is a job (customer). The arrival event simulates the initial arrival of a job into the system. The departure event controls the departure of a job from the facility and its possible subsequent arrival back into the system.

Conceptually, the simulation program flow is partitioned into four tasks:

1. *Initiation* of the simulation is performed in the routine MAIN. MAIN reads the simulation parameters for a given run and initializes storage accordingly. The *first* ARRIVAL is also scheduled in MAIN. The program flow is illustrated in Figure 5-3.

2. *Arrivals.* An arrival creates new jobs and inputs them into the queue of the server. It not only schedules both the departure of the job from the server, but also reschedules another arrival. The program flow in the event ARRIVAL is shown in Figure 5-4.

3. *Departures.* The departure event from the server performs several tasks. It removes a job from the server and attempts to reinput it to the server (or destroys it if it is to leave the system). If the server is not busy, the DEPARTURE places the job in the server and schedules DEPARTURE. The departure event also

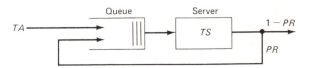

FIGURE 5-1 Simple Feedback Queue

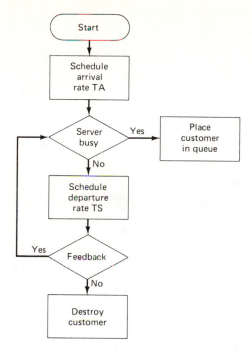

FIGURE 5-2　Flowchart of Simple Feedback Queue

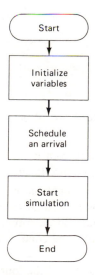

FIGURE 5-3　Main

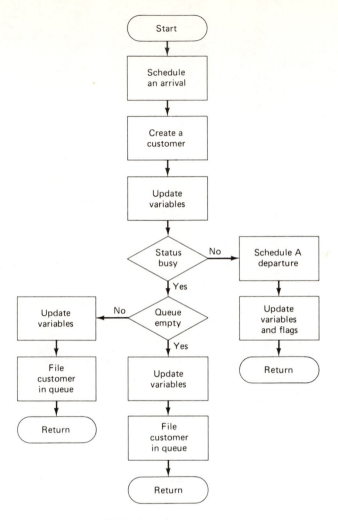

FIGURE 5-4 Event Arrival

removes the next job (if any) from its own queue, places it in the server, and schedules its departure. Figure 5-5 illustrates the control flow in DEPARTURE.

4. *Statistical collection and evaluation.* This consists of the routine STOP.SIMULATION (plus logic in ARRIVAL and DEPARTURE) that accumulates the desired statistics and determines when the simulation is to be terminated. Figure 5-6 illustrates the control flow in STOP.SIMULATION.

Figure 5-7 illustrates the interaction of the four classes of events in the simulation. Most of the events and entities possess attributes which either are necessary for program

122

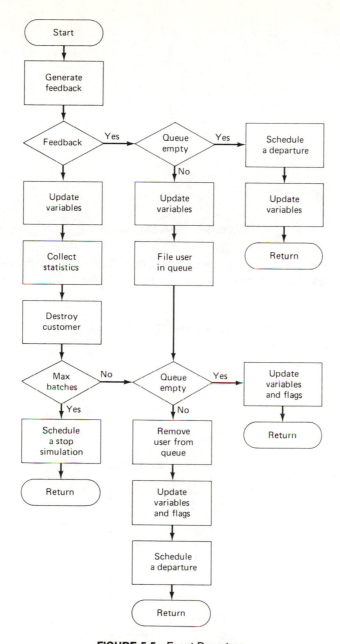

FIGURE 5-5 Event Departure

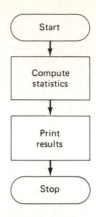

FIGURE 5-6 Event Stop.Simulation

execution or are designed to aid statistical collection. Table 5-1 lists the more important of these attributes. The activities in the simulation model are relatively few and straight-forward. These are

1. Entering the system (i.e., arriving)
2. Leaving the system
3. Waiting for service
4. Receiving service

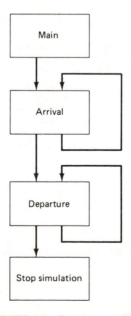

FIGURE 5-7 Event Interaction

124

TABLE 5-1

Entity	Attributes
Server	Mean service time, status numerous statistical attributes
Queue	Length
Customer	Time of arrival, waiting time, number times through the system

The model structure has been established. The system boundary has been determined and the entities, attributes, and activities of the system have been identified. The next task of deriving a model of a system is that of supplying the data. The data provide the values the attributes can have and define the relationships involved in the activities. Part of the data have already been supplied, since Figure 5-7 illustrates the interaction of the four classes of events in the simulation.

From Figure 5-1 we see that the three pieces of data that must be supplied a priori to the simulation are (1) the interarrival time of jobs, (2) the service time of jobs, and (3) the probability of a feedback for any given job. Typically, these attributes are supplied by observing a real system in operation and using that data to parameterize the simulation.

SIMULATION AND MODEL VERIFICATION

veracity of the model

After discussing a simulation model, we must address the question of simulation validation. The literature pertaining to problems of simulation model validation is diverse and full of debate.

The precise definition of a simulation model's veracity is elusive, but may be described as those parts of the simulation process that increase the user's confidence that his model provides (1) a good representation of the real-world system he wishes to simulate, and (2) provides an acceptable level of detail. The precise procedure for demonstrating a model's veracity is just as elusive as its definition. It is impossible to prove that a simulation model is a correct or true model of the real system. Fortunately, we are not concerned with proving truth, but rather to validate the insights gained (or the insights to be gained) through the entire modeling process. Thus, it is the operational utility of the model and not the proven truth of its structure that primarily concerns us.

In many cases the discussions of simulation model validation in the literature have lost sight of this important aspect. What is the purpose of the simulation model and why was it created? This is well stated by Forrester as follows:

The validity (or significance) of a model should be judged by its suitability for a particular purpose. A model is sound and dependable if it accomplishes what is expected of it. This means that validity, as an abstract concept divorced from purpose, has no useful meaning. What may be an excellent model for one purpose may be misleading and worse than useless for another purpose.[1]

The next section presents the various measures that need to be taken to validate the simulation model.

validation guidelines and tests

Influence of Validation Concerns upon the Design.

The experience of modelers has been that the most useful and valid models are those that most closely emulate the interactions and the cause-and-effect relationships of the real system. Although it may be difficult to find the exact mechanisms that control a system, a simulation that is based upon underlying logical relationships will usually be better than one based upon aggregate statistical or empirical descriptions or extrapolations.

Reasonableness Tests.

Before the final detailed statistical tests, but following initial verification, the model must show that its results are reasonable. It must be consistent with common sense in terms of such things as continuity, consistency, and degeneracy. This form of testing is especially important to those aspects of the model that cannot be validated by comparing to either real-world data or theoretical results.

A model is tested for continuity by performing sensitivity analysis on the input parameters. Small changes in input parameters cause consequential small changes in the output variables. This result is dictated by common sense.

The consistency of a model is confirmed by demonstrating that similar simulation cases yield similar results even through stated to the computer model with differing combinations of descriptive parameters.

The reasonableness of a model in a degenerate situation is shown by selecting parameters to eliminate the effect of a particular feature in a model and then checking to see that the computer simulation acted as if the characteristic modeled by the eliminated feature is totally absent. A priori determination of the model objectives dictates the level of model detail required. This in turn affects the accuracy of the model's behavior and the degree to which the model parallels the system being modeled.

There is no such thing (for a simulation model) as "the test for validity." Rather there have developed certain empirical guidelines and sets of tests. The simulator follows the guidelines and conducts applicable tests in the process of developing the model in order to build up his or her confidence. Validation of a simulation study is a continuous process that begins from the start of the study. Confidence is built into the model as the study proceeds. It is not just something done at the end.

[1]J. W. Forrester, *Industrial Dynamics*, MIT Press, Cambridge, Mass., 1961, p. 117.

Broadly, the validation process is (conceptually) divided into two parts. We will refer to these parts hereafter as *verification,* which is concerned with the implementation of the design specifications of the conceptual model, and *validation,* which is concerned with the applicability and fit of the conceptual model to the real problem. Each of the guidelines and tests are concerned with either verification or validation.

verification

The verification process assures the software integrity of the model. This is the determination that the software statement of the conceptual model is equivalent to the design statement of the conceptual model. This is necessary since there is a high probability (if not a certainty) that the model will initially contain errors. In terms of time required, verification represents roughly 30% of the total model development effort [16]. This percentage is based on the author's own experience in model development. This includes the time spent debugging the code as it is implemented and time spent testing the completed code. Thus, verification represents a major part of this simulation study.

verification guidelines and tests

Structured Programming.

The software used to simulate a real-world situation typically contains hundreds of lines of code. In programs of this size, complexity arises out of the large number of interactions within and among routines. If this complexity were not controlled, the software used to simulate the real system would become virtually unintelligible. Coding errors due to misunderstandings or the sheer numbers of things would tend to creep into the program in spite of every precaution.

For these reasons, top-down structured programming is employed [17]. First, a conceptual model is designed and then it is coded into a structured computer program. The program is written to be readable so that it can quickly be understood. There is a structural framework furnished by internal algorithm descriptions and topic headings, which serve to organize and isolate ideas into recognizable patterns. The program is constructed in a stepwise manner with each new piece being fitted into the existing program after it is checked out by itself. Each structure in the program, from the smallest IF structures to entire routines, is designed to do something exactly where it appears with no side effect elsewhere in the program. The result of using structured programming, in terms of model verification, is that the number of programming errors are kept to a minimum.

Event Trace.

There are several activities that the job may engage in, according to the specific event interactions that occur. It is necessary to show that the model does indeed perform the interactions as claimed in the conceptual model. This means that for the model one must trace customers from the time they arrive until the time they depart and show each interaction and event. This customer event trace will quickly reveal gross programming errors, oversights, and omissions. Furthermore, one can watch individual customers and see, step by step, how the model works. Therefore, an event trace is included as an integral part of the model verification package.

Upon completion of coding the simulation, several short runs with various representative input parameters can be made. The resulting event trace can be manually analyzed and shown that the job did indeed follow a logical path determined by the random variates generated. Hence, one can ascertain whether the events interact in the manner specified in the design statement of the conceptual model.

The user is encouraged, however, not to merely accept this statement as fact, since all possible input parameters could not be checked. For this reason, an event trace of the first few occurrences of each event should be made on every simulation run. A manual analysis of the event trace would then verify the event interaction for that particular configuration. Verification of event interaction in this manner would be an ongoing process that would be performed each time the model is used for as long as the simulation program is useful in a production mode.

Numerical Test Cases.

There are certain special conditions in the simulation model that may be easily checked by the use of specially constructed data sets. These are used to ensure that the numerical computations were properly calculated. These data sets produce a predictable behavior that is monitored through the output statistics and the event trace. Any deviation between the predicted behavior and the simulated behavior would point to a potential software problem. This verification test is different from the validation test of comparing the model's output to the results predicted by queuing theory (which will be done in the model validation section). In this case the simulation's results are checked by hand for simple correctness of numerical results. A simple check is to run a simulation using a specific random number generator, say R, and compare the results with the simulation run using $1 - R$. These results should be very close and, if not, the simulation has a problem.

validation

The validation process is designed to increase the user's confidence that the conceptual model is applicable or useful by demonstrating an acceptable correspondence between the computational results of the model and actual data (if they exist) or theoretical data. Although this can be a time-consuming and costly process (even on a limited basis), it is necessary before the model can be used to predict results or select alternatives.

The validation process begins with the development of the conceptual model. The concern for model validation should directly influence the model design. The extent of this influence depends upon a number of factors, including the objectives of the model, the scope of the model, and the real system performance data available.

After the conceptual model has been successfully implemented as a computer program, the rest of the model validation process occurs. There are theoretical models of queuing systems similar to the simulation model used here. The analytical results of these queuing models (the reader should review Chapter 4) can be shown to experimentally agree with the results observed from the simulation model for many configurations. Then the limited amount of real-world data should be compared as closely as possible and in as many different ways as possible to the simulation model. The number and depth of these tests will be limited to some reasonable amount of testing because of the cost and time required. While complete confidence cannot be attained no matter how much is performed, each test that is performed will provide a higher level of confidence. The simulator is responsible for determination of how much is enough.

An example of one technique used to demonstrate reasonableness is to selectively "zero out" certain parameters of the data set and determine that the proper simulation features were not used.

Testing Closeness to the Theoretical Model.

The most powerful method for validating the normal operations of the simulation model is to predict and verify the simulation's main results, such as grade of service and waiting time, by the analytical queuing model under ideal conditions. Two models, using different techniques but employing the same basic input information and operating with the same configuration, should provide comparable results.

By correctly choosing the input parameters to a model, it may be configured to closely conform to the standardized ideal conditions of queuing theory. This is valuable as there are several analytical equations describing the overall statistical characteristics of many systems. These analytical results may be used to confirm that the simulation model performs as predicted by queuing theory. The technique is to run the model and collect the statistics, which can also be calculated from equations. This is done for several different measures. Batched confidence intervals[2] are computed for each measure, and if the predicted value and the observed values coincide for at least $(1 - p)\%$ of the measures when using $(1 - p)\%$ confidence intervals, then the simulation run may be considered valid. Thus what is actually being done is that separate models are constructed operating upon completely different principles; one is an analytical model based upon equations and the other is a simulation model based upon the interaction of discrete events. The two models are run with the same conditions, and we look to see if they obtain the same results. This is a very reliable check if both models agree.

The actual execution of this test is an involved process. First, the ideal conditions

---

[2]Batched confidence intervals are regular confidence intervals employing a special method to avoid auto-correlation errors (see the section on batched confidence intervals.)

of queuing theory require several things, of which one requirement is that the system be in steady state, which is not easy to determine. Thus, a routine must be written to determine when the system is out of its period of initial transient. Second, the construction of confidence intervals is not a straightforward process since the simulation observations are sometimes autocorrelated. Thus, batched confidence intervals must be collected.

Removal of Initial Bias.

The elimination of initial bias is concerned with eliminating the effect of observations during the period at the start of the simulation when transient fluctuations in the system's behavior occur due to starting the system from an idle state. The period at the start of a simulation run, which is considered unacceptable due to transient fluctuations in the system's behavior or that of a parameter of the system, is termed the *initial bias period*. During the initial bias period the system changes from its initial conditions and approaches its steady-state conditions. (This of course assumes that the mechanisms and driving statistical distributions are unchanged over time.) In terms of computer-time requirements, the duration of the transient period is affected not only by simulation considerations, reliability of random number generators, and so on, and the required level of accuracy, but depends heavily also on the level of traffic intensity, the characteristics of the system being modeled, that is, the system configuration, number of servers, type, and so on.

There are several methods for overcoming the initial bias. One could allow the simulation to run for a long enough period that the effect of the initial observations are negligible, or one could choose initial starting conditions to be typical of steady state, or one might simply exclude some appropriate part of the initial period from consideration.

The last method is the simplest technique for reducing unwanted transient effects. The run is started from an idle state and stopped after a certain number of observations have occurred. The entities existing in the system at that time are left as they are. The run is then restarted with statistics being gathered from the point of restart. As a practical matter, it is usual to program the simulation so that statistics are gathered from the beginning and simply wipe out the statistics gathered up to the point of restart.

In removing the initial bias of the system, one wishes to determine a time, T_b, such that the long-run distribution adequately describes the system for any time $> T_b$. Once T_b is known, it is a simple matter to disregard all simulation results collected prior to T_b. (T_b may be expressed as time units or may be in terms of events, such as the number of changes in queue size since the system started, number of completed services, etc.)

To determine T_b, the method of batched means [8] will be used. Waiting time in the queue is collected in batches of size n ($n = 5, 10, 15, 20, \ldots, N$). For each batch size n, the mean waiting time, $X_j(n)$, is calculated.

$$X_j(n) = \sum_{i=1}^{n} \frac{x_{ij}}{n},$$

where x_{ij} is the ith observation in the jth batch and $X_j(n)$ is the value of the sample mean for the jth batch. A sampling interval of size N (i.e., N changes in waiting time) is used to obtain one each of the mean waiting time of a batch of size n, $X_j(n)$, where j is fixed. The simulation is continued until p of these sample intervals is obtained. By the central limit theorem, the mean of the $X_j(n)$, $m(n)$, for each n is approximately normally distributed, provided that the batch mean (of the same size) is identically and independently distributed.

$$m(n) = \frac{1}{p} \sum_{j=1}^{p} X_j(n) = \frac{1}{np} \sum_{j=1}^{p} \sum_{i=1}^{n} x_{ij}.$$

Approximate independence of the batch means should have been achieved, since for small n the $X_j(n)$'s are widely separated, and for large n dependence effects are swamped out [8]. The batch means are not identically distributed, however, unless the long-run distribution applies. As the batch size exceeds T_b, the effect of the initial bias on the first sampling interval becomes minimized, and thus batch mean becomes approximately distributed as the rest of the $X_j(n)$. Thus, as t exceeds T_b, the distribution of $m(n)$ approaches the normal. As the sample mean $m(n)$ approaches its theoretical (population) mean, the standard deviation of $m(n)$, $\sqrt{V(n)/p}$ approaches 0 as n approaches infinity [18].

$$V(n) = \frac{1}{p - 1} \sum_{j=1}^{p} [X_j(n) - m(n)]^2.$$

Then, where these assumptions hold, $\sqrt{V(n)/p}$ should be decreasing or $\sqrt{V(n)}$ should be inversely proportional to n [8]. It follows, therefore, that one estimate of T_b is that value of n at which $\sqrt{V(n)/p} = S(n, p)$ demonstrates a definite decreasing behavior. Figure 5-8 and Table 5-2 illustrate the decreasing behavior of $S(n, p)$ for waiting time.

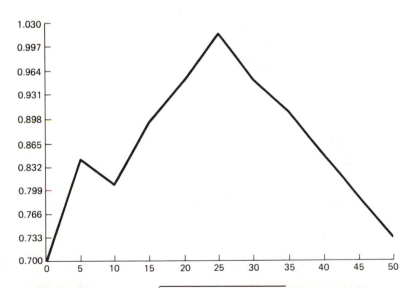

FIGURE 5-8 Graph of $\sqrt{\text{Var (WT)}}$/Number Batches Versus Batch Size

TABLE 5-2

Initial Bias Graph Points with $P = 100$, $PR = 0.20$, and Utilization $= 0.40$

Batch size	S(n, p)	m(n)
5	0.8416	5.9638
10	0.8036	6.0571
15	0.8928	6.5747
20	0.9539	7.1339
25	1.0088	7.3889
30	0.9579	7.4191
35	0.9078	7.4465
40	0.8537	7.6347
45	0.7838	7.8339
50	0.7294	7.8706

At a batch size of 25 to 30, the decrease of $S(n, p)$ is pronounced. Thus, 30 waiting time changes appears to be a sufficient estimate of T_b. In practice, T_b should be established for each simulation run.

Batched Confidence Intervals.

Once the effect of the initial bias period has been adequately reduced, the model can be assumed to be in a steady state. One would now like to compare the results of the model (now configured under ideal conditions) to the results predicted by the analytical model.

The results from a model can show a certain amount of experimental variability, which creates a problem in gauging the significance of the results. The values measured are no more than a sample, and they must be used to estimate the parameters of the distribution from which they are drawn. Typically, experimentalists have used confidence intervals and tests of hypothesis to decide if the mean value results from two experiments are statistically equivalent (Chapter 6). This requires, however, that the individual observations used to form the mean must be independent (as well as identically distributed).

The observations collected in the simulation are often autocorrelated, and so if one wishes to compute a confidence interval for the mean of the observations, then the method of batched confidence intervals [8] or some other suitable method must be used.

Under broad conditions that can normally be expected to hold in a simulation run, the distribution of the sample mean of autocorrelated data can be shown to approximate a normal distribution as the sample size increases. The usual formula for estimating the mean value of the distribution remains a satisfactory estimate for the mean of autocor-

132

related data. However, the variance of the autocorrelated data is not related to the population variance by the simple expression (variance/n) as occurs for independent data. Thus, we would like to collect our observations in such a manner that they will be independent so that the normality assumptions will hold.

The approach adopted uses a single long run, with the initial bias removed. The run is divided into a number of segments to separate the measurements into batches of equal size. The mean of each batch is taken, and the individual batch means are regarded as independent observations. The estimated mean value of the variable being measured is the mean of the batch means. This, of course, is exactly the same as the mean of all the measurements. However, the assumption that the batch means are independent, together with the application of the central limit theorem, allows the batch mean observations to be treated as normally distributed. The usual formula can then be applied to estimate the variance of the overall mean and so compute a confidence interval.

This method cannot be directly applied to a time-dependent accumulated statistic, such as the queue length, because the distribution of the sample mean depends upon time, and successive batch means cannot be treated as observations from the same population. The method used in measuring an accumulated statistic such as queue length is to conduct the experiment by sampling the queue length at uniform intervals of time so that each observation is an individual measure of the same random variable.

A complete run consists of N observations that are broken into p batches of size n so that $N = np$. (It is assumed that N is exactly divisible by p.) In effect, the experiment is equivalent to repeating an experiment of length n a total of p times, with the final state of one run becoming the initial state of the next run. This way of repeating a run is preferable to starting each run from an initial idle state, since the state at the end of a batch is a more reasonable initial state than the idle state. However, the connection between the batches introduces correlation. The batches could be separated by intervals in which measurements are discarded in order to eliminate the correlation. Clearly, this throws away useful information. The variance to be expected by using all the data and accepting the correlation between batches is less than that obtained from the reduced amount of data obtained by separating the batches. It seems to be preferable, therefore, to work with adjoining batches [8].

As was mentioned earlier, it is necessary to assume that the individual batch means are independent. The assumption can be justified if the batch length is sufficiently long. The effect of autocorrelation is that the value of one piece of data effects the value of following data. The effect diminishes as the separation between the data increases, and beyond some interval size it may reasonably be ignored. If the batch size is greater than this interval, the batch means may be treated as independent. It remains a matter of judgment to choose a suitable batch size. It might reasonably be speculated that the interval over which the batch is measured should be at least as great as the interval excluded from the beginning of a run to remove initial bias. If that has been determined, it can also be used as a batch size and input to the model. Another approach is to repeat the simulation with several batch sizes and test for consistency of results.

With the batch method there is a trade-off between batch size and number of batches. Since the number of batches corresponds to the number of samples of an assumed normal distribution, it is advisable to hold this number to a reasonable minimum limit of 30 to meet the normality assumption and it is advisable to maximize the batch size in order to reduce the correlation between batches.

An important practical aspect of the batch method is that it does not entail the simultaneous presence of all the data to carry out the calculations. The batch means can be calculated as the simulation run proceeds. Computer space is only required to accumulate the sum of the batch means and the sums of their squares, together with an accumulation of the numbers forming the current batch mean.

Once confidence intervals are computed, it is easy to test the hypothesis that the observed and predicted means are equivalent and the simulation results agree with the analytical results.

Comparison with the Real-World Data.

If real-world data are available, comparisons can be made between the results of a model and the real world. Typical kinds of real-world data are (1) empirical distribution, such as service time, (2) values that can be compared to statistics produced by the simulation model, such as mean queue length, and (3) values that represent the internal aspects of the simulation model, such as event interaction.

Alternate Stopping Rules.

When using confidence intervals based on batch means, we assume that the correlation between parts of batch means becomes smaller as the batch size increases. Hence, we assume that it is possible to find a fixed batch size such that a departure from independence in a sequence of batch means is not detectable by statistical testing. Thus, if initial bias has been removed, one can assume that this sequence of batch means is independent and identically distributed. This is an essential assumption, since we wish to utilize the central limit theorem after computing the overall mean and the variance of the batch means.

A second method for estimating the variance of the batch means, and hence computing a confidence interval is called the *autoregressive approach* [6]. The basic assumption is that one can take a sequence of dependent observations and transform them into a sequence of independent and identically distributed observations. These new observations are based on a linear regression model of the dependent observations.

A third method for computing a confidence interval for observations that are *not* necessarily independent and identically distributed is called the *regeneration method* [2, 4, 5]. In this method a batch (cycle) is based on the concept of a regeneration point, that is, a state to which the system returns at intervals of finite length. It is assumed that the behavior of the system in one such interval must be independent of the system in preceding intervals. An example of a regeneration point in the systems we have looked at is the times the server becomes idle. Using this method, one can implement a stopping rule, which stops the simulation once a predetermined level of confidence has been obtained.

example of model verification using queuing theory and batch means

The result of investigating a multiserve queuing system (Theorem 16) will be reported here. A figure of this model is given in Chapter 4. The study is divided into two steps: (1) remove *initial bias* on waiting time, and (2) *collect statistics* on a theoretically known model and compare the simulation results to the analytical results. In this model, the same notation will be used as defined in Chapter 4.

Nine statistics are of interest, and their steady-state expected values are listed in Table 5-3. For various values of λ and μ, it is fairly straightforward to compute the expected values.

Table 5-4 gives the theoretical expected values when $m = 5$, $\lambda = 0.1$, and $\mu = 0.04$. Figure 5-9 illustrates the decreasing behavior of $\sqrt{V(n)/n}$ for waiting in the queue ($n = 50$). At a batch size of somewhere between 40 and 50, the decrease of

TABLE 5-3

Statistics of Interest	Expected Value
Utilization of server	$\rho_s = \lambda T_s/m$
Mean waiting line	$L_w = P_0 \dfrac{(\lambda/\mu)^m(\lambda\mu)}{(m-1)!(m\mu - \lambda)^2}$
Mean waiting time	$T_w = L_w/\lambda = P_0 \dfrac{(\lambda/\mu)^m(\mu)}{(m-1)!(m\mu - \lambda)^2}$
Mean queuing line	$L_q = L_w + L_s$
Mean queuing time	$T_q = T_w + T_s$
Mean waiting line (length of nonempty queue)	$L_w(>0) = \dfrac{L_w}{1 - Q_0} = \dfrac{L_w}{1 - (P_0 + P_1 + \cdots + P_m)}$
Mean waiting time, given waiting time > 0	$T_w(>0) = \dfrac{T_w}{P(w>0)} = \dfrac{T_w}{1 - (P_0 + P_1 + \cdots + P_{m-1})}$
Mean number in service facility	$L_s = \lambda T_s$
Mean service time	$T_s = 1/\mu$
Mean arrival time	$T_a = 1/\lambda$

$$\text{where } P_0 = \left[\sum_{k=0}^{m-1} \frac{(\lambda/\mu)^k}{k!} + \frac{(\lambda/\mu)^m}{m!\,(1 - \frac{\lambda}{\mu m})} \right]^{-1}, \qquad \lambda/\mu < m$$

m = number of servers

TABLE 5-4

Theoretical Statistics of the Multiserver
Queuing System with $m = 5$, $\lambda = 0.1$, and $\mu = 0.04$

Utilization of server	= 0.500000
Mean waiting line	= 0.130371
Mean waiting time	= 1.303713
Mean queuing line	= 2.630371
Mean queuing time	= 26.303713
Mean waiting line (>0)	= 2.000000
Mean waiting time (>0)	= 9.999999
Mean service line	= 2.500000
Mean service time	= 25.000000
Mean arrival time	= 10.000000

$\sqrt{V(n)/n}$ is pronounced. Thus 40 waiting time changes appear to be a sufficient estimate of T_b. In practice, T_b should be established for each simulation run.

To verify the correctness of the simulation model, the simulation estimates obtained from a multiserver queuing system with Poisson input and exponential service are compared with the theoretical value. Table 5-5 illustrates this comparison. For those statistics

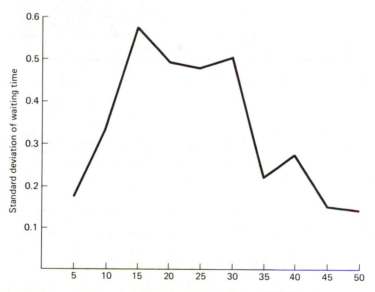

FIGURE 5-9 Variation of Sample Standard Deviation $\sqrt{V(N)/P}$ of Mean Waiting Time (T_w) with the Various Batch Sizes

TABLE 5-5

Expected and Observed Values of Statistics for a Poisson Arrival/Exponential Service Simulation

Statistic	Expected Value	Observed Value	95% Confidence Interval for Expected Value		
T_a	10	10.066	9.935	10.197	Accept
L_s	2.5	2.382	2.238	2.525	Accept
T_s	25.	25.083	24.778	25.338	Accept
L_w	0.1303	0.120	0.099	0.141	Accept
T_w	1.3037	1.300	1.109	1.491	Accept
L_q	2.6303	2.505	2.352	2.657	Accept
T_q	26.3037	26.389	25.947	26.831	Accept
$L_w (>0)$	2.000	1.795	1.474	2.117	Accept
$T_w (>0)$	9.9999	9.559	8.501	10.618	Accept

$$\text{where} \quad \lambda = 0.1$$
$$\mu = 0.04$$
$$m = 5$$
$$\rho = \lambda T_s/m = 0.5$$

that did not involve a time average (e.g., T_w, T_q), 50 observations were collected and their batch means were calculated. These batch means were then accumulated and their mean variance were calculated at the end of the simulation. For time-average statistics (e.g., L_w, L_q), batch means were calculated as the average value within a specified time interval. These batch means were accumulated as the others. Confidence intervals for the statistics were calculated using the normal approximation

$$Pr\left[\overline{X} - a\frac{\sigma}{\sqrt{n}} < \mu < \overline{X} + a\frac{\sigma}{\sqrt{n}}\right] = 1 - \alpha$$

where $\alpha = 0.05$ and $a = 1.96$, since $N(1.96) = 0.975$ from Table 1 of Appendix C. Table 5-4 gives a complete summary for the system simulation. It is obvious that the theoretical values fall within the confidence interval, thus supporting the correctness of the simulation model.

To use the preceding normal approximation, the assumption of independence and identical distribution must be fulfilled. The pairwise correlation coefficient can be calculated using the formula

$$\frac{\sum_{i=1}^{n-1} (X_i - \overline{X})(X_{i+1} - \overline{X})}{\sum_{i=1}^{n} (X_i - \overline{X})^2}$$

where X_i denotes the ith batch mean and $\overline{X}$ denotes the overall mean. The calculated value of the correlation coefficient for waiting time is 0.021. To verify independence, this value must be statistically tested against 0.0. If 0.021 is significantly different from 0.0, then the assumption of independence must be rejected. With $n = 50$, the assumption of independence is not rejected. The assumption of identical distribution is satisfied by the removal of initial bias.

EXERCISES

5-1. The statistical problems associated with a simulation study have been conveniently classified into two broad classes: (a) strategic planning problems and (b) tactical planning problems. Briefly explain each of these two broad classes.

5-2. (a) Justify the procedure for removing initial bias in a simulation experiment.
(b) Why may it be important to remove initial bias? (Give at least two reasons.)

5-3. Assume you have a simulation experiment to estimate a performance parameter (mean waiting time, say) for a queuing model of a computer system. The experiment gives 10% accuracy with 95% confidence; that is, $P[|x - \mu| < 0.1] = 0.95$.
(a) How would you alter the experiment to obtain 1% accuracy with the same confidence? Be as quantitative as possible, discussing whether you would increase the length of each sample run or increase the number of sample runs, by how much, and why?
(b) Assume you also have an iterative numerical procedure that solves the same model to the same 10% accuracy at the same cost as the originally designed experiment. Without knowing precisely what numerical algorithm is being applied, would you use the simulation determined in (a) or the numerical algorithm to obtain the result to 1% accuracy. Explain why, in your judgment, you made a good choice.

5-4. A software system consisting of 12 program modules has been instrumented to measure the frequencies of transitions of control among modules, producing relative frequencies (f_{ij}) for $i, j = 1, 2, \ldots, 12$. The variables f_{ij} represent the relative frequency that an exit for module i causes invocation of module j, normalized so that

$$\sum_{j=1}^{12} f_{ij} = 1$$

I have modeled this transition process by a Markov chain, with the f_{ij} as transition probabilities, and I compute the state probabilities $(p_j, j = 1, 2, \ldots, 12)$. A student proposed to verify the validity of my Markov model by measuring the relative frequency of actual entries to modules, and comparing these frequencies with the calculated probabilities. Discuss the reasonableness of such a "verification" and explain (as analytically as possible) what it is that is being verified.

5-5. Two modelers, Mr. A and Ms. B, are working on models of the same real system. A claims his model is better because it is more detailed, hence more valid. B disagrees that detail necessarily implied validity, and in addition claims superiority for her model on the basis of its simplicity. Judge the worthiness of the claims and counterclaims. (What does it mean for a simulation model to be valid?)

5-6. State the central limit theorem and explain how it is important in simulation experimentation and verification.

REFERENCES

1. ANNINO, J. S., and RUSSELL, E. C., "The Ten Most Frequent Causes of Simulation Analysis Failure—and How to Avoid Them," *Simulation,* Vol. 32, No. 6, June 1979, pp. 137–140.

2. BASKET, F., "Confidence Intervals for Simulation Results: A Case Study of Buffer Pool Performance," *Proceedings of Computer Science and Statistics: 7th Annual Symposium on the Interface,* Iowa State University, Oct. 1973, pp. 53–64.

3. CHAN, T. F., and LEWIS, J. G., "Computing Standard Deviation: Accuracy," *Communications of the ACM,* Vol. 22, No. 9, Sept. 1979, pp. 526–531.

4. CRANE, M. A., and IGLEHART, D. I., "Simulating Stable Stochastic Systems, I: General Multiserver Queues," *Journal of the ACM,* Jan. 1974, pp. 103–113.

5. CRANE, M. A., and IGLEHART, D. I., "Simulating Stable Stochastic Systems, II: Markov Chains," *Journal of the ACM,* Jan. 1974, pp. 114–123.

6. FISHMAN, G. S., *Principles of Discrete Event Simulation,* John Wiley & Sons, Inc., New York, 1978.

7. FRANTA, W. R., *The Process View of Simulation,* North-Holland Publishing Co., Amsterdam, 1977.

8. GORDON, G., *System Simulation* (2nd ed.), Prentice-Hall, Inc., Englewood Cliffs, N.J., 1978.

9. MAISEL, H., and GNUGNOLI, G., *Simulation of Discrete Stochastic Systems,* Science Research Associates, Chicago, 1976.

10. SHANNON, R. E., *Systems Simulation: The Art and Science,* Prentice-Hall, Inc., Englewood Cliffs, N.J., 1975.

11. TEOREY, T. J., "Validation Criteria for Computer System Simulation," *Simuletter,* Vol. 6, No. 4, July 1975, pp. 9–20.

12. VAN HORN, R. L., "Validation of Simulation Results," *Management Science,* Vol. 17, No. 5, Jan. 1971, pp. 247–258.

13. WEST, D. H. D., "Updating Mean and Variance Estimates: An Improved Method," *Communications of the ACM,* Vol. 22, No. 9, Sept. 1979, pp. 532–535.

14. WIRTH, N., "Program Development by Stepwise Refinement," *Communications of the ACM,* Vol. 14, No. 4, Apr. 1971, pp. 221–227.

15. ZEIGLER, B. P., *Theory of Modeling and Simulation,* John Wiley & Sons, Inc., New York, 1976.

16. SMOTHERS, N. P., *Simulation of Local Switched Data Communications Network,* M.S. Dissertation, University of Kansas, 1978.

17. RYAN, K. T., "Validating a Bus Operations Simulation Model," *1979 Winter Simulation Conference,* San Diego, Calif.

18. HOGG, R. V. and CRAIG, A. T., *Introduction To Mathematical Statistics* (3rd ed.), Macmillan, Inc., New York, 1968.

6

WHICH
TEST
STATISTIC?

Even though you have had a course in statistics, you may still be bewildered by the question of which test statistic to use after collecting an extensive set of simulation data. The flow chart in Figure 6-1 ([7], p. 300) is to assist you in determining which test statistic is appropriate for a particular set of data. A list of references will be given at the end of the chapter to assist if further study is still needed.

The flow chart is organized by a series of questions. In the area of simulation, we will be making decisions about populations based on large samples. For example, we may wish to decide on the basis of sample data whether one simulation procedure is better

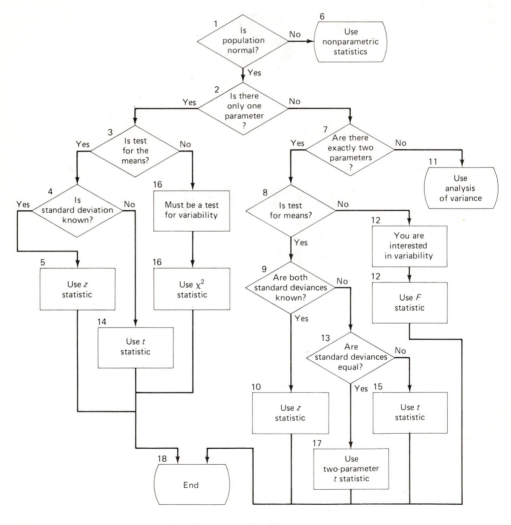

FIGURE 6-1

than another. Because of the large samples, the sampling distributions of many statistics are normally distributed (or at least nearly normal). The only nonnormal populations (block 6) considered in this text are discussed in Chapter 7. In the case where the normal distribution (block 1) is reasonable, one can use this fact to formulate decision rules on tests of hypotheses. In attempting to reach decisions, it is useful to make assumptions about the parameters of the populations involved. Such assumptions (which may not be true) are called statistical hypotheses and are usually statements about the probability distribution of the population. Block 2 asks the question concerning whether we are going to make assumptions about one or more parameters of the normal population. If it is the population mean that is of interest (block 3), then we proceed to block 4. If the population standard deviation is known, then we proceed to block 14; otherwise, we proceed to block 5. Let us assume block 5.

As the reader will note from the information contained in block 5, only the hypotheses and test statistics are given. One must still make a decision on the basis of the test statistic computed from the sampling data. For any tests of hypothesis (rules for decisions) to be good, they must be designed so as to minimize errors of decisions. If we reject a hypothesis when it should be accepted, we say a *type I error* has been made.

If, on the other hand, we accept a hypothesis when it should be rejected, we say that a *type II error* has been made. In either case, an error or wrong decision has been made. It is not a simple matter to minimize these errors. For a given sample, an attempt to decrease one error will result in an increase in the other type of error. The only way to reduce both errors is to increase the sample size.

In tests of hypothesis, the (maximum) probability of a type I error is called the *level of significance* and is denoted by α. In practice, a level of significance of 0.05 or 0.01 is typical. If a level of significance of 0.05 is chosen, then there is a 5% chance that we would reject the hypothesis when it should be accepted.

On the basis of the level of significance and the distribution of the test statistic, we can construct a critical region (region of rejection of the hypothesis) for the hypothesis. For example, in block 5, if $\alpha/2 = 0.025$, the critical values for a two-tailed test are -1.96 and $+1.96$ since $N(1.96) = 0.975 = 1 - 0.025$ (Table 1 of Appendix C). Hence we can formulate the following rule of decision or test of hypothesis.

1. Reject the hypothesis at a 0.05 level of significance if the z statistic value falls outside the range -1.96 to 1.96 (i.e., if $|z| > 1.96$).
2. Accept the hypothesis (or make no decision at all) otherwise.

The values of z and $N(z)$ are found in Table 1 of Appendix C. This means we are assuming that the z test statistic has a standard normal distribution.

In blocks 14, 15, and 17, we must determine the critical values from a table of the t distribution. In block 16, we must determine the critical values from a table of the chi-square distribution. In block 12, we must determine the critical values from a table of the F distribution. There are examples at the end of this chapter that illustrate the use of the various test statistics. The tables are found in Appendix C.

Block 1. The underlying assumption in most hypothesis testing is the assumption that the sample data are nearly normally distributed. Duncan [3] devotes a chapter to tests of normality. Is the population normal?

1. *Yes,* go to block 2.
2. *No,* go to block 6.

Block 2. The number of parameters of interest is an important piece of information. If one is concerned with one population mean, then there is only one parameter. If one is concerned with the equality of two population means, then there are two parameters. Is there only one parameter in your test?

1. *Yes,* go to block 3.
2. *No,* go to block 7.

Block 3. The population mean tends to be the parameter that is most often studied. Is this a test concerning the mean?

1. *Yes,* go to block 4.
2. *No,* go to block 16.

Block 4. The important parameter here is the standard deviation. If you are taking a sample from a population that has been sampled many times before, you might feel you have accurate knowledge about the population standard deviation. On the other hand, it is conceivable that the sample that you are currently testing is from a population never sampled before. Do you know the standard deviation of the population?

1. *Yes,* go to block 5.
2. *No,* go to block 14.

Block 5. You are interested in a single parameter test for the mean from a normal population with known standard deviation σ.

Hypothesis: Mean of a normal population has a specified value μ_0.

Test statistic

$$z = \frac{(\bar{x} - \mu_0)\sqrt{n}}{\sigma},$$

where $\bar{x}$ is the sample mean and n is the sample size. References [1, 2, 3, 4, 5] suggest some sources where this information can be found. Tables of the normal distribution are found in Appendix C.
Go to block 18.

Block 6. This area is outside the scope of this book. When the normality assumption is not true, nonparametric methods must be used. Another name for nonparametric methods is "distribution-free" methods. Although much has been written on this subject in recent years, Siegel [6] is one of the better references.

Go to block 18.

Block 7. You have stated an interest in two population parameters. Suppose, for example, you are interested in the productivity of two computer systems. There would be two parameters, one for each computer system. If you were comparing the productivity of three computer systems, then you would be interested in three parameters.

Are there exactly two parameters in your test?

1. *Yes,* go to block 8.
2. *No,* go to block 11.

Block 8. If you are interested in measures of central tendency, then the two parameters of interest are probably the population means. On the other hand, the variability might be of interest since the spread of output data is important information. Is this a test concerning two means?

1. *Yes,* go to block 9.
2. *No,* go to block 12.

Block 9. You are interested in comparing the means of two normal distributions. How much is known about the variability of the two populations? As in block 4, do you feel that the standard deviations of both populations are known?

1. *Yes,* go to block 10.
2. *No,* go to block 13.

Block 10. You are interested in a two-parameter test concerning the difference between two means, $\mu_1 - \mu_2$, whose standard deviations, σ_1 and σ_2, are known.

Hypothesis: The difference of the means of two normal populations is equal to a constant, D_0.

Test Statistic

$$z = \frac{(\bar{x}_1 - \bar{x}_2) - D_0}{\sqrt{\dfrac{\sigma_1^2}{n_1} + \dfrac{\sigma_2^2}{n_2}}},$$

where $\bar{x}_1$ is the sample mean, of size n_1, from the first population and $\bar{x}_2$ is the sample mean, of size n_2, from the second population. References [1, 2, 3, 4, 5] suggest some sources where this information can be found. Tables of the normal distribution are found in Appendix C.
Go to block 18.

Block 11. You are concerned with a problem involving three or more population parameters. This area is outside the scope of this book. This area is called *analysis of variance* and is concerned with some very powerful techniques. References [1, 2, 4, 6] suggest sources where this information can be found.

Go to block 18.

Block 12. You are concerned with comparing the variability (spread) of two populations: σ_1^2 and σ_2^2.

Hypothesis: Standard deviations of two normal populations are equal; $\sigma_1^2 = \sigma_2^2$

Test Statistic

$$F = \frac{S_1^2}{S_2^2},$$

where
$$S_1^2 = \frac{\sum_{i=1}^{n_1} (x_{1i} - \bar{x}_1)^2}{n_1 - 1}$$

is the sample variance based on a sample (x_{1i}) of size n_1 and

$$S_2^2 = \frac{\sum_{i=1}^{n_2} (x_{2i} - \bar{x}_2)^2}{n_2 - 1}$$

is the sample variance based on a sample (x_{2i}) of size n_2. Tables for the F distribution with degrees of freedom $n_1 - 1$, $n_2 - 1$ are found in Appendix C.
Go to block 18.

Block 13. You are interested in comparing the mean of two normal populations whose standard deviations are unknown. Even though the standard deviations may not be known, there is an effective test statistic if the variances of the two populations are the same.
Is the standard deviation of the first population equal to the standard deviation of the second population?

1. *Yes,* go to block 17.
2. *No,* go to block 15.

3. *Don't know.* Go to block 12, conduct the test suggested there, and return to block 13.

Block 14. You are interested in comparing the mean of a normal population to a particular value, μ_0, when the population standard deviation is unknown.

Hypothesis: Mean of a normal population equals a specified number, μ_0.

Test Statistic

$$t = \frac{(\bar{x} - \mu_0)\sqrt{n}}{S},$$

where

$$S^2 = \frac{\sum\limits_{i=1}^{n}(x_i - \bar{x})^2}{n-1}$$

is the sample variance and $\bar{x}$ is the sample mean based on a sample size of n. Tables for the t distribution with degrees of freedom $n-1$ are found in Appendix C. When $n > 30$, the standard normal distribution is an excellent approximation to the t distribution.
Go to block 18.

Block 15. If you have reached this block, your knowledge about the populations of interest is very little. You have no confidence in your knowledge about the variances of the two populations. In addition, you doubt whether they are equal. Although there is no exact procedure available, there is an approximate statistic, $\hat{t}$, which has an approximate t distribution.

Hypothesis: Means of two normal populations are equal.

Test Statistic

$$\hat{t} = \frac{\bar{x}_1 - \bar{x}_2}{\sqrt{\dfrac{s_1^2}{n_1} + \dfrac{s_2^2}{n_2}}},$$

where $\bar{x}_1$, $\bar{x}_2$, s_1^2, and s_2^2 are defined in block 12. The degrees of freedom for this approximate t distribution are

$$\frac{\left(\dfrac{s_1^2}{n_1} + \dfrac{s_2^2}{n_2}\right)^2}{\dfrac{(s_1^2/n_1)^2}{n_1+1} + \dfrac{(s_2^2/n_2)^2}{n_2+1}} - 2.$$

This is a complicated test, but it is the price you pay for having so little information. References [1, 3] suggest where more information may be found.

Go to block 12.

Block 16.   Since you are not interested in a test of central tendency, we have concluded that you are interested in a test of variability. In particular, the standard deviation is the most effective measure of variability.

Hypothesis: Standard deviation of a normal population has a specified value, σ_0.

Test Statistic

$$\chi^2 = \frac{(n - 1)s^2}{\sigma_0^2},$$

where s^2 is the sample variance (block 14) based on a sample size of n. Tables for the χ^2 (chi-square) distribution based on $n - 1$ degrees of freedom are found in Appendix C.
Go to block 18.

Block 17.   You want to compare the means of two normal populations and the standard deviations are equal but unknown. The appropriate test statistic follows a t distribution.

Hypothesis: The difference of the means of two normal populations is equal to a constant, D_0.

Test Statistic

$$t = \frac{(\bar{x}_1 - \bar{x}_2) - D_0}{s\sqrt{\dfrac{1}{n_1} + \dfrac{1}{n_2}}}$$

where $$s = \sqrt{\frac{(n_1 - 1)s_1^2 + (n_2 - 1)s_2^2}{n_1 + n_2 - 2}}$$

is a pooled estimate of σ and s_1^2 and s_2^2 are defined in block 12. Tables for the t distribution with $n_1 + n_2 - 2$ degrees of freedom are found in Appendix C.

Go to block 18.

Block 18.   Congratulations! You have made it through the flow chart, which has helped you in selecting an appropriate test statistic.

Example 1.

In block 14, we are interested in comparing the mean of a normal distribution to a particular value, μ_0, when the population standard deviation is *unknown*. In the example at the end of Chapter 5, we found that the expected value of mean waiting time (T_w) was 1.3037, and the observed average value of waiting time was 1.300. Hence $\mu_0 = 1.3037$ and $\bar{x} = 1.300$. We are interested in the hypothesis $\mu = 1.3037$. From a sample of size 50, we found the sample variance $s^2 = 0.4748$. Hence $t = (\bar{x} - \mu_0)\sqrt{n}/s = (1.3 - 1.3037)\sqrt{50}/0.689 = -0.0551$. From the t table with $\alpha = 0.05 =$ probability of rejecting $\mu = 1.3037$ when in truth $\mu = 1.3037$ (type I error), $n = 50$, $t_{0.025} = 1.96$. Since $|0.0551| < 1.96$, we cannot reject the hypothesis that $\mu = 1.3037$.

Example 2.

In block 5, we are interested in comparing the mean of a normal distribution to a particular value, μ_0, when the population standard deviation is *known*. In the example at the end of Chapter 5, we found the value of $\bar{x} = 1.300$ from a sample of size 50. If we had known the value of σ^2 before obtaining the sample (theoretically derived), it would not have been necessary to estimate it by computing s^2. If σ^2 is known, then $z = (\bar{x} - \mu_0)\sqrt{n}/\sigma$ is computable. From a z table with $\alpha/2 = 0.025$, $N(1.96) = 1.96$ (Appendix C). If $|z| > 1.96$, we reject the hypothesis $\mu = 1.3037$; otherwise, we accept. *Note:* Percentiles from a normal distribution and a t distribution are the same when $n \geq 30$.

Example 3.

In block 16, we are interested in comparing the variance of a normal distribution to a particular value, σ_0^2. In the example at the end of Chapter 5, we found that for a sample size of $n = 50$, the sample variance of waiting time was 0.4748. Let us assume we are interested in the hypothesis that $\sigma^2 = 1.00$. Hence $\chi^2 = 49(0.4748)/1.00 = 23.27$. If we reject $\sigma^2 = 1.00$, then we accept $\sigma^2 \neq 1.00$ (i.e., $\sigma^2 > 1.00$ or $\sigma^2 < 1.00$). From the table of critical values of chi-square (Appendix C), $\chi^2(0.025) = 71.4204$ and $\chi^2(0.975) = 32.3574$ with degrees of freedom $= 49$. We would reject $\sigma^2 = 1.0$ if $\chi^2 = 23.27$ is greater than 71.4204 or less than 32.3574. In this example $23.27 < 32.3574$; hence we accept $\sigma^2 \neq 1.00$ and, in particular, we accept $\sigma^2 < 1.00$.

Example 4.

In block 17, we are interested in comparing the means of two independent normal populations, where the variances are equal, but unknown. We are interested in the hypothesis that $D_0 = \mu_1 - \mu_2 = 0$ or $\mu_1 = \mu_2$. If we reject this hypothesis, we accept the alternative hypothesis $\mu_1 \neq \mu_2$ (i.e., $\mu_1 < \mu_2$ or $\mu_1 > \mu_2$). Let us assume we have taken a sample of size $n_1 = 50$ from population 1 and obtained $\bar{x}_1 = 1.3$ and $s_1^2 = 0.4748$ (as in Example 1). Let us assume we have taken an independent sample of size $n_2 = 50$ from population 2 and obtained $\bar{x}_2 = 1.5$ and $s_2^2 = 0.6165$. Hence, $t = (x_1 - x_2)/s \sqrt{1/n_1 + 1/n_2} = -1.35$. From a t table with $\alpha = 0.05$ and degrees of freedom $= 98$, $t_{0.025} = 1.96$ and $t_{0.975} = -t_{0.025}$. We would reject $\mu_1 = \mu_2$ if $t > 1.96$ or $t < -1.96$, which is the same as $|t| > 1.96$ (see Example 1). In this example $|-1.35| < 1.96$; hence we accept $\mu_1 = \mu_2$ (we cannot reject $\mu_1 = \mu_2$).

REFERENCES

1. BOWKER, A. H., and LIEBERMAN, G. J., *Engineering Statistics,* Prentice-Hall, Inc., New York, 1959.

2. BRUNK, H. D., *An Introduction of Mathematical Statistics,* Xerox College Publishing, Lexington, Mass., 1965.

3. DUNCAN, A. J., *Quality Control and Industrial Statistics* (3rd ed.), Richard D. Irwin, Inc., Homewood, Ill., 1965.

4. HOGG, R. V., and CRAIG, A. T., *Introduction to Mathematical Statistics* (3rd ed.), Macmillan, Inc., New York, 1968.

5. LINGREN, B. W., and MCELRATH, G. W., *Introduction to Probability and Statistics,* Macmillan, Inc., New York, 1969.

6. SIEGEL, S., *Nonparametric Statistics for the Behavioral Sciences,* McGraw-Hill Book Co., New York, 1956.

7. MOORE, J. M., "Which Test Statistic?—A Scramble Book Approach," *The Journal of Industrial Engineering,* **5,** (1967), pp. 300–305.

7

GENERATING PSEUDO-RANDOM NUMBERS

Random number generators are widely used in computer science and related disciplines. The numbers they produce are used in simulation, numerical analysis, games, and decision making. To supply these needs, the algorithm for the generator must essentially duplicate the effect of flipping a coin or rolling a dice. This need for random numbers and the algorithms to generate them sparked interest in the generation of pseudo-random, or quasi-random, numbers by means of algorithms that used the arithmetical operations available on the computer. Such numbers are called pseudo-random because, while they are certainly not random since they are produced by a mathematical function, they appear to be random and satisfy most of the tests of randomness.

Many such algorithms have been developed, one of which is the additive method. Exactly what kind of numbers are to be produced by these algorithms and what criteria those numbers must meet to be considered sufficiently random are our first concerns.

Arithmetical random number generators are commonly designed to yield numbers that are uniformly distributed between zero and one, inclusively. This means that every real number within the desired range that is representable by the computer being used is equally likely to be the result of the algorithm. The numbers must also be statistically independent; that is, just as when rolling dice the values of the previous rolls have no effect on the value of the current roll, we want the previous numbers to have as little as possible an effect on the current number. For example, in the sequence 1, 2, 3, 4, 5, 6, 1, 2, . . . each number appears the same number of times, but each number is just one more than the previous number, while after the 6, the sequence returns to the beginning.

Another requirement of the sequence of numbers produced is that they must have sufficiently long period. If some application requires 10,000 random numbers, a sequence that begins repeating after 5000 numbers is useless for that application. The algorithm must also be executable in a minimum of statements so that it requires very little time for execution. The algorithm should also require very few memory locations. If either of the last two requirements is not met, the cost of producing very large quantities of random numbers becomes exorbitant. The last requirement is that the sequence of numbers must be reproducible. This allows programs using random numbers to be tested and it allows results to be compared to previous results.

It should be noted that for many applications we need numbers from some probability distribution other than the uniform distribution between zero and one. This need is easily met, for numbers from other distributions can be produced from our original numbers without difficulty. For a detailed treatment of this topic, see Chapter 8.

HISTORY

Arithmetic methods of random number generators became popular because the alternatives were impractical and unworkable. Mechanical devices to produce random numbers at the speeds required and in the quantities desired were expensive to build and difficult to maintain. Furthermore, they did not allow reproduction of a sequence of numbers for program test. Tables of random numbers required far too much time to retrieve the numbers from auxiliary memory, there might not be enough numbers in the table for a particular application, and the tables allowed no variety in the sequence of numbers. Arithmetical random number generators solved these problems. They were fast, reproducible, had extremely long periods, and could produce different sequences just by altering a few initial parameters.

Von Neumann's middle-square method was the first widely used [6] arithmetic generator. In it, each successive number is the middle digits of the previous number squared. It met all the criteria except that its period was dependent on the initial value and quite often degenerated into cycles of very short length. Because of this degeneration, the middle-square method has largely been discarded in favor of some form of the linear congruential generator.

Linear congruential generators are of the form

$$X_n = (C_1X_{n-1} + \cdots + C_jX_{n-j} + C_0) \text{ modulus } M.$$

Multiplicative generators, mixed congruential generators, and additive generators are all special cases of the linear congruential generator.

For the multiplicative generator, $j = 1$ and $C_0 = 0$. So it can be stated as

$$X_n = (CX_{n-1}) \text{ modulus } M.$$

There are two important parameters for the multiplicative generator, C and X_0. They must be chosen to meet certain requirements to guarantee that the sequence of numbers generated has the maximum period. The value of M is generally taken to be the word size of the computer being used, so the modulus operation can be accomplished by simply ignoring overflow. The values of the X_n's generated this way will not be between zero and one, but numbers in the desired range can be obtained by simply dividing X_n by M. Since each X_n is between zero and M, X_n/M will be between zero and one. The length of the period for the multiplicative generator achieves a maximum of 2^{r-2} when $M = 2^r$, (C) modulus $8 = 3$ or 5 and X_0 is odd (Theorem 1).

This method was introduced in 1948 by D. H. Lehmer [6] and has since become the most popular method. This method requires only two memory locations, the arithmetic involved is just multiplication as long as M equals the computer's word size, and its period is very long. For example, when working with a computer that uses 35 bits to represent an integer, it is quite simple to obtain a sequence with a period of length 2^{33}.

The mixed congruential generator resembles the multiplicative method. However, it requires three initial parameters and is of the form

$$X_n = (C_1X_{n-1} + C_0) \text{ modulus } M.$$

The chief advantage of the mixed congruential method is that it is possible to increase the period length of the derived sequence greatly by merely adding in the constant C_0. The maximum period possible with the mixed congruential generator is equal to M. It is obtained whenever C_0 is relatively prime to M and (C_1) modulus $P = 1$, for all P such that P is a prime factor of M, and also (C_1) modulus $4 = 1$, if 4 is a factor of M (Theorem 2). In a sequence from the mixed congruential generator, with a period of length M, every number between 0 and $M - 1$ occurs exactly once, so the initial value of X_0 has no effect on the length of the period. The mixed congruential method is also popular, but it does not always satisfy the desired statistical properties as well as does the multiplicative method.

The additive method is a subclass of the linear congruential that can be specified as

$$X_n = (X_{n-1} + X_{n-j}) \text{ modulus } M.$$

That is, C_1 and C_j are equal to one while C_0 and C_2 through C_{j-1} are equal to zero. A special case of the additive method is the Fibonacci method, in which $j = 2$.

$$X_n = (X_{n-1} + X_{n-2}) \text{ modulus } M.$$

It is called the Fibonacci method after its resemblance to the Fibonacci series in which each successive number is the sum of the two numbers immediately preceding it. The Fibonacci method has been given more attention than the additive method, but neither has been studied extensively. The chief drawback of these methods is their requirement for additional storage and their failure to perform well on the runs tests. Their chief attraction is the great increase in period length independent of the computer word size that they allow.

MULTIPLICATIVE GENERATOR

Given an initial starting value x_0, a constant multiplier λ, then $x_{i+1} = \lambda x_i$ (modulus P) yields a multiplicative relationship (modulus P) for any value of i over the sequence $\{x_1, x_2, \ldots, x_i, \ldots\}$. Hence, we have formed a sequence of integer numbers $\{x_1, x_2, \ldots, x_i, \ldots\}$. We also have that $x_i < P$ for all x_i. From the sequence of integers $\{x_i\}$, rational numbers in the unit interval $(0, 1)$ can be obtained by forming the sequence $\{r_i\} = \{x_i/P\}$. Our computer program to generate random numbers in the unit interval will employ a modulus $P = 2^m$, where m represents the word size of the binary computer in bits. The following are examples of P for commonly used computers.

$$P = 2^{31} = 214783648 \qquad \text{for IBM,}$$

$$P = 2^{35} = 34359738368 \qquad \text{for Honeywell or Univac,}$$

$$P = 2^{48} = 2^{35} \times 8192 \qquad \text{for CDC.}$$

Since we desire to write a program to generate $\{r_i\} = \{x_i/P\}$, we shall write $r_i = X_i \cdot 2^{-m}$. As an example, for $m = 31$,

$$r_i = X_i \cdot (0.46566613E - 9)$$

or for $m = 35$,

$$r_i = X_i \cdot (0.29103805E - 10).$$

The multiplicative procedure for generating random numbers on an m-bit binary machine may be summarized as follows:

1. Choose any odd number x_0 (integer) as a starting value that is less than $P = 2^m$.

2. Choose an integer λ, which is the constant multiplier. (As suggested in the reference of footnote 1 of Chapter 5, $\lambda = 5^{13} = 1220703125$ is a good selection.)

3. Compute λx_0 using integer arithmetic. This product consists of $2m$ bits of which the high-order m bits are discarded and the low-order m bits represent x_1. (This discarding bits in integer arithmetic is done automatically in FORTRAN.)

4. Calculate $r_1 = x_1 \cdot 2^{-m}$ to obtain a pseudo-random number on the unit interval.

5. Each successive random number x_{i+1} is obtained from the low-order bits of the product λx_i.

The following is a FORTRAN subroutine utilizing the preceding algorithm with $m = 35$.

```
FUNCTION RCM(IST)
IST = IST*1220703125
RCM = IST
RCM = RCM*0.291038305E-10
RETURN
END
```

Examples of other values of λ are given by Coveyou and MacPherson [1]. The output RCM is a floating-point random number between 0 and 1. The main program that calls this generator must provide an initial odd integer value of IST, which must be less than P. The function RCM(IST) can be called in an expression in any place where a variable is permitted.

The following are criteria for "acceptable" methods for generating random numbers. These methods must yield sequences of numbers that are:

1. Uniformly distributed
2. Statistically independent
3. Reproducible
4. Nonrepeating for any desired length (period)
5. Capable of generating random numbers at high rates of speed
6. Requiring a minimum amount of computer memory capacity

The prior two theorems on the maximum period possible for mixed congruential generators address the question of whether there exists a smallest positive value of $i = h$, such that $x_h = x_0$, where h is called the *period* of the sequence $\{x_i\}$. If such an h does exist, what conditions can be imposed on x_0, λ, c, and P so that the period of $\{x_i\}$ is as large as possible.

STATISTICAL TESTS OF PSEUDO-RANDOM NUMBERS

The statistical properties of pseudo-random numbers generated by the methods outlined in the previous section should coincide with the statistical properties of numbers generated by an idealized chance device that selects numbers from the unit interval (0, 1) independently and with all numbers equally likely. Clearly, the pseudo-random numbers produced by computer programs are not random in this sense, since they are completely determined by the starting data and have limited precision. But as long as our pseudo-random numbers can pass the set of statistical tests implied by the aforementioned idealized chance device, these pseudo-random numbers can be treated as "truly" random numbers, even though they are not.

the frequency test

The frequency test is used to check the uniformity of a sequence of M consecutive sets of N pseudo-random numbers. For each set of N random numbers $r_1, r_2, \ldots r_N$, we divide the (0, 1) unit interval into x subintervals.

$$0 = \frac{0}{x} \quad \frac{1}{x} \quad \frac{2}{x} \quad \frac{3}{x} \quad \frac{4}{x} \ldots \frac{x-1}{x} \quad \frac{x}{x} = 1.$$

The expected number of random numbers in each subinterval is N/x. Next let f_j, where $j = 1, 2, 3, \ldots, x$, denote the actual number of pseudo-random numbers r_i ($i = 1, 2, \ldots, N$) in the subinterval $(j - 1)/x \leqslant r_i < j/x$. The statistic

$$\chi_1^2 = (\frac{x}{N}) \sum_{j=1}^{x} (f_j - \frac{N}{x})^2$$

has approximately a $\chi^2(x - 1)$ for a sequence of "truly" random numbers. This statement is then computed for all M consecutive sets of N pseudo-random numbers. Next, let F_j denote the number of the resulting M values of χ_1^2, which lie between the $(j - 1)$th and the jth quantile of a χ^2-distribution with $x - 1$ degrees of freedom ($j = 1, 2, 3, \ldots, u$), and compute the statistic

$$\chi_F^2 = \frac{u}{M} \sum_{j=1}^{u} (F_j - \frac{M}{u})^2.$$

The hypothesis that the pseudo-random numbers in the sequence consisting of M sets of pseudo-random numbers are uniform is rejected if χ_F^2 with $u - 1$ exceed the critical values. For example, let $x = u = 10, M = 100, N = 1000$. N/x and M/u should always be 75. For example with $\alpha = 0.05$, the hypothesis is rejected if $\chi_F^2 > 16.919$, where $u = 10$. Table 6, Appendix C yields $\chi^2(0.05) = 16.919$.

serial tests

Serial tests are used to check the degree of randomness between successive numbers in a sequence. A serial test is usually applied to pairs of numbers where the pseudo-random numbers are taken as the coordinate of a point in a unit square divided into x^2 cells. The idea can be extended to a unit cube.

Begin by generating a sequence of M consecutive sets of N pseudo-random numbers and compute x_1^2 statistic for each of the M sets of pseudo-random numbers. Then for each set of N pseudo-random numbers, we let f_{jh} denote the number of pseudo-random numbers r_i ($i = 1, 2, \ldots, N - 1$), which satisfies $(j - 1)/x \leqslant r_i < j/x$ and $(h - 1)/x \leqslant r_{i + 1} < h/x$, where $j, h = 1, 2, \ldots, x$. Next compute

$$\chi_2^2 = \frac{x^2}{N - 1} \sum_{j = 1}^{x} \sum_{h = 1}^{x} (f_{jh} - \frac{N - 1}{x^2})^2$$

for each set of N pseudo-random numbers. It has shown that $\chi_2^2 - \chi_1^2$ has approximately a χ^2 distribution with $x^2 - x = $ df, for a "truly" random sequence of numbers [6].

Next, calculate $\chi_2^2 - \chi_1^2$ for each of the M sets of N pseudo-random numbers, and let s_j denote the number of the resulting M values of $\chi_2^2 - \chi_1^2$ that lie between the $(j - 1)$th and the jth quantile ($j = 1, 2, \ldots, u$) of a $\chi^2(\alpha)$ with df $= x^2 - x$.

Finally, we compute

$$\chi_s^2 = \frac{u}{M} \sum_{j = 1}^{u} (s_j - \frac{M}{u})^2, \qquad df = u - 1$$

Serial randomness of a sequence of pseudo-random numbers is acceptable if $\chi_s^2 < \chi^2(\alpha)$ with df $= u = 1$.

the lagged product test

If k is the length of lag, the lagged product coefficient C_k for sequence r_i ($i = 1, 2, \ldots, N$) is defined as

$$C_k = \frac{1}{N - k} \sum_{i = 1}^{N - k} r_i r_{i + k}.$$

It can be shown that, if there is no correlation between r_i and $r_{i + k}$, the values of C_k will be approximately normally distributed with expected value equal to 0.25 and standard deviation equal to $\sqrt{13N - 19k/12(N - k)}$ for $k > 0$. The χ^2 goodness of fit test can be applied to test for normality.

tests of runs

Runs Up and Down

For a sequence of N pseudo-random numbers $r_1, r_2, \ldots, r_N$, we define an $N - 1$ bit binary sequence, where the ith term is equal to zero if $r_i < r_{i + 1}$ and is equal to one if $r_i > r_{i + 1}$. A subsequence of k zero, bracketed by ones at each end, forms a run of zeros of length k, and similarly for runs of ones. The test involves counting the actual number of occurrences of runs of different lengths and comparing these counts with their corresponding expected theoretical values. The expected values based on a "truly" random samples are

$$\frac{(2N - 1)}{3} \quad \text{for total number of runs,}$$

$$\frac{(5N + 1)}{12} \quad \text{for runs of length 1,}$$

$$\frac{(11N - 14)}{60} \quad \text{for runs of length 2,}$$

$$\frac{2[(k^2 + 3k + 1)N - (k^3 + 3k^2 - k - 4)]}{(k + 3)!} \quad \text{for runs of length } k \text{ for } k < N - 1,$$

$$\frac{2}{N!} \quad \text{for runs of length } N - 1.$$

Again, a χ^2 goodness of fit test may be used to check whether a pseudo-random number generator is acceptable. A common characteristic of nonrandom sequences is an excess of long runs.

Example of Runs Up and Down

Consider the following $N - 1 = 20$ bit binary sequence:

$$10111010010110100011.$$

Table 7-1 illustrates the expected and observed values of runs.

$$\chi^2 = (13.66 - 13)^2/13.66 + (0.333)^2/8.333 + (0.616)^2/3.616 + (1.411)^2/0.489$$

$$+ 0$$

$$= 5.895, \quad \text{with degrees of freedom} = 20.$$

From a table of percentiles of the chi-square distribution, we find $\chi^2(0.95) = 31.4$. Hence, one cannot reject the hypothesis of randomness.

TABLE 7-1

Statistics of Interest	Expected Value	Observed Value
Total number of runs	$(2N - 1)/3 = 13.66$	13
Runs of length 1	$(5N + 1)/12 = 8.33$	8
Runs of length 2	3.616	3
Runs of length 3	0.489	2
Runs of length $i, 4 \leq i \leq 20$	Approx. zero	0

Runs Above and Below the Means

For a sequence of N pseudo-random numbers $r_1, r_2, \ldots, r_N$, we define an N-bit binary sequence S, where the ith term is equal to zero if $r_i < \frac{1}{2}$ and is equal to one if $r_i > \frac{1}{2}$. Again the runs of S are counted, the expected number of runs of length k is $(N - k + 3)2^{-k-1}$, and the expected total number of runs is $(N + 1)/2$. Use a χ^2 test. (A very large or very small number of runs in a sequence indicates nonrandomness; e.g., let R = number of runs in a sequence of pseudo-random numbers and reject randomness if $R < k_1$ or $R > k_2$.)

the gap test

Although the preceding tests have been concerned with the randomness of sequences of numbers where each number consisted of some fixed number of digits, for example, 10 digits, the gap test is concerned with the randomness of the digits in a sequence of numbers. For any given digit d, we are interested in the lengths of gaps of non-d digits between any two of the given digits. A gap of length k occurs when k non-d digits occur between two d's. Two consecutive d's produce a gap of length $k = 0$. For a "truly" random sequence of digits, the probability of obtaining a gap of length k is

$$P(k) = (0.9)^k(0.1).$$

For a given sequence of digits, tallies are made of gaps occurring for each length. A χ^2 goodness of fit test can be used to compare the expected and actual number of gaps of length k, and the χ^2 values for several samples can be treated in a manner similar to before (like χ_1^2 and χ_s^2).

the maximum test

For a set of N independent uniform random numbers on the $(0, 1)$ unit interval, we define a random variable $R = \max(r_1, r_2, \ldots, r_N)$, which has a probability distribution defined by order statistics. R^N, is uniformly distributed over $(0, 1)$.

$$g(R) = NR^{N-1}, \qquad 0 \leqslant R \leqslant 1,$$

$$= 0, \quad \text{elsewhere.}$$

Let $z = R^N$

$$h(z) = 1, \qquad 0 \leqslant z \leqslant 1,$$

$$= 0, \quad \text{elsewhere.}$$

The test of the observed values for R^N is a simple frequency test that can be repeated with several sets of N random numbers. The maximum test of N uniform random numbers is also called the test of N-tuples $(r_1, r_2, \ldots, r_N)$ and is considered to be a more stringent test than the basic test.

EXERCISES

7-1. What are the (a) additive, (b) multiplicative, (c) mixed congruential methods for generating uniform random variates? What are the advantages and/or disadvantages of each technique?

7-2. State the general form of the congruential method for generating pseudo-random numbers. Given $n_0 = 5$, $c = 2$, $a = 4$, and $m = 3$, generate five numbers using this method.

7-3. Consider the mixed congruential generator $X_{n+1} \equiv aX_n + c \pmod{M}$. Find a set of values for a and c in the mixed congruential generator (other than $c = a = 1$) that will assure a period of 256 in a computer of word length $2^8 = 256$. Generate the first few numbers in this sequence and comment on their behavior.

7-4. *Prove:* Let $x_{i+1} \equiv \lambda x_i + c \pmod{P}$. If $\lambda = 10^a + 1$ ($a \geqslant 2$) and if c is not divisible by 2 or 5, $P = 10^{10}$, then the sequence $x_0, x_1, x_2, \ldots$ has a full period of 10^{10} elements.

7-5. Let $X_{i+1} \equiv aX_i + c \pmod{m}$. With $m = 10$, find values of a, c, X_0 that will result in a mixed congruential generator that produces all the even digits and no odd digits (comment on its period). Once more with $M = 10$, find values of a and c (other than $a = c = 1$) that will give a period of 10. Generate these ten numbers and comment on their sequential behavior.

7-6. Describe the criteria you would use in judging a random number generator acceptable.

7-7. Describe a statistic to test the uniformity of a sequence of random numbers.

7-8. Given $X_{i+1} \equiv 3X_i \pmod{7}$ and $X_0 = 3$, determine the period.

7-9. Find a set of values for a and c in the mixed congruential generator $X_{i+1} \equiv aX_i + c \pmod{m}$ that will assure a period of $m = 1024$ in a computer of word length $m = 2^{10} = 1024$. Generate the first three numbers in this sequence.

7-9. Describe at least four criteria you would use in judging a random number generator acceptable *and* discuss a test for one criteria in judging a random number generator acceptable.

7-10. A random number generator is to be tested for (a) uniformity of distribution, (b) runs above and below the mean, and (c) autocorrelation between the first, fifth, ninth, and so on, numbers. The probability of rejecting the generator as nonrandom if in fact it is random is to be 0.02. Describe in detail each of these tests. At what α level should each of the tests be conducted?

7-11. It has been suggested that the last four digits of telephone numbers constitute a reasonable source for random numbers. Discuss in detail how you would test this assertion.

REFERENCES

1. COVEYOU, R. R., and MACPHERSON, R. D., "Fourier Analysis of Uniform Random Number Generators," *Journal of ACM*, XIV(1967), pp. 100–119.

2. GORENSTEIN, S., "Testing a Random Number Generator," *Communications of ACM*, X(1967), pp. 111–117.

3. GREEN, B. F., SMITH, J. E., and KLEM, L., "Empirical Tests of an Additive Random Number Generator," *Journal of ACM*, VI(1959), pp. 527–537.

4. HULL, T. E., and DOBELL, A. R., "Random Number Generators," *SIAM Review*, 3(1962), pp. 230–254.

5. JANSSON, B., *Random Number Generators*, Victor Pettersons Bokindustri, Aktiebolag, Stockholm, 1966.

6. KNUTH, D. E., *The Art of Computer Programing*, Vol. 2, *Seminumerical Algorithms*, Addison-Wesley Publishing Co., Reading, Mass., 1969.

7. MACLAREN, M. D., and MARSAGLIA, G., "Uniform Random Number Generators," *Journal of ACM*, XII(1965), pp. 83–89.

8. SEDGEWICK, R., and SZYMANSKI, T. G., "The Complexity of Finding Periods," *ACM* (1979), pp. 74–80.

9. WALL, D. D., "Fibonacci Series Modulo M," *American Mathematics Monthly*, 67(1960), pp. 525–532.

10. ZIERLER, N., "Linear Recurring Sequences," *Journal of the Society of Industrial and Applied Mathematics*, 7(1959), pp. 31–48.

8

GENERATION OF STOCHASTIC VARIATES

The purpose of this chapter is to provide the practitioner a set of techniques for generating random variates on the computer from some of the widely used probability distributions. Some general methods for generating random variates from any empirical distribution are provided.

To generate random variates from probability distributions, a point function must be defined. This point function is denoted by $F(x) = P[X \leq x]$ and is called the cumulative distribution function of the random variable X. The cumulative distribution function can be stated mathematically as

$$F(x) = \sum_{w \leq x} f(w), \quad \text{(discrete)}$$

$$F(x) = \int_{-\infty}^{x} f(w) \, dw, \quad \text{(continuous)}$$

Some of the properties of $F(x)$ include

1. $0 \leq F(x) \leq 1$.
2. $F(x)$ is a nondecreasing function of x.
3. $F(\infty) = 1, F(-\infty) = 0$.
4. $F(x)$ is continuous to the right at each point x.

In the continuous case, $f(x) = F'(x)$ is called a probability density function (pdf) and in the discrete case $f(x) = P[X = x]$ is called a probability function (pf).

I. THREE BASIC METHODS FOR GENERATING VARIATES FROM PROBABILITY DISTRIBUTIONS

a. inverse transformation method

If we want to generate random variates x_i from some particular statistical population whose pdf is given by $f(x)$, then we must first obtain $F(x)$. Since $F(x)$, the distribution function, is defined over the range 0 to 1, we can generate uniformly distributed random numbers and set $F(x) = R$. It is clear that x is uniquely determined by $R = F(x)$, since $F(x)$ is a nondecreasing function of x. R denotes the uniform random variate.

Therefore, for $R = R_0$ (Figure 8-1), it is possible to find $x = x_0$; that is,

$$x_0 = F^{-1}(R_0),$$

where $F^{-1}(R)$ is the inverse transformation of R on the unit interval into the domain of x. Set

$$R = F(x) = \int_{-\infty}^{x} f(t) \, dt.$$

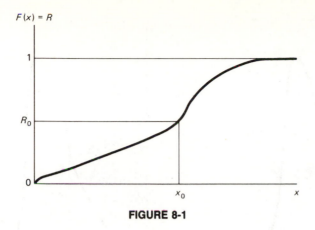

$F(x) = R$

1

R_0

0

x_0

x

FIGURE 8-1

Then $P[X \leq x] = F(x) = P[R \leq F(x)] = P[F^{-1}(R) \leq x]$ and, hence, $F^{-1}(R)$ is a variate that has $f(x)$ as its pdf.

Example:

$$f(x) = 2x, \qquad 0 < x < 1$$
$$= 0, \qquad \text{elsewhere}$$

$$R = F(x) = \int_0^x 2t \, dt = x^2, \qquad 0 < x < 1$$

$$\therefore x = F^{-1}(R) = \sqrt{R}, \qquad 0 < R < 1$$

b. the rejection technique

Suppose we want a random sample (RS) from a pdf $f(x)$, $a < x < b$, $0 < f(x) < M$. Then

$$0 < \frac{f(x)}{M} < 1.$$

If R_1 is a random number from the standard uniform density, then (from the definition of a uniform density) the probability that $R_1 \leq f(x)/M$ is $f(x)/M$.

Suppose now that we choose x_1 at random (Figure 8-2) from the interval $a < x < b$ by selecting a second random number, say R_2, and setting $x_1 = a + (b - a)R_2$. We use this number if and only if $R_1 \leq f(x_1)/M$. This procedure is called the rejection technique.

$$E[\text{No. of trials before a successful pair is found}] = M(b - a)$$

Therefore, the method may be very inefficient.

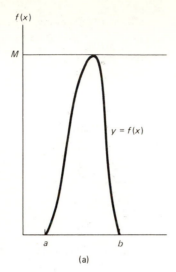

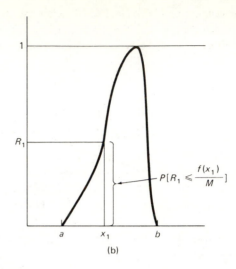

(a)   (b)

FIGURE 8-2

Example:

Generate x from $f(x) = 2x$, $0 < x < 1$, and zero elsewhere. $0 < f(x) \leq 2$. $M = 2$.

1. Obtain two random numbers R_1, R_2.
2. If $R_1 \leq f(R_2)/2$. Let $x = R_2$.
3. If $R_1 > f(R_2)/2$, start all over again.
4. Repeat until RS has been obtained.

c. the composition, or mixture method

Suppose that $F(x)$ can be expressed in the following form:

$$F(x) = \sum_{i=1}^{n-1} a_i F_i(x) + \left(1 - \sum_{i=1}^{n-1} a_i\right) F_n(x)$$

with $a_1, a_2, \ldots, a_{n-1} > 0$ and $\sum_{i=1}^{n-1} a_i < 1$.

A random number R_1 is drawn from the standard uniform distribution. Because of the restriction on a_i, if

$$S_j = \sum_{i=1}^{j} a_i \qquad \text{for } j = 1, 2, \ldots, n$$

then there is a value m of j such that

$$S_{m-1} < R_1 < S_m.$$

166

The random number to be used then is generated using a procedure that generates numbers with distribution F_m. *Note: F_m should be an easy distribution. Typical easy distributions are those for which the inverse transformation can be utilized.

Example:

$n = 2$, $F(x) = pF_1(x) + (1 - p)F_2(x)$. If $R < p$, then x is chosen from $F_1(x)$ (by either rejection or inverse transformation). If $R \geqslant p$, then x is chosen from $F_2(x)$.

Example:

The probability density function for the hyperexponential distribution is

$$f(x) = p_1\alpha_1 e^{-\alpha_1 x} + p_2\alpha_2 e^{-\alpha_2 x}, \qquad x > 0,\ \alpha_1 > 0,\ \alpha_2 > 0,\ = 0,$$

$$= 0, \qquad \text{elsewhere.}$$

The distribution function for X is

$$F(x) = p_1[1 - e^{-\alpha_1 x}] + p_2[1 - e^{-\alpha_2 x}], \qquad p_1 = 1 - p_2.$$

Hence, the distribution function is the form

$$F(x) = p_1 F_1(x) + (1 - p_1)F_2(x).$$

II. GENERATION OF STOCHASIC VARIATES: CONTINUOUS TYPE

a. uniform distribution

$$f(x) = 1/(b - a), \qquad a < x < b,$$

$$= 0, \qquad \text{elsewhere.}$$

$$F(x) = \int_a^x \frac{1}{b - a}\, dt = \frac{x - a}{b - a},$$

$$E(x) = \frac{b + a}{2},$$

$$V(x) = \frac{(b - a)^2}{12}.$$

By inverse transformation technique,

$$X = a + (b - a)R, \qquad 0 < R < 1$$

b. exponential distribution

$$f(x) = \alpha e^{-\alpha x}, \qquad \alpha > 0, x \geq 0,$$
$$= 0, \qquad \text{elsewhere.}$$

$$F(x) = \int_0^x \alpha e^{-\alpha t}\, dt = 1 - e^{-\alpha x}$$

$$E(x) = \frac{1}{\alpha}$$

$$V(x) = \frac{1}{\alpha^2} = [E(x)]^2$$

By inverse transformation technique,

$$R = 1 - e^{-\alpha x} \quad \text{or} \quad 1 - R = 1 - e^{-\alpha x}$$

$$\therefore X = -\left(\frac{1}{\alpha}\right) \ln R, \qquad \text{since } R \text{ is as likely to occur as } 1 - R.$$

$$= -E(x) \ln R$$

c. generalized exponential (number of populations finite)

The exponential distribution is based on the assumption that α is constant; that is, all events are assumed to have been generated by a single random process. This condition is frequently violated in the real world when we deal with *indistinguishable* events that are the result of different but intermixed random processes. It is possible, indeed likely, that a sample may be taken from two or more exponential distributions each having a different value of α. For example, arrival rates α_i with probabilities p_i, where α_i is the parameter of the ith population ($i = 1, 2, \ldots, s$) such that $\alpha_i \neq \alpha$, and $\sum_{i=1}^{s} p_i = 1$. When $s = 2$ it is called a *hyperexponential*, and when $s > 2$ it is called *generalized exponential*.

To generate a given mixture of s exponential variates, we merely introduce a probability switch before the call to exponential. Generate $R \; \varepsilon \; (0, 1)$ and set $X = 1/\alpha_i$ if $p_0 + \cdots + p_{i-1} < R \leq p_1 + \cdots + p_i$ where $p_0 = 0$ and $i = 1, \ldots, s$. In practice, p_i are difficult to estimate.

d. weibull distribution

$$f(x) = \frac{c}{b}\left(\frac{x}{b}\right)^{c-1} e^{-(x/b)^c},$$

$$F(x) = 1 - e^{-(x/b)^c}, \qquad x \geq 0, b > 0, c > 0.$$

where b is a scale parameter

c is a shape parameter

$\dfrac{1}{b}$ is similar to that of α in the exponential distribution

With $c = 1$, we have exponential with $\alpha = \dfrac{1}{b}$:

$$E(x) = b\Gamma\left(\frac{1}{c} + 1\right)$$

$$V(x) = b^2\Gamma\left(\frac{2}{c} + 1\right) - [E(x)]^2, \qquad \text{where } \Gamma(\alpha) = \int_0^\infty x^{\alpha-1}e^{-x}\, dx$$

By inverse transformation technique,

$$X = b(-\ln R)^{1/c}$$

e. the gamma distribution

The sum of k independent exponential variates with parameter α. This is also called an Erlang distribution.

$$f(x) = \frac{\alpha^k x^{(k-1)} e^{-\alpha x}}{(k-1)!}, \qquad \alpha > 0, k > 0, x > 0$$

$F(x)$ does not exist in explicit form, but is well tabled (Appendix C).

$$E(x) = \frac{k}{\alpha}$$

$$V(x) = \frac{k}{\alpha^2}$$

If $k = 1$, the gamma is exponential. As $k \to \infty$, gamma approaches normal distribution.

To generate a gamma random variate X, take the sum of independent k exponential variates $x_1, x_2, \ldots, x_k$ with $E(x_i) = \dfrac{1}{\alpha}$; then

$$X = \sum_{i=1}^{k} x_i = -\frac{1}{\alpha}\sum_{i=1}^{k} \ln R_i$$

$$= -\frac{1}{\alpha}\ln\left(\prod_{i=1}^{k} R_i\right)$$

f. the chi-square distribution

A gamma with $\alpha = \dfrac{1}{2}$:

$$f(x) = \frac{x^{k-1} e^{-x/2}}{2^k \Gamma(k)}, \qquad lx \geqslant 0$$

Usually, $k = r/2$ and r is called the degree of freedom. $F(x)$ does not exist in explicit form, but is well tabled (Appendix C).

$$E(x) = 2k = r$$

$$V(x) = 4k = 2r$$

To generate a chi-square random variate:

Case i: If $E(x) = 2k = r$ is an even number, then the generation technique is

$$x = -\frac{1}{\alpha} (\ln \prod_{i=1}^{r/2} R_i), \qquad \alpha = \frac{1}{2}.$$

A gamma with $\alpha = \dfrac{1}{2}$:

and the generation technique is

$$x = -\frac{1}{\alpha} (\ln \prod_{i=1}^{r-1} R_i) + Z^2,$$

where Z is a normal variate with mean 0 and variance 1.

g. beta distribution

Let x_1 and x_2 be two stochastic independent random variables that have gamma distribution and the joint pdf

$$f(x_1, x_2) = \frac{1}{\Gamma_{(a)} \Gamma_{(b)}} x_1^{a-1} x_2^{b-1} e^{-x_1 - x_2}, \qquad x_1 > 0, x_2 > 0,$$

$$a > 0, b > 0.$$

The *beta* variable is given by

$$x = \frac{x_1}{x_1 + x_2}, \qquad 0 < x < 1$$

and

$$f(x) = \frac{\Gamma(a + b)}{\Gamma_{(a)} \Gamma_{(b)}} x^{a-1}(1 - x)^{b-1},$$

$$E(x) = \frac{a}{(a + b)},$$

$$V(x) = \frac{E(x)b}{(a + b + 1)(a + b)}.$$

To generate a beta variate, x, set

$$x = \frac{x_1}{x_1 + x_2}$$

where x_1 is the gamma distribution with $\alpha = 1$ and $k = a$, and x_2 is the gamma distribution with $\alpha = 1$ and $k = b$.

h. normal distribution

$$f(x) = \frac{1}{\sigma \sqrt{2\pi}} \exp\left[-\frac{1}{2}\left(\frac{x - \mu}{\sigma}\right)^2\right], \qquad -\infty < x < \infty.$$

Let $z = (x - \mu)/\sigma$; then z has a normal distribution with $\mu = 0$ and $\sigma^2 = 1$. $F(x)$ does *not* exist in explicit form, but can be approximated as follows.

Central Limit Theorem:
If $x_1, x_2, \ldots, x_N$ are independent random variables each having the same probability distribution with $E(x_i) = \theta$ and $V(x_i) = \sigma^2$, then

$$\lim_{N \to \infty} Pr\left[a < \frac{\sum_{i=1}^{N} x_i - N\theta}{\sqrt{N}\,\sigma} < b\right] = \frac{1}{\sqrt{2\pi}} \int_a^b e^{-(1/2)z^2} dz,$$

where $E(\sum_1^N x_i) = N\theta, \ V(\sum_1^N x_i) = N\sigma^2$.

Note
$$z = \frac{\sum_1^N x_i - N\theta}{\sigma \sqrt{N}}$$

is approximately $N(0, 1)$.

Method 1. To generate normal random variates x, which are $N(\mu_x, \sigma_x^2)$: Let $R_1, R_2, \ldots, R_K$ be K independent uniformly distributed random variates defined over the interval $0 < R_i < 1$. Now

$$\theta = \frac{1}{2}, \qquad \sigma = \frac{b - a}{\sqrt{12}} = \frac{1}{\sqrt{12}}.$$

Therefore,

$$z = \frac{\sum\limits_{i=1}^{K} R_i - \frac{K}{2}}{\sqrt{\frac{K}{12}}}$$

is approximately $N(0, 1)$.

Now

$$z = \frac{X - \mu_x}{\sigma_x}$$

set

$$X = \sigma_x \left(\frac{12^{1/2}}{K}\right) \left(\sum_{i=1}^{K} R_i - \frac{K}{2}\right) + \mu_x.$$

Important: How large should K be to satisfy the central limit theorem? Minimum value of K is 10. $K = 12$ is nice since $\sqrt{\frac{12}{K}} = 1$. $K = 12$ truncates the distribution at $\pm 6\sigma$ limits and is reliable only at $\pm 3\sigma$ limits. In order to have reliable $\pm 6\sigma$ limits, set $K = 24$.

Method 2. To generate two normal random variates x_1, x_2 that are independent and each $N(0, 1)$: Let R_1 and R_2 be two uniformly distributed independent random variates defined over $(0, 1)$. Then

$$x_1 = (-2 \ln R_1)^{1/2} \cos 2\pi R_2,$$

$$x_2 = (-2 \ln R_1)^{1/2} \sin 2\pi R_2,$$

are two standard normal random variates. Since this method is exact, it is usually recommended.

i. normal related distribution

To generate *chi-square* variate x, set

$$x = \sum_{i=1}^{m} z_i^2$$

where z_i are $N(0, 1)$ and $m = $ degrees of freedom.

$$E(x) = m$$

$$V(x) = 2m$$

For $m < 30$, we could use this or previous techniques. For $m > 30$, we use

$$z = \sqrt{2x_m^2} - \sqrt{2m - 1}$$

or

$$x = \frac{(z + \sqrt{2m - 1})^2}{2},$$

where z is $N(0, 1)$.

To generate *t-distribution* variate t, set

$$T = \frac{z}{\sqrt{\chi_m^2/m}}, \qquad df = m.$$

Note

$$f(t) = \frac{\Gamma\left(\dfrac{m + 1}{2}\right)}{\Gamma\left(\dfrac{m}{2}\right)} \left[\pi m(1 + \frac{t^2}{m})^{m + 1} \right]^{-1/2},$$

$$E(T) = 0, \qquad V(T) = \frac{2}{m - 2}.$$

For $m > 30$, we can use normal approximation since T is approximately $N(0, 1)$.

To generate *F-distribution* variate F,

$$\text{set } F = \frac{\chi_m^2/m}{\chi_n^2/n}, \qquad df = m, n,$$

$$E(F) = \frac{n}{n - 2}, \qquad n > 2$$

$$V(F) = \frac{2n^2 (m + n - 2)}{m(n - 2)^2 (n - 4)}, \qquad n > 4$$

Alternate Technique: Set

$$F = \frac{n}{m} (\frac{1}{Y} - 1), \qquad df = m, n,$$

where Y has a beta distribution with $a = m$ and $b = n$.

j. lognormal distribution

Let

$$f(y) = \frac{1}{\sigma_y \sqrt{2\pi}} \, e^{-1/2 \left(\frac{y - \mu_y}{\sigma_y} \right)^2}, \quad -\infty < y < \infty,$$

and

$$y = \ln x, \quad x \geqslant 0$$

Then x is said to have a lognormal distribution.

$$E(x) = e^{\mu_y} + \sigma_y^2/2,$$

$$V(x) = [E(x)]^2 \, [e^{\sigma_y^2} - 1].$$

$$\mu_y = \ln E(x) - \frac{1}{2} \ln \left[\frac{-V(X)}{[E(x)]^2} + 1 \right],$$

$$\sigma_y^2 = \ln \left[\frac{V(x)}{[E(x)]^2} + 1 \right].$$

To generate lognormal variate x, note that the standard normal variate z can be expressed as

$$z = \frac{\ln x - \mu_y}{\sigma_y}, \quad \ln x = \mu_y + \sigma_y z.$$

Therefore $\qquad x = e^{\mu_y} + \sigma_y \, z$, where z is $N(0, 1)$.

III. GENERATION OF STOCHASTIC VARIATES: DISCRETE TYPE

In this section, we are concerned only with random variables that take on only discrete, nonnegative integer values.

$$F(x) = p[X \leqslant x] = \sum_{j=0}^{x} f(j),$$

where

$$f(j) = P[X = j], \quad j = 0, 1, 2, \ldots.$$

Discrete probability distributions are *appropriate models* of random phenomena only if the values of the random variables are measured by counting.

Definition: *Bernoulli trials* are chance experiments in which the outcome of each trial is expressed as either a success or failure. The $P[\text{success}] = p$, where p is constant for a particular sequence of trials. Set $q = 1 - p$.

a. geometric distribution

Assume Bernoulli trials.

Definition: The variate generated by counting the number of failures in a sequence of trials (events) before the first success occurs are variates, x, from a geometric probability function (pf).

The probability function can be expressed as

$$f(x) = pq^x, \qquad x = 0, 1, 2, \ldots ,$$

$$F(x) = P_r[X \leq x] = \sum_{j=0}^{x} pq^x = 1 - q^{x+1},$$

$$p \leq F(x) \leq 1, \text{ since } F(0) = p$$

$$Pr[X > 0] = q.$$

$$E(x) = \frac{q}{p}$$

$$V(x) = \frac{q}{p^2} = \frac{E(x)}{p}$$

Method 1: To generate geometric variate x. Note that $p \leq F(x) \leq 1$ or $0 \leq \frac{[1 - F(x)]}{q} \leq 1$. Therefore,

$$R = q^x = P[X \geq x]$$

and by inverse transform technique,

$$x = \left[\frac{\ln R}{\ln q} \right],$$

where x is rounded to the next smallest integer.

Method 2: To generate geometric variate x. This method is exact, whereas method 1 is an approximation. If p is large, use method 2. Generate a sequence $R_1, R_2, \ldots ,$ $R_i, \ldots$. Terminate the sequence when we reach a value of $R_i \leq p$.

Procedure

$i = 1, 2, \ldots$, and $x = 0$.

If $R_i > p$, set $x \leftarrow x + 1$.

If $R_i \leq p$, stop.

The x generated is defined as the number of failures occurring before the first success.

Method 1 is recommended when $p < 0.8$. The disadvantage of method 1 is that it is an approximate method.

b. negative binomial distribution

When Bernoulli trials are repeated until k successes occur ($k \geq 1$), then the random variable, x, denoting the number of failures will have a negative binomial distribution. *Note:* Negative binomial variates are the sum of k geometric variates.

$$f(x) = \binom{k + x - 1}{x} p^k q^x, \qquad x = 0, 1, 2, \ldots ,$$

where k is the total number of successes out of $k + x$ trials, and x is the number of failures that occur before k successes occur.

$$E(x) = \frac{kq}{p}, \qquad V(x) = \frac{kq}{p^2}.$$

To generate variate, X, take the sum of k geometric variates, k integer.

$$x = \sum_{i=1}^{k} \left[\frac{\ln R_i}{\ln q} \right].$$

c. binomial distribution

The random variable is defined by the number of successful events in a sequence of n independent Bernoulli trials, where the probability of a success is p for each trial. *Note:* Sampling with replacement: The random variable equals the number x of success in n trials.

$$f(x) = \binom{n}{x} p^x q^{n-x}, \qquad x = 0, 1, 2, \ldots , n,$$

$$E(x) = np$$

$$V(x) = npq \quad \text{and} \quad V(x) < E(x)$$

Method 1: For generation of binomial variate x. When n is large, use normal approximation. Since it is possible to have negative values with the normal distribution, the probability of negative observations must be negligibly small.

In practice,

$$E(x) = np \geqslant 3 \sqrt{V(x)} = 3 \sqrt{npq}$$

which implies $n \geqslant 9q/p$.

$$\therefore z = \frac{x - np}{\sqrt{npq}}$$

$$\text{or } X = [z \sqrt{npq} + np],$$

where z is $N(0, 1)$ and x is rounded to the next smallest integer.

Method 2: For generation of binomial variate X. For moderate n, use the reproduction of Bernoulli trials via the rejection technique. Assume n and p are known. Set $x_0 = 0$. Generate r_i, $i = 1, 2, \ldots, n$.

x_i is incremented as follows:

$$x_i = x_{i-1} + 1, \quad \text{if } r_i \leqslant p,$$

$$x_i = x_{i-1} \quad \text{if } r_i > p.$$

$$x_n = \text{binomial variate } x.$$

Since method 1 is approximate, it is recommended when $n > 9q/p$ and $n < 30$. When $n \geqslant 30$, method 2 is recommended.

d. hypergeometric distribution

Consider a population consisting of N elements such that each element belongs either to class I or class II. Let Np be the number of elements in class I and Nq be the number of elements in class II.

If a random sample of n ($< N$) is taken from the population of N elements *without replacement*, the x, the number of class I elements in the sample of n elements, has a hypergeometric probability distribution.

$$f(x) = \frac{\binom{Np}{x} \binom{Nq}{n-x}}{\binom{N}{n}}, \quad \begin{aligned} &0 \leqslant x \leqslant Np, \\ &0 \leqslant n - x \leqslant Nq, \end{aligned}$$

where x, n, and N are integers.

$$E(x) = np, \qquad V(x) = npq \left(\frac{N - n}{N - 1} \right)$$

Method 1: for generation of hypergeometric variate x. We merely alter the Bernoulli trials method of generating binomial variates so that N and p vary, depending respectively on the total number of elements that have been previously drawn from the population and the number of class I elements that have been drawn. As each element in a sample of n elements is drawn, the original value of $N = N_0$ is reduced according to the formula

$$N_i = N_{i-1} - 1, \qquad i = 1, 2, \ldots, n.$$

In a similar manner, the value of $p = p_0$ when the ith element in a sample of n elements is drawn becomes

$$p_i = \frac{N_{i-1}p_{i-1} - s}{N_{i-1} - 1}, \qquad i = 1, 2, \ldots, n,$$

where $s = 1$ when sample elements $i - 1$ belongs to class I and $s = 0$ when sample element $i - 1$ belongs to class II.

Procedure: Set $N_0 = N, p_0 = p, x_0 = 0$. Generate $R_i, i = 1, 2, \ldots, n$.

If $R_i \leq p_{i-1}$, set $x_i = x_{i-1} + 1$, $s = 1.0$. Compute p_i and N_i.
If $R_i > p_{i-1}$, set $x_i = x_{i-1}$, $s = 0.0$. Compute p_i and N_i. $x_n =$ hypergeometric variate x.

Rule of Thumb: The hypergeometric distribution can be approximated by the binomial distribution when $N > 50$ and $n < 0.10N$.

e. poisson distribution

If we take a series of n independent trials Bernoulli trials, in each of which there is a small probability of an event occurring, then use $n \to \infty$. The probability of x occurrences is given by the Poisson distribution

$$f(x) = e^{-\lambda}\frac{\lambda^x}{x!}, \qquad x = 0, 1, 2, \ldots,$$

$$\lambda > 0,$$

when we allow $p \to 0$ in such a manner that $\lambda = np$ remains fixed.

$$E(x) = \lambda$$

$$V(x) = \lambda$$

Theorem: If

(i) The total number of events occurring during any given time interval is independent of the number of events that have already occurred prior to the beginning of the interval, and

(ii) the probability of an event occurring in the interval t to $t + \Delta t$ is approximately $\lambda \Delta t$ for all t,

(iii) probability of more than one event occurring in the interval t to $t + \Delta t$ is negligible.

Then

(a) The pdf of the interval t between the occurrence of consecutive events is $f(t) = \lambda e^{-\lambda t}$, and

(b) The probability of x events occurring during time T is

$$f(x) = e^{-\lambda T}\frac{(\lambda T)^x}{x!}, \qquad x = 0, 1, 2, \ldots$$

Method 1:   For generation of Poisson variate x. Consider a time horizon that has been divided into time intervals $T = \lambda$ (see Figure 8-3). Events are assumed to occur along the time horizon and are denoted by the symbol (Δ). The time interval t between events is assumed to have an exponential distribution with expected value equal to 1. This implies that the number of events x occurring during a time interval $T = \lambda$ follows a Poisson distribution with expected value equal to λ.

Generate exponential distributed time intervals, $t_1, t_2, t_3, \ldots$, with expected value equal to 1. Poisson variate x is determined by

$$\sum_{i=0}^{x} t_i \leq \lambda < \sum_{i=0}^{x+1} t_i, \qquad x = 0, 1, 2, \ldots,$$

where

$$t_i = -\ln R_i \quad \text{and} \quad t_0 = 0.$$

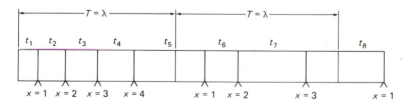

FIGURE 8-3

This could be written as

$$\prod_{i=0}^{x} R_i > e^{-\lambda} \geqslant \prod_{i=0}^{x+1} R_i.$$

Method 2:   For generation of Poisson variate x. If x is a Poisson variable with parameter λ, then for large values of λ ($\lambda > 10$), the normal distribution with $E(x) = \lambda$ and $V(x) = \lambda$ can be used to approximate the distribution of x. That is,

$$x = \left[\sqrt{\lambda} z + \lambda \right],$$

where x is rounded to the next smallest integer.

This method is applicable when $\lambda > 10$. When $\lambda < 10$, use method 1. *Rule of Thumb:* The Poisson is an excellent approximation of the binomial when $n \geqslant 50$, $p < 0.10$, and $\lambda = np$.

empirical discrete distributions

This is a more general method that can be used to simulate

1. Any empirical distribution.
2. Any discrete distribution.
3. Any continuous distribution that can be approximated by a discrete distribution.

(Use this method when no other method is available.)
    Let X be a discrete random variable with $P(X = b_i) = p_i$, such as the random variable in the following:

b_i	$P(X = b_i) = p_i$
b_1	p_1
b_2	p_2
b_3	p_3
b_4	p_4
b_5	p_5
.	.
.	.
.	.
b_n	p_n

Method of Generating x: Generate R (0, 1) and set $x = b_i$ if

$$p_0 + p_1 + \cdots + p_{i-1} < R \leqslant p_1 + \cdots p_i,$$

where $p_0 = 0$.

IV. COMMENTS ON VARIOUS DISTRIBUTIONS

uniform distribution

The value of the uniform distribution (Figure 8-4) for simulation is that it is used to simulate almost any kind of probability function and probability density function. It also has the advantage of being simple to use.

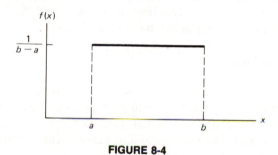

FIGURE 8-4

exponential distribution

Throughout the area of simulation and modeling, we are involved with observing time intervals between the occurrence of distinct random events. Examples include births, deaths, arrivals, and accidents. As pointed out previously, if the probability that an

FIGURE 8-5

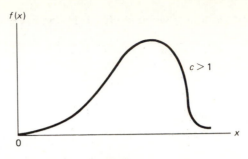

FIGURE 8-6

occurrence of a change in a small time interval is very small, and if the occurrence of this event is statistically independent of the occurrence of other events, then the time interval between the occurrence of events is exponentially distributed (Figure 8-5). Whether a process in the real world actually fits the Poisson assumption or not is an empirical question and cannot be solved here. In the real world, there are a large number of time-dependent processes that satisfy these assumptions.

weibull distribution

The Weibull distribution (Figure 8-6) is a generalization of the exponential distribution. The role of $1/b$ is very similar to α in the exponential distribution. If $c = 1$, then the Weibull distribution is the exponential distribution. If $c > 1$, then the Weibull distribution is bell-shaped (like the normal distribution). The Weibull random variate is very useful in the area of life-testing and reliability.

gamma distribution

The gamma distribution (Figure 8-7) is very useful if the process under consideration is the sum of K independent exponential random variates with parameter α. Since the probability density function is positively skewed, many empirical distributions may be fitted to it.

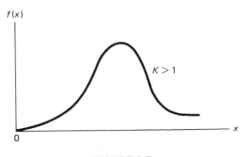

FIGURE 8-7

182

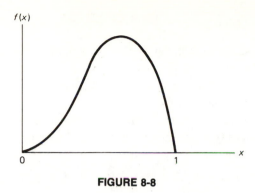

$f(x)$

0   1 x

FIGURE 8-8

beta distribution

The beta distribution (Figure 8-8) is very useful if the process under consideration is the ratio of gamma variates. Since the probability density function is defined in the interval 0 to 1, some empirical distributions may be fitted to it.

normal distribution

The normal distribution (Figure 8-9) is important in many areas. First, many random variates are approximately bell shaped. Second, many processes when sampled in large numbers approximate the normal distribution due to the central limit theorem. Finally, the normal distribution is used in generating other random variates.

lognormal distribution

If a random variable, X, has a positively skewed probability density function, then the logarithm of the random variable, Y, has a normal distribution. A random process that has this property is one which is the product of several independent events; that is, the distribution of the product is positively skewed. Areas where the lognormal is important include sales analysis (income) and profit analysis.

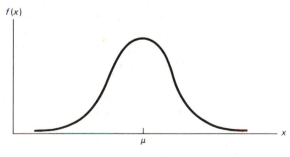

$f(x)$

μ x

FIGURE 8-9

183

EXERCISES

8-1. Use the inverse transformation method to generate stochastic variates from an exponential distribution with mean α.

8-2. Use the rejection method to generate stochastic variates from a binomial distribution with mean np and variance $np(1 - p)$.

8-3. Give the correct value of the constant A that makes the following equation for $f(x)$ a probability density function. Derive a formula for generating random numbers having this distribution.

$$
\begin{aligned}
f(x) &= 0.25 + A(x - 1), & 1 \leqslant x \leqslant 2, \\
&= 0.25 - A(x - 3), & 2 < x \leqslant 3, \\
&= 0, & \text{elsewhere.}
\end{aligned}
$$

8-4. Derive a formula for generating random numbers having the following probability density function:

$$
\begin{aligned}
f(x) &= 1, & 0 \leqslant x < \tfrac{1}{4}, \\
&= 3/7, & \tfrac{1}{4} \leqslant x < 2.
\end{aligned}
$$

8-5. (a) Set up (do not calculate) the probability of there being n arrivals in an interval of 10 seconds when the arrivals have a Poisson distribution with a mean number of arrivals per second of 0.4.

(b) Describe a method for generating stochastic variates from a Poisson distribution with parameter λ.

8-6. Describe how to compute the area of the final quadrant of a unit circle using the rejection method.

8-7. Justify one method of how to generate random Poisson variates.

8-8. Justify a method to generate N pseudo-random numbers having a normal distribution with mean value 50 and standard deviation 5.

8-9. The number of orders X (where an order is defined as 1000 yards of finished cloth) received each day (24 hours) by a cotton textile mill has a Poisson distribution with mean 250 orders. To transfer raw cotton into a completed order, a four-stage process is required. The four stages of production are spinning, weaving, finishing, and packaging. The process time required to *spin* a sufficient amount of cotton to produce 1000 yards of finished cloth has an exponential distribution with expected value equal to 3 minutes. The process time required to *weave* 1000 yards of cloth has an exponential distribution with expected value equal to 6 minutes. The process time required to *finish* 1000 yards of cloth is exponentially distributed with expected value equal to 8 minutes. The *packaging* time for an order is also exponentially distributed with expected value equal to 1 minute. The firm operates three shifts per day, seven days a week. Formulate and implement a computer simulation model of the cotton textile mill's production system.

8-10. The computer simulation model derived in Problem 8-9 can be validated by a theoretical queuing model. Assume that the steady-state probability has been reached and that you have shown that the probability of exactly N orders in any given process is geometric with parameter λ/μ, where λ denotes the arrival rate and μ denotes the service rate of a specific process. Also assume that you have shown that the total time spent in any given process has an exponential distribution with mean $1/(\mu - \lambda)$.

    (a) State and derive as many theoretical expected values as you can about the model described in Problem 8-9.

    (b) Discuss how you would use the results in (a) to validate your computer simulation model.

8-11. Generate random numbers for the random variables with the following density function:

    (a) Use the inverse method:

$$f(x) = 1/x^2, \qquad \text{if } 1 < x < \infty,$$
$$= 0, \qquad \text{otherwise.}$$

    (b) Use the rejection method:

$$f(x) = x \qquad \text{if } 0 < x < 1,$$
$$= 2 - x, \qquad \text{if } 1 < x < 2,$$
$$= 0 \qquad \text{otherwise.}$$

8-12. State the central limit theorem and explain how it is important in generating various distributions.

8-13. A company manufactures personal computers at a rate of 10,000 per year. Each computer is guaranteed for a period of four years. The cost of manufacturing a computer that has a mean life of m years, C_m, is

$$C_m = a + bm + cm^2,$$

where $a = \$50$, $b = \$40$, $c = \$2$. Time until failure for each computer is exponentially distributed with a mean of m. Each failure that occurs during the guarantee period costs the manufacturer an average of $50. Describe in detail how to determine the optimal value of m.

8-14. The distribution of daily production for a particular item is given by a normal distribution with mean 6000 and variance 40,000. Each day a certain portion, p, of the total production is scrapped. That is, if the percentage of scrap is $p100\%$ and x is the day's production, the total scrap is px. New production, y, is then $y = x - px$. The density function of the proportion scrap is given by

$$gp(p) = 99(1 - p)^{98}, \qquad 0 < p < 1.$$

Develop a random number generator for net daily production, Y. Describe a test to determine whether the distribution of net daily production can be assumed to be normal.

8-15. Generate random numbers for the random variable with the following density function:

$$f(x) = \frac{x}{100}, \qquad 0 < x \leq 10,$$

$$\frac{20 - x}{100}, \qquad 10 < x \leq 20,$$

$$0, \qquad \text{elsewhere.}$$

Discuss how to verify that the values generated are from the pdf $f(x)$.

8-16. The XYZ Company plans to study its shipping practices through simulation. One of the products involved is shipped to customers by truck. However, more than one truckload may be shipped at one time. The following data have been recorded on the number of truckloads per shipment.

Truckloads/Shipments	Frequency
1	77
2	90
3	35
4	8
5	1

Develop a random number generator for the number of trucks required per shipment.

9

EXAMPLES

The task of deriving a model of a system can be classified into two very interrelated categories. The first is that of establishing the model structure and the second is that of supplying the data. The purpose of this chapter is to illustrate through example the task of deriving a model and supplying the data.

The examples are the result of student projects that were assigned through Appendix B. In this type of project, arrival and service distributions are developed from theoretically known distributions, not by observation. The examples not only illustrate the concept of validation and verification, but also illustrate the reproducibility of the queuing theory results in Chapter 4. This property allows the programmer to easily test the correctness of the simulation program. By a slight deviation of the assumptions of queuing theory, it can be seen that simulation is the only way to solve many problems.

EXAMPLE 1

This example was a result of a semester project as outlined in Appendix B. The author of the project was Larry Holden.

introduction

Single-server queuing systems with exponentially distributed service times and Poisson arrivals (exponential interarrival times) have been well investigated. Such studies have provided a considerable volume of theoretical literature [2, 3, 4, 5]. In addition, these results can be easily extended to multiple-server systems including, perhaps the simplest of such, the tandem queuing system. For non-Poisson arrivals, however, an analytical approach is not, in general, as rewarding, although Karlin [3, pp. 445-461] discusses an embedding, Markov chain approach to obtain characterizations of systems with generally distributed arrivals.

An alternative, albeit less elegant, approach is to use simulation techniques to elucidate the effects of non-Poisson input. Such an approach is used here to investigate the performance of an exponential-service tendem queuing system with uniformly distributed interarrival times.

With regard to uniform input to a system, two important questions will be considered:

1. How does the single-server queuing system with uniform input compare with its Poisson-input counterpart regarding the various long-run statistics (i.e., waiting time, etc.)?
2. Is the behavior of the single-server units (SSUs), when placed in tandem (i.e., with the output of one the input of the next), predictable from their performance as single units?

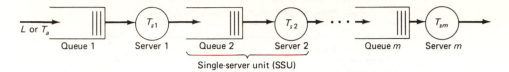

FIGURE 9-1 Multiple Tandem Queue Model (L = mean arrival rate; T$_a$ = mean interarrival time; T$_s$ = mean service time)

Both questions are only briefly considered here to provide information for further study. No attempt is made at either producing analytic solutions or at performing exhaustive simulations.

the model

The general tandem queue model is diagrammed in Figure 9-1. Jobs enter the system (to queue 1) with a mean rate L. If the first service facility (server 1) is not presently in use, then the job enters the facility; otherwise, it must wait (in the queue). When the job leaves the server (after a random time with mean T_1), it enters the next queue in line, and so on. After the job departs from the last service facility (server m), it leaves the system.

The long-run distributions of single-server queuing systems with Poisson input and exponential service time are well known. Utilizing this single-server information, the long-run distribution of such a tandem queuing system is also easily found [2]. With these facts, the expected values of selected statistics can be derived. These statistics will be used both for the verification of the accuracy of the Poisson-input model with the uniform-input tandem-queue model. These long-run statistics and their expected values for the Poisson-input tandem queue system are given in Table 9-1.

simulation

A SIMSCRIPT II.5 simulation of the tandem queue model is driven primarily by the execution of two classes of events: arrivals and departures. The arrival event simulates the initial arrival of a job into the system. The departure event controls the departure of a job from a particular service facility *and* its subsequent arrival into the next service facility in the tandem chain. Figure 9-2 illustrates the interaction of these two classes of events in the simulation.

Conceptually, the simulation program flow is partitioned into four tasks:

1. *Initiation* of the simulation is performed in the routine MAIN. MAIN reads the simulation parameters for a given run and initializes storage accordingly. The *first* ARRIVAL is also scheduled in MAIN.

189

TABLE 9-1

Expected Values of Various Long-run Statistics for a
Poisson-Arrival/Exponential-Service Tandem Queue
System[a]

Statistic	Expected Value
For a single-server unit (SSU) i	
Server utilization (u_i)	T_s/T_a
Queuing time (T_{qi})	$(T_sT_a)/(T_a - T_{si})$
Waiting time (T_{wi})	u_iT_{qi}
Conditional waiting time (T_{ci}) (given $T_{wi} > 0$)	T_{qi}
Total number in unit (R_i)	$u_i/(1 - u_i)$
Queue length (Q_i)	$u_i^2/(1 - u_i)$
Nonempty queue length (C_i)	$1/(1 - u_i)$
For the entire system (m SSU's)	
Total queuing time (*TIS*)	$\sum\limits_{i=1}^{m} T_{qi}$
Total waiting time (*TWT*)	$\sum\limits_{i=1}^{m} T_{wi}$
Total number in the system (*NIS*)	$\sum\limits_{i=1}^{m} R_i$

[a]T_s = mean service time; T_a = mean interarrival time.

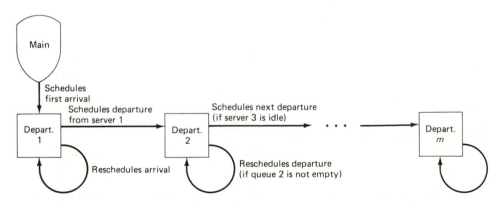

FIGURE 9-2 Event interaction in the Simulation Model (the directed lines imply control, not flow)

2. *Arrivals.* An arrival creates new jobs and inputs them into the queue of server 1. It not only schedules both the departure of the job from server 1, but also reschedules another arrival. The program flow in the event ARRIVAL is shown in Figure 9-3.

3. *Departures.* The departure event from server N (DEPARTURE(N)) performs several tasks. It removes a job from server N and attempts to input it to server $N + 1$ (or destroys it if N is the last server). If server $N + 1$ is not busy, then DEPARTURE(N) places the job in server $N + 1$ and schedules a DEPARTURE($N + 1$). The departure event also removes the next job (if any) from its own queue, places it in the server, and schedules its departure. Figure 9-4 illustrates the control flow in DEPARTURE(N).

4. *Statistical collection and evaluation.* This consists of several events and routines (plus coding in ARRIVAL and DEPARTURE) that accumulate the desired statistics and determine when the simulation is to be terminated.

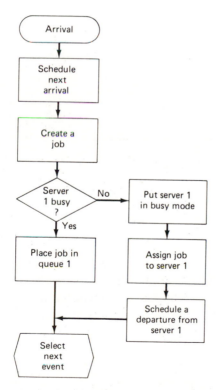

FIGURE 9-3 Flowchart for the Event Arrival in the Simulation Program

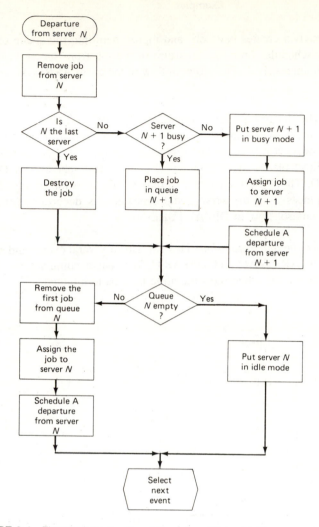

FIGURE 9-4 Flowchart for the Event Departure (N) in the Simulation Program

Most of the events and entities possess attributes that either are necessary for program execution or are designed to aid statistical collection. Table 9-2 lists the more important of these attributes. The activities in the simulation model are relatively few and straightforward. These are as follows:

1. Entering the system (i.e., arriving).
2. Leaving the system.
3. Waiting for service (from a given server).
4. Receiving service (from a given server).

TABLE 9-2

Entities, and Their Associated Attributes Used in the Simulation Model

Entity (or Event)	Attributes
DEPARTURE	Server number (DNR)[a]
SERVER	Mean service time (SVT), status (STATUS), numerous statistical attributes
QUEUE (1 per server)	Length (N.QUEUE)
PLACE (1 per server)	None
JOB	Time of arrival (T.OF.A), time entered queue (QINN), time spent waiting in last queue (QWAIT), total time spent waiting (TWAIT)

[a]Symbols in parentheses represent the name used in the SIMSCRIPT program.

simulation and model verification

Removal of Initial Bias

Although the long-run expected values for various statistics in a tandem queuing system with arrival and exponential service are known, the simulation system will not initially be in this "steady state." This inability of the system to adequately represent the theoretical long-run distribution is its initial bias of the system.

It is certain [3, 4] that for utilization values less than 1, a long-run distribution exists. However, it is less certain as to the time required to "attain" it. In removing the initial bias of the system, one wishes to determine a time interval, T_b, such that the long-run distribution adequately describes the system for any time $t > T_b$. Once T_b is known, it is a simple matter to disregard all simulation results collected prior to T_b. (T_b may be either expressed as time units or may be in terms of number of events, such as the number of changes in queue size since the system started, number of completed services, etc.).

To determine T_b for a 3-SSU tandem queue system, the method of batched means [1] was used. Waiting time in queue 3, T_{q^3}, was collected in batches of size n ($n = 5$, 10, 15, . . . , 50). For each batch size n, the mean waiting time was calculated. A sampling "interval" of size 50 (i.e., 50 changes in T_{w^3}) was used to obtain one each of the mean waiting times for a batch of size n, $X(n)$. The simulation was continued until 100 of these sampling intervals were obtained. By the central limit theorem, the mean of $X(n)$, $m(n)$, for each n is approximately normally distributed, provided that the batch means (of the same size) are identically and independently distributed. Approximate

193

independence of the batch means should have been achieved, since for small n the $X(n)$'s are widely separated, and for n large, dependence effects are "swamped out." The batch means are *not* identically distributed, however, unless the long-run distribution applies. As batch size exceeds T_b (in terms of T_{w^3} changes), the effect of the initial bias on the first sampling interval becomes minimized, and that batch mean becomes approximately distributed as the rest of the $X(n)$. Thus, as n exceeds T_b, the distribution of $M(n)$ approaches the normal. Under central limit theory, the standard deviation of $m(n)$, $D(n)$, $[D(n) = S(n)/10]$ approaches 0 as n approaches infinity.

Then, where these assumptions hold, $D(n)$ should be decreasing. It follows, therefore, that one estimate of T_b is that value of n at which $D(n)$ demonstrates a definite decreasing behavior. Figure 9-5 illustrates the decreasing behavior of $D(n)$ for waiting time at queue 3. At a batch size of 20 to 25, the decrease of $D(n)$ is pronounced. Thus, 20 waiting time changes appears to be a sufficient estimate of T_b.

In practice, T_b should be established for each simulation run. However, this time-consuming practice was eliminated and an alternative, although crude, substitute was used. Another event, RESTART, was included in the simulation model. When this event was executed, all statistical counters were reset to their initial values and accumulation of data was restarted. The time at which RESTART was scheduled was an input parameter to the program.

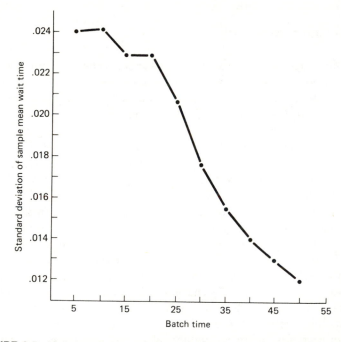

FIGURE 9-5 Variation of Sample Standard Deviation of Mean Wait Time with Batch Size (wait time was collected on the last queue of a 3-SSU tandem system)

Testing Closeness to the Theoretical Model

To verify the correctness of the simulation model, the simulation estimates obtained from a 3-SSU tandem system with Poisson input were compared with the theoretical values. Several techniques of statistical collection were employed. For those statistics that did *not* involve a time average (waiting time, time in system, conditional wait time), 20 observations were collected and their batch means calculated. These batch means were then accumulated and their mean and variance were calculated at the end of the simulation. For time-average statistics (number in system, queue length, conditional queue length,

TABLE 9-3.

Expected and Observed Values of Statistics for a Poisson-Arrival/Exponential-Service 3-SSU Simulation[a]

Statistic	Exp. Value	Obs. Value	95% Confidence Interval for Expected Value	
u_1	0.5	0.510	0.454 to	0.565
u_2	0.4	0.397	0.359	0.435
u_3	0.3	0.293	0.260	0.327
T_{w1}	0.250	0.295	0.208	0.381
T_{w2}	0.133	0.119	0.082	0.155
T_{w3}	0.064	0.054	0.040	0.069
Q_1	0.5	0.554	0.407	0.701
Q_2	0.267	0.254	0.193	0.315
Q_3	0.129	0.112	0.079	0.145
T_{c1}	0.5	0.527	0.427	0.626
T_{c2}	0.333	0.313	0.265	0.363
T_{c3}	0.214	0.217	0.185	0.250
C_1	2.0	1.953	1.722	2.185
C_2	1.667	1.583	1.454	1.711
C_3	1.429	1.421	1.316	1.526
TIS	1.048	1.083	0.948	1.217
TWT	0.447	0.466	0.363	0.570
NIS	2.095	2.057	1.908	2.205

[a] $T_a = 0.5$, $T_{s1} = 0.25$, $T_{s2} = 0.2$, $T_{s3} = 0.15$.

utilization), batch means were calculated as the average value within a specified time interval. These batch means were then accumulated like the others. The total number of batch means collected, p, was input before each simulation run. After the p batch means were accumulated for each statistic, the statistics were calculated and printed, and the program terminated. Confidence intervals for the statistics were calculated using the normal approximation.

The expected and observed values for one 3-SSU system simulation are shown in Table 9-3. It is obvious that the fit of observed to theoretical is very good, thus supporting the correctness of the simulation model. Further results using various utilization values are equally as close to the theoretical model.

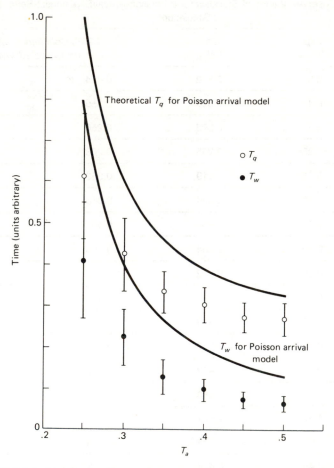

FIGURE 9-6   Variation of Mean Queuing Time and Mean Wait Time with Increasing Interarrival Time (T_s = 0.2) for a Single-Server with Uniform Arrivals (vertical lines represent 95% confidence limits)

results

Single-Server Simulations

Before investigating the effects of queues (and servers) in tandem with uniform input it was first necessary to obtain information for the single-server case. These results were then compared with that expected for the Poisson-input case. Figure 9-6 shows the effects of varying the mean interarrival time (T_a) on both waiting time (T_w) and queuing time (T_q). Clearly, T_q and T_w are higher for the Poisson-input system. It is also interesting to note that the differences between T_w and T_q appear smaller for the Poisson-input system than for the uniform input. That is, for the exponential system the proportion of total queuing time spent waiting, F_w, is equal to u, the utilization. However, from the simulation results shown in Figure 9-6 it appears that the uniform-input system as $F_w < u$, especially for small T_a. Admittedly, however, these two estimates are less reliable at the higher utilizations (lower T_a) owing to greater variance.

Figure 9-7 shows that much the same trend is generated by varying the mean service

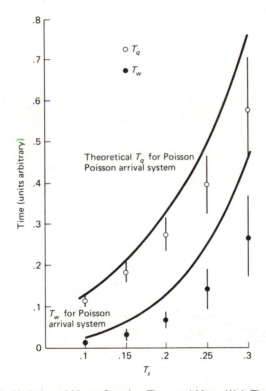

FIGURE 9-7 Variation of Mean Queuing Time and Mean Wait Time with Mean Service Time for a Single-Server System with Uniform Arrivals (T_a = 0.5), (vertical lines represent 95% confidence limits)

time T_s. Again, both T_w and T_q are lower in the uniform-input system. At low utilizations (in this case low T_s), the difference between the two systems is minimal. The lower F_w for the uniform-input model is also evident here, although it is, perhaps, not as striking as in Figure 9-6.

The variance of mean interarrival time for the Poisson and uniform input cases, V_{ae} and V_{au}, respectively, are related by

$$V_{au} = 1/3 \; V_{ae}$$

It may be reasonable to speculate, then, that the effect of decreasing the variance in interarrival time is to reduce waiting and queuing times. Further support for this speculation can be provided by examining the single-server system with exponential service but regular arrivals [2]. With regular arrivals, the variance in interarrival time is equal to zero. By hypothesis, then, the queuing time in the regular-input system should be less

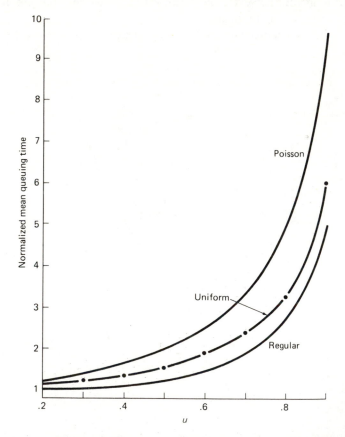

FIGURE 9-8 Variation of Normalized Mean Queuing Time (T_q/T_s) with Server Utilization *(u)* for the Poisson, Regular, and Uniform (simulated) Arrival Models (confidence intervals for the uniform model are omitted; data for the regular model was obtained from [2]).

than for the uniform input model. Normalized mean queuing time, T_q/T_s, for the Poisson, regular, and uniform input systems is compared in Figure 9-8. Clearly, the uniform input system is intermediate between the regular and Poisson.

Tandem Queue Simulations

From the previous section, it is clear that the primary difference shown by the uniform-input model over the Poisson-input model is the lower value of all the statistics except utilization (or, alternatively, that for any value of the statistics higher utilization is attainable). However, the exact form of the distribution of output from the system has still not been determined. Although a direct investigation of the output from the single server was possible, a simpler, but less conclusive, test was employed. If, like the Poisson-input system, the output from the single server in the uniform system is also uniform with the same mean, then the long-run statistics for queues in tandem should be identical with the single-server results. Using a 3-SSU tandem system with $T_a = 0.5$ and several configurations of mean service times, the standard set of statistics was obtained. No differences between each single-server system and its tandem server counterpart were found. This implies that either the output from each queue is also uniform (with the same mean as the input) or that it produces results in successive SSUs as though it were uniform. The latter alternative appears very unlikely.

conclusions

This brief investigation of uniform input queuing systems has, I feel, yielded two interesting results. First, it has shown that, compared with Poisson-input, uniform-input systems have lower values of queuing time, waiting time, queue length, and nonempty queue length. This occurs without sacrificing server utilization. It is likely that this increased efficiency property of the system may also be characteristic of other interarrival distributions that have lower variances than the Poisson.

Second, the uniform input distribution seems to be preserved by the exponential service facility. This results in tandem queue behavior (at steady state) identical to that of single-server system.

Although most tests of the various hypotheses considered here were of an indirect nature, I feel that more rigorous test of, at least, the uniform output would not be really necessary. It would be much more productive to investigate the effects of both more complex systems and the effects of other interarrival distributions.

One possible practical application of this type of investigation concerns scheduling of system input. Since the reduction of variances appears to reduce waiting time while maintaining high server utilizations, it then follows that a "properly" programmed scheduling facility (one that reduces the variance of output) can improve system efficiency. This certainly is associated with many, more complex problems (e.g., wait time in the scheduling queue can also be great), but it is surely one justification for the use of system schedulers in operating systems.

EXAMPLE 2

This example was a result of a semester project as outlined in Appendix B. The author of the project was Ann Sanner.

introduction

The model studied herein is that of machine minding. The model will be validated using the known results for Poisson arrivals and exponential service. A uniform service and Poisson arrivals system will be investigated in order to determine how the long-run statistics of the uniform model compare with those of the exponential model.

the model

The machine-minding model is diagrammed in Figure 9-9. This model has a finite number of customers, K, arriving randomly at a single server; the customers correspond to K machines, each of which is in one of two states: either "up" (operating) or "down" (requiring service). When a machine goes "down," it joins the queue or is serviced immediately. The queue is assumed to be first-in, first-out; the arrival rate of machines to be serviced is proportional to the number still operating.

The long-run statistics and their expected values for the Poisson arrival/exponential service model are theoretically known and are derived in the following. The tabulated results of these derivations are found in Table 9-4.

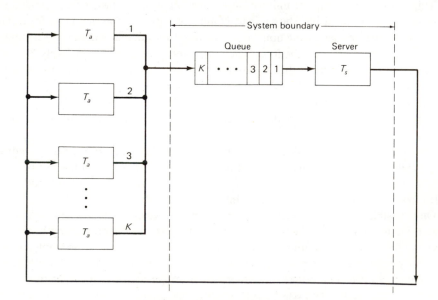

FIGURE 9-9 Machine Minding Model

TABLE 9-4.

Expected Values of Various Long-run Statistics for a Poisson-Arrival/Exponential Service Machine Minding System[a]

Statistic	Expected Value
Expected number in the queue: L_w	$K - (\frac{T_a}{T_s} + 1)(1 - P_0)$
Expected number in system: L_q	$K - (1 - P_0)\frac{T_a}{T_s}$
Expected number in service: L_s	$1 - P_0$
Expected time in queue: T_w	$\frac{KT_s}{1 - P_0} - T_a - T_s$
Expected time in system: T_q	$T_w + T_s$
Expected length of nonempty queue: $L_w\ (>0)$	$\frac{L_w}{1 - (P_0 + P_1)}$
Expected waiting time given it is nonzero: $T_w\ (>0)$	$\frac{T_w}{1 - P_0}$

[a] T_a = "up" time for *each* machine.
T_s = mean service time.

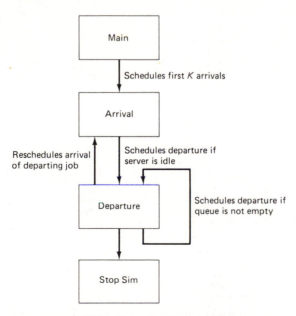

FIGURE 9-10 Event Interaction

201

TABLE 9-5.

Entities and Their Attributes Used in the
Simulation Model

Entity	Attributes
Departure	Mean service time STATUS Numerous statistical attributes

Server	Length
	Max length
	   time of last change
	   in queue

Queue	Time of arrival
Customer	Time spent waiting in queue Time spent in system

simulation

The simulation of the machine-minding queue model is driven primarily by the execution of two classes of events: arrivals and departures (see Figure 9-10). Table 9-5 illustrates the entities and their attributes in the simulation model.

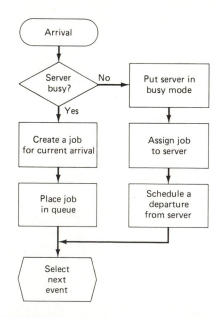

FIGURE 9-11 Flowchart for the Event Arrival

The main program schedules (SIMSCRIPT II.5) an initial arrival for each of the *K* machines. *Main* also initializes all the simulation parameters.

Arrival creates a job and puts it in the queue if the server is busy; otherwise, arrival puts the server in the busy mode and schedules a departure (see Figure 9-11).

Departure schedules an arrival ("up" time) for the job (machine) that is departing. If the queue is not empty, *Departure* removes the first job from the queue and schedules a departure from the server for that job (see Figure 9-12).

The previous discussion is presented in terms of SIMSCRIPT II.5 terminology.

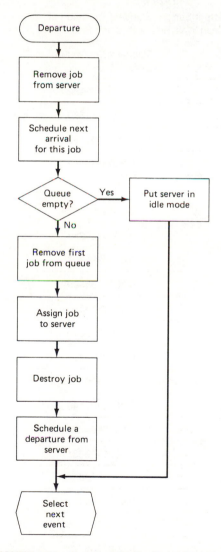

FIGURE 9-12 Flowchart for the Event Departure

simulation and model verification

Removal of Initial Bias

Waiting time was collected in batches of size n ($n = 5, 10, 15, \ldots, 50$). For each batch size n, the mean waiting time was calculated. A sampling interval of size 50 was used to obtain each of the mean waiting times for a batch of size n, $X(n)$. The mean of the batch means, $m(n)$, and the standard deviation, $D(n)$, of $m(n)$ was calculated for

TABLE 9-6.

Variation of Sample Standard Deviation of
Mean Wait Time with Batch Size

Batch Size	Standard Deviation of Sample Mean Wait Time
5	0.0005152282
10	0.0004544689
15	0.0003099183
20	0.0003436069
25	0.0004013083
30	0.0003996873
35	0.0003829257
40	0.0003391707
45	0.0003035599
50	0.0002885355
55	0.0002755506
60	0.0002566767
65	0.0002320070
70	0.0002207149
75	0.0002104721
80	0.0001912331
85	0.0001910832
90	0.0001905395
95	0.0001793755
100	0.0001736277

TABLE 9-7.

Expected and Observed Values of Statistics for a Poisson-arrival/Exponential Service Machine Minding Simulation[a]

Statistic	Exp. Value	Obs. Value	Z	Accept/Reject α = 0.05
LW	0.2401298	0.2572872	1.051158	Accept
LQ	0.6823643	0.6805058	0.0559865	Accept
LS	0.4422345	0.4458083	0.3136643	Accept
TQ	0.0108009	0.01093175	0.4027046	Accept
TS	0.007	0.007112909	0.7985868	Accept
TW	0.0038009	0.003818840	0.0808174	Accept
LW(>0)	1.4214802	1.4330807	0.3868136	Accept
TW(>0)	0.0085948	0.009998805	3.946451	Reject
TA	0.1	0.1016652	0.948027	Accept

[a]$T_s = 0.007$, $T_a = 0.1$, $K = 7$.

each n, since the value of n at which $D(n)$ demonstrates a definite decreasing behavior is an estimate of T_b. The information in Table 9-6 is of special interest. It reveals a definite decreasing behavior between $n = 25$ and $n = 30$. Thus, 25 waiting time changes appear to be a reasonable estimate of T_b.

Testing Closeness to the Theoretical Model

The expected and observed values for one simulation run are shown in Table 9-7. The z statistic was calculated. The fit of the observed value to the theoretical value was good, except for waiting time greater than zero.

TABLE 9-8.

Variation of Mean Queuing Time and Mean Wait Time with Increasing Interarrival Time[b]

Poisson ρ	TA	Poisson TW	Service TQ	Uniform TW	Service TQ
0.76	0.05	0.0092	0.016	0.0068	0.014
0.45	0.1	0.0038	0.011	0.0024	0.0094
0.32	0.15	0.0024	0.0095	0.0015	0.0084
0.24	0.2	0.0017	0.0088	0.0011	0.0080

[b]$T_s = 0.007$.

TABLE 9-9.

Variation of Mean Queuing Time and Mean Wait Time with Increasing Service Time

Poisson ρ	TS	Poisson TW	Service TQ	Uniform TW	Service TQ
0.14	0.002	0.00024	0.0023	0.00016	0.0021
0.45	0.007	0.0038	0.011	0.0024	0.0094
0.82	0.017	0.028	0.046	0.023	0.039

$T_a = 0.1$.

results

The primary difference exhibited by the uniform service model over the exponential service model is the lower value of all the statistics except utilization. Slightly higher service utilization was achieved with the uniform service model.

Table 9-8 shows the effect of varying the mean time T_a on waiting time, T_w, and queuing time, T_q. Table 9-9 shows the effect of varying the mean service time T_s on waiting time, T_w, and queuing time, T_q.

conclusions

We have seen that uniform service systems have lower statistical values than exponential service systems without sacrificing server utilization. This result was counter to my intuition based upon the higher percentage of service times less than the mean in the exponential. Apparently, the greater variance in the exponential distribution accounts for the higher values here. It would be interesting to run the model with regular service times to see if this increased efficiency holds true for a system with even lower variance than either the Poisson or the uniform system.

Another entertaining possibility would be to change the model to handle different T_a's for the machines. It would be interesting to see the effect of abandoning the assumption of identical machines.

REFERENCES

1. GORDON, G., *System simulation (2nd ed.)*, Prentice-Hall, Inc., Englewood Cliffs, N.J., 1978.
2. IBM, *Analysis of Some Queuing Models in Real-time Systems.* IBM Technical Publications Department, White Plains, N.Y., 1971.
3. KARLIN, S., *A First Course in Stochastic Processes*, Academic Press, Inc., New York, 1968.
4. PARZEN, E., *Stochastic Processes*, Holden-Day, Inc., San Francisco, 1962.
5. SAATY, T. L., *Elements of Queueing Theory with Applications.* McGraw-Hill Book Co., New York, 1961.

A

APPENDIX: PROOFS FOR CHAPTER 4

PROOF OF THEOREM 1 OF CHAPTER 4

Let $P_N(t)$ denote the probability of N units in the system at time t. We first wish to compute $P_0(t + h)$. The event [0 units in the system at time $t + h$] could have occurred as follows: [0 units at time t, no arrivals] or [1 unit at time t, 1 service during h, no arrivals during h] or [0 units at time t, 1 arrival during h, 1 service during h] or [2 units at time t, 2 services during h, no arrivals during h], and so forth. All the events, except the first two, will have probabilities of order $(h)^2$. The event [0 units at time t, no arrivals during h] could be written as $P_0(t)(1 - \lambda h)$, because what happens in one time interval is independent of what happens in another time interval, and the probability of no arrivals during h is $1 - \lambda h$. Therefore,

$$P_0(t + h) = P_0(t)(1 - \lambda h) + P_1(t)(\mu h) + 0(h) \tag{1}$$

where $0(h)/h \to 0$ as $h \to 0$. Hence, solving equation (1), one obtains

$$\frac{P_0(t + h) - P_0(t)}{h} = \frac{-\lambda P_0(t) + \mu P_1(t) + 0(h)}{h}.$$

Taking $\lim h \to o$, we obtain

$$\frac{dP_0(t)}{dt} = -\lambda P_0(t) + \mu P_1(t) \tag{2}$$

For $N \geq 1$, an analysis similar to the preceding will show the event [N units in the system at time $t + h$] could have occurred as follows:

[N units at time t, no arrivals during h, no services during h] or

[N units at time t, 1 arrival during h, 1 service during h] or

[$N + 1$ units at time t, 1 service during h, 0 arrivals during h] or

[$N - 1$ units at time t, 1 arrival during h, 0 services during h], and so forth.

We have assumed that the probability of more than one unit arriving (or being serviced) during h tends to zero as $h \to 0$. Therefore,

$$P_N(t + h) = P_N(t)(1 - \lambda h)(1 - \mu h) + P_N(t)(\lambda h)(\mu h) + P_{N + 1}(\mu h)(1 - \lambda h)$$
$$+ P_{N - 1}(t)(\lambda h)(1 - \mu h) + 0(h),$$

or

$$P_N(t) = P_N(t)[1 - \lambda h - \mu h] + P_{N + 1}(t)(\mu h) + P_{N - 1}(t)(\lambda h) + 0(h).$$

Solving, we obtain

$$\frac{P_N(t + h) - P_N(t)}{h} = \frac{-\lambda P_N(t) - \mu P_N(t) + \lambda P_{N - 1}(t) + \mu P_{N + 1}(t) + 0(h)}{h}$$

Taking $\lim_{h \to o}$, we obtain

$$\frac{dP_N(t)}{dt} = -(\lambda + \mu)P_N(t) + \lambda P_{N-1}(t) + \mu P_{N+1}(t). \tag{3}$$

Since we assume that $P_N(t)$ does not depend upon t, $dP_N(t)/dt = 0$. In particular, from (2), $0 = -\lambda P_0 + \mu P_1$ or

$$P_1 = \left(\frac{\lambda}{\mu}\right)P_0. \tag{4}$$

Similarly, from (3), we obtain $dP_N(t)/dt = 0$, and by solving we find

$$P_{N+1} = \left[\frac{(\lambda + \mu)}{\mu}\right]P_n - \left(\frac{\lambda}{\mu}\right)P_{N-1}, \qquad N \geq 1. \tag{5}$$

It can be easily shown by induction, using (4) and (5), that

$$P_N = \left(\frac{\lambda}{\mu}\right)^N P_0. \tag{6}$$

Using the assumption that $\lambda/\mu < 1$ and that P_N is a probability function, that is, $\sum_{1}^{\infty} P_N = 1$, we obtain from (6) that $P_0 = (1 - \lambda/\mu)$ and

$$P_N = \left(\frac{\lambda}{\mu}\right)^N\left(1 - \frac{\lambda}{\mu}\right), \qquad N \geq 1.$$

PROOF OF THEOREM 2 OF CHAPTER 4

$$E(N) = \sum_{0}^{\infty} nP_n = \sum_{0}^{\infty} n(1 - \rho)\rho^n = (1 - \rho)\sum_{0}^{\infty} n\rho^n$$

$$= \frac{(1 - \rho)\rho}{(1 - \rho)^2} = \frac{\rho}{(1 - \rho)}, \qquad \rho < 1.$$

PROOF OF THEOREM 3 OF CHAPTER 4

There are 0 units in the queue if and only if there are 0 or 1 units in the system. Thus, $Q_0 = P_0 + P_1 = (1 - \rho) + (1 - \rho)\rho = (1 - \rho)(1 + \rho)$. For $N \geq 1$, there are N units in the queue if and only if there are $N + 1$ units in the system. Thus,

$$Q_N = P_{N+1} = (1 - \rho)\rho^{N+1}, \qquad N \geq 1.$$

B

APPENDIX:
SEMESTER
PROJECTS

The purpose of a semester project is to give the student practical experience and insight in the area of simulation. The first approach is to assign a hypothetical project, which includes all the elements discussed in Chapter 5. The following is an outline of such a project. It can also be used as a table of contents.

I. Outline

    A. Introduction

        1. Purpose

        2. State at least one hypothesis

    B. Model Description

        1. Detail model

        2. Flow chart

        3. Statistics of interest (will be specified in class)

    C. Simulation

        1. Event interaction

        2. Program flow chart

        3. Description of entities, attributes, and activities

    D. Model Verification

        1. Removal of initial bias

        2. Closeness to theoretical model

    E. Conclusions

        1. Result of hypothesis

        2. Further work

In this type of project, arrival and service distributions are developed from theoretically known distributions, not by observation. Typically, hypotheses might include (1) the effect of varying the service or arrival rate, (2) the effect of various service distributions (e.g., uniform, normal, and exponential) on mean wait time in queue, and (3) the effect of various server disciplines (e.g., FIFO and LIFO) on mean time in the system. Some examples of basic models include the multiserver queue with no loss; three or more queues in tandem; machine interference; simple feedback queue; two queues in tandem in which the second queue has traffic merging from the outside. Chapter 4 discusses the theoretical statistics of interest such as mean queue time, mean time in the system, and so forth. These models can be parameterized relatively easily so the experimenter can compare the simulation results to the theoretically known values. The other important component of this type of project is for the student to document the final results, following the previous outline.

The second approach is for the student to contact a business person in the community and develop a simple model of a real system. These systems might include a bank, drugstore, service station, supermarket, governmental agency, traffic intersection, airport, and so forth. A short proposal by the student is absolutely necessary with these projects, since it is very easy to make them too difficult. As in the other more theoretical projects, a final write-up is a necessary element.

These types of projects help integrate the various chapters of the book and help encourage student feedback and interaction in the teaching process.

C

APPENDIX: TABLES

TABLE 1
Normal Curve Areas

$$N(z) = \int_{-\infty}^{z} \frac{1}{\sqrt{2\pi}} e^{-w^2/2} dw$$

$$[N(-z) = 1 - N(z)]$$

z	N(z)	z	N(z)
.0	0.500	1.645	0.950
.1	.540	1.7	.955
.2	.579	1.8	.964
.3	.618	1.9	.971
.4	.655	1.96	.975
.5	.691	2.0	.977
.6	.726	2.1	.982
.7	.758	2.2	.986
.8	.788	2.3	.989
.9	.816	2.326	.990
1.0	.841	2.4	.992
1.1	.864	2.5	.994
1.2	.885	2.576	.995
1.282	.900	2.6	.995
1.3	.903	2.7	.997
1.4	.919	2.8	.997
1.5	.933	2.9	.998
1.6	.945	3.0	.999

Table 2 Critical Values of t

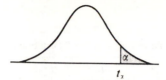

t_α

n	$t_{.100}$	$t_{.050}$	$t_{.025}$	$t_{.010}$	$t_{.005}$	d.f.
2	3.078	6.314	12.706	31.821	63.657	1
3	1.886	2.920	4.303	6.965	9.925	2
4	1.638	2.353	3.182	4.541	5.841	3
5	1.533	2.132	2.776	3.747	4.604	4
6	1.476	2.015	2.571	3.365	4.032	5
7	1.440	1.943	2.447	3.143	3.707	6
8	1.415	1.895	2.365	2.998	3.499	7
9	1.397	1.860	2.306	2.896	3.355	8
10	1.383	1.833	2.262	2.821	3.250	9
11	1.372	1.812	2.228	2.764	3.169	10
12	1.363	1.796	2.201	2.718	3.106	11
13	1.356	1.782	2.179	2.681	3.055	12
14	1.350	1.771	2.160	2.650	3.012	13
15	1.345	1.761	2.145	2.624	2.977	14
16	1.341	1.753	2.131	2.602	2.947	15
17	1.337	1.746	2.120	2.583	2.921	16
18	1.333	1.740	2.110	2.567	2.898	17
19	1.330	1.734	2.101	2.552	2.878	18
20	1.328	1.729	2.093	2.539	2.861	19
21	1.325	1.725	2.086	2.528	2.845	20
22	1.323	1.721	2.080	2.518	2.831	21
23	1.321	1.717	2.074	2.508	2.819	22
24	1.319	1.714	2.069	2.500	2.807	23
25	1.318	1.711	2.064	2.492	2.797	24
26	1.316	1.708	2.060	2.485	2.787	25
27	1.315	1.706	2.056	2.479	2.779	26
28	1.314	1.703	2.052	2.473	2.771	27
29	1.313	1.701	2.048	2.467	2.763	28
30	1.311	1.699	2.045	2.462	2.756	29
inf.	1.282	1.645	1.960	2.326	2.576	inf.

From "Table of Percentage Points of the *t*-Distribution." Computed by Maxine Merrington, *Biometrika*, Vol. 32 (1941), p. 300. Reproduced by permission of Professor E. S. Pearson.

TABLE 3
Percentage Points of the F-Distribution ($\alpha = .10$)

v_2 \ v_1	1	2	3	4	5	6	7	8	9
1	39.86	49.50	53.59	55.83	57.24	58.20	58.91	59.44	59.86
2	8.53	9.00	9.16	9.24	9.29	9.33	9.35	9.37	9.38
3	5.54	5.46	5.39	5.34	5.31	5.28	5.27	5.25	5.24
4	4.54	4.32	4.19	4.11	4.05	4.01	3.98	3.95	3.94
5	4.06	3.78	3.62	3.52	3.45	3.40	3.37	3.34	3.32
6	3.78	3.46	3.29	3.18	3.11	3.05	3.01	2.98	2.96
7	3.59	3.26	3.07	2.96	2.88	2.83	2.78	2.75	2.72
8	3.46	3.11	2.92	2.81	2.73	2.67	2.62	2.59	2.56
9	3.36	3.01	2.81	2.69	2.61	2.55	2.51	2.47	2.44
10	3.39	2.92	2.73	2.61	2.52	2.46	2.41	2.38	2.35
11	3.23	2.86	2.66	2.54	2.45	2.39	2.34	2.30	2.27
12	3.18	2.81	2.61	2.48	2.39	2.33	2.28	2.24	2.21
13	3.14	2.76	2.56	2.43	2.35	2.28	2.23	2.20	2.16
14	3.10	2.73	2.52	2.39	2.31	2.24	2.19	2.15	2.12
15	3.07	2.70	2.49	2.36	2.27	2.21	2.16	2.12	2.09
16	3.05	2.67	2.46	2.33	2.24	2.18	2.13	2.09	2.06
17	3.03	2.64	2.44	2.31	2.22	2.15	2.10	2.06	2.03
18	3.01	2.62	2.42	2.29	2.20	2.13	2.08	2.04	2.00
19	2.99	2.61	2.40	2.27	2.18	2.11	2.06	2.02	1.98
20	2.97	2.59	2.38	2.25	2.16	2.09	2.04	2.00	1.96
21	2.96	2.57	2.36	2.23	2.14	2.08	2.02	1.98	1.95
22	2.95	2.56	2.35	2.22	2.13	2.06	2.01	1.97	1.93
23	2.94	2.55	2.34	2.21	2.11	2.05	1.99	1.95	1.92
24	2.93	2.54	2.33	2.19	2.10	2.04	1.98	1.94	1.91
25	2.92	2.53	2.32	2.18	2.09	2.02	1.97	1.93	1.89
26	2.91	2.52	2.31	2.17	2.08	2.01	1.96	1.92	1.88
27	2.90	2.51	2.30	2.17	2.07	2.00	1.95	1.91	1.87
28	2.89	2.50	2.29	2.16	2.06	2.00	1.94	1.90	1.87
29	2.89	2.50	2.28	2.15	2.06	1.99	1.93	1.89	1.86
30	2.88	2.49	2.28	2.14	2.05	1.98	1.93	1.88	1.85
40	2.84	2.44	2.23	2.09	2.00	1.93	1.87	1.83	1.79
60	2.79	2.39	2.18	2.04	1.95	1.87	1.82	1.77	1.74
120	2.75	2.35	2.13	1.99	1.90	1.82	1.77	1.72	1.68
∞	2.71	2.30	2.08	1.94	1.85	1.77	1.72	1.67	1.63

From "Tables of Percentage Points of the Inverted Beta (F) Distribution," *Biometrika,* Vol. 33 (1943), pp. 73–88, by Maxine Merrington and Catherine M. Thompson. Reproduced by permission of Professor E. S. Pearson and the *Biometrika* Trustees.

10	12	15	20	24	30	40	60	120	∞	v_1 \ v_2
60.19	60.71	61.22	61.74	62.00	62.26	62.53	62.79	63.06	63.33	1
9.39	9.41	9.42	9.44	9.45	9.46	9.47	9.47	9.48	9.49	2
5.23	5.22	5.20	5.18	5.18	5.17	5.16	5.15	5.14	5.13	3
3.92	3.90	3.87	3.84	3.83	3.82	3.80	3.79	3.78	3.76	4
3.30	3.27	3.24	3.21	3.19	3.17	3.16	3.14	3.12	3.10	5
2.94	2.90	2.87	2.84	2.82	2.80	2.78	2.76	2.74	2.72	6
2.70	2.67	2.63	2.59	2.58	2.56	2.54	2.51	2.49	2.47	7
2.54	2.50	2.46	2.42	2.40	2.38	2.36	2.34	2.32	2.29	8
2.42	2.38	2.34	2.30	2.28	2.25	2.23	2.21	2.18	2.16	9
2.32	2.28	2.24	2.20	2.18	2.16	2.13	2.11	2.08	2.06	10
2.25	2.21	2.17	2.12	2.10	2.08	2.05	2.30	2.00	1.97	11
2.19	2.15	2.10	2.06	2.04	2.01	1.99	1.96	1.93	1.90	12
2.14	2.10	2.05	2.01	1.98	1.96	1.93	1.90	1.88	1.85	13
2.10	2.05	2.01	1.96	1.94	1.91	1.89	1.86	1.83	1.80	14
2.06	2.02	1.97	1.92	1.90	1.87	1.85	1.82	1.79	1.76	15
2.03	1.99	1.94	1.89	1.87	1.84	1.81	1.78	1.75	1.72	16
2.00	1.96	1.91	1.86	1.84	1.81	1.78	1.75	1.72	1.69	17
1.98	1.93	1.89	1.84	1.81	1.78	1.75	1.72	1.69	1.66	18
1.96	1.91	1.86	1.81	1.79	1.76	1.73	1.70	1.67	1.63	19
1.94	1.89	1.84	1.79	1.77	1.74	1.71	1.68	1.64	1.61	20
1.92	1.87	1.83	1.78	1.75	1.72	1.69	1.66	1.62	1.59	21
1.90	1.86	1.81	1.76	1.73	1.70	1.67	1.64	1.60	1.57	22
1.89	1.84	1.80	1.74	1.72	1.69	1.66	1.62	1.59	1.55	23
1.88	1.83	1.78	1.73	1.70	1.67	1.64	1.61	1.57	1.53	24
1.87	1.82	1.77	1.72	1.69	1.66	1.63	1.59	1.56	1.52	25
1.86	1.81	1.76	1.71	1.68	1.65	1.61	1.58	1.54	1.50	26
1.85	1.80	1.75	1.70	1.67	1.64	1.60	1.57	1.53	1.49	27
1.84	1.79	1.74	1.69	1.66	1.63	1.59	1.56	1.52	1.48	28
1.83	1.78	1.73	1.68	1.65	1.62	1.58	1.55	1.51	1.47	29
1.82	1.77	1.72	1.67	1.64	1.61	1.57	1.54	1.50	1.46	30
1.76	1.71	1.66	1.61	1.57	1.54	1.51	1.47	1.42	1.38	40
1.71	1.66	1.60	1.54	1.51	1.48	1.44	1.40	1.35	1.29	60
1.65	1.60	1.55	1.48	1.45	1.41	1.37	1.32	1.26	1.19	120
1.60	1.55	1.49	1.42	1.38	1.34	1.30	1.24	1.17	1.00	∞

Table 4 *Percentage Points of the F Distribution*

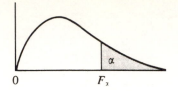

$$\alpha = .05$$

Degrees of Freedom

ν_1

ν_2	1	2	3	4	5	6	7	8	9
1	161.4	199.5	215.7	224.6	230.2	234.0	236.8	238.9	240.5
2	18.51	19.00	19.16	19.25	19.30	19.33	19.35	19.37	19.38
3	10.13	9.55	9.28	9.12	9.01	8.94	8.89	8.85	8.81
4	7.71	6.94	6.59	6.39	6.26	6.16	6.09	6.04	6.00
5	6.61	5.79	5.41	5.19	5.05	4.95	4.88	4.82	4.77
6	5.99	5.14	4.76	4.53	4.39	4.28	4.21	4.15	4.10
7	5.59	4.74	4.35	4.12	3.97	3.87	3.79	3.73	3.68
8	5.32	4.46	4.07	3.84	3.69	3.58	3.50	3.44	3.39
9	5.12	4.26	3.86	3.63	3.48	3.37	3.29	3.23	3.18
10	4.96	4.10	3.71	3.48	3.33	3.22	3.14	3.07	3.02
11	4.84	3.98	3.59	3.36	3.20	3.09	3.01	2.95	2.90
12	4.75	3.89	3.49	3.26	3.11	3.00	2.91	2.85	2.80
13	4.67	3.81	3.41	3.18	3.03	2.92	2.83	2.77	2.71
14	4.60	3.74	3.34	3.11	2.96	2.85	2.76	2.70	2.65
15	4.54	3.68	3.29	3.06	2.90	2.79	2.71	2.64	2.59
16	4.49	3.63	3.24	3.01	2.85	2.74	2.66	2.59	2.54
17	4.45	3.59	3.20	2.96	2.81	2.70	2.61	2.55	2.49
18	4.41	3.55	3.16	2.93	2.77	2.66	2.58	2.51	2.46
19	4.38	3.52	3.13	2.90	2.74	2.63	2.54	2.48	2.42
20	4.35	3.49	3.10	2.87	2.71	2.60	2.51	2.45	2.39
21	4.32	3.47	3.07	2.84	2.68	2.57	2.49	2.42	2.37
22	4.30	3.44	3.05	2.82	2.66	2.55	2.46	2.40	2.34
23	4.28	3.42	3.03	2.80	2.64	2.53	2.44	2.37	2.32
24	4.26	3.40	3.01	2.78	2.62	2.51	2.42	2.36	2.30
25	4.24	3.39	2.99	2.76	2.60	2.49	2.40	2.34	2.28
26	4.23	3.37	2.98	2.74	2.59	2.47	2.39	2.32	2.27
27	4.21	3.35	2.96	2.73	2.57	2.46	2.37	2.31	2.25
28	4.20	3.34	2.95	2.71	2.56	2.45	2.36	2.29	2.24
29	4.18	3.33	2.93	2.70	2.55	2.43	2.35	2.28	2.22
30	4.17	3.32	2.92	2.69	2.53	2.42	2.33	2.27	2.21
40	4.08	3.23	2.84	2.61	2.45	2.34	2.25	2.18	2.12
60	4.00	3.15	2.76	2.53	2.37	2.25	2.17	2.10	2.04
120	3.92	3.07	2.68	2.45	2.29	2.17	2.09	2.02	1.96
∞	3.84	3.00	2.60	2.37	2.21	2.10	2.01	1.94	1.88

$$\nu_1$$

10	12	15	20	24	30	40	60	120	∞	ν_2
241.9	243.9	245.9	248.0	249.1	250.1	251.1	252.2	253.3	254.3	1
19.40	19.41	19.43	19.45	19.45	19.46	19.47	19.48	19.49	19.50	2
8.79	8.74	8.70	8.66	8.64	8.62	8.59	8.57	8.55	8.53	3
5.96	5.91	5.86	5.80	5.77	5.75	5.72	5.69	5.66	5.63	4
4.74	4.68	4.62	4.56	4.53	4.50	4.46	4.43	4.40	4.36	5
4.06	4.00	3.94	3.87	3.84	3.81	3.77	3.74	3.70	3.67	6
3.64	3.57	3.51	3.44	3.41	3.38	3.34	3.30	3.27	3.23	7
3.35	3.28	3.22	3.15	3.12	3.08	3.04	3.01	2.97	2.93	8
3.14	3.07	3.01	2.94	2.90	2.86	2.83	2.79	2.75	2.71	9
2.98	2.91	2.85	2.77	2.74	2.70	2.66	2.62	2.58	2.54	10
2.85	2.79	2.72	2.65	2.61	2.57	2.53	2.49	2.45	2.40	11
2.75	2.69	2.62	2.54	2.51	2.47	2.43	2.38	2.34	2.30	12
2.67	2.60	2.53	2.46	2.42	2.38	2.34	2.30	2.25	2.21	13
2.60	2.53	2.46	2.39	2.35	2.31	2.27	2.22	2.18	2.13	14
2.54	2.48	2.40	2.33	2.29	2.25	2.20	2.16	2.11	2.07	15
2.49	2.42	2.35	2.28	2.24	2.19	2.15	2.11	2.06	2.01	16
2.45	2.38	2.31	2.23	2.19	2.15	2.10	2.06	2.01	1.96	17
2.41	2.34	2.27	2.19	2.15	2.11	2.06	2.02	1.97	1.92	18
2.38	2.31	2.23	2.16	2.11	2.07	2.03	1.98	1.93	1.88	19
2.35	2.28	2.20	2.12	2.08	2.04	1.99	1.95	1.90	1.84	20
2.32	2.25	2.18	2.10	2.05	2.01	1.96	1.92	1.87	1.81	21
2.30	2.23	2.15	2.07	2.03	1.98	1.94	1.89	1.84	1.78	22
2.27	2.20	2.13	2.05	2.01	1.96	1.91	1.86	1.81	1.76	23
2.25	2.18	2.11	2.03	1.98	1.94	1.89	1.84	1.79	1.73	24
2.24	2.16	2.09	2.01	1.96	1.92	1.87	1.82	1.77	1.71	25
2.22	2.15	2.07	1.99	1.95	1.90	1.85	1.80	1.75	1.69	26
2.20	2.13	2.06	1.97	1.93	1.88	1.84	1.79	1.73	1.67	27
2.19	2.12	2.04	1.96	1.91	1.87	1.82	1.77	1.71	1.65	28
2.18	2.10	2.03	1.94	1.90	1.85	1.81	1.75	1.70	1.64	29
2.16	2.09	2.01	1.93	1.89	1.84	1.79	1.74	1.68	1.62	30
2.08	2.00	1.92	1.84	1.79	1.74	1.69	1.64	1.58	1.51	40
1.99	1.92	1.84	1.75	1.70	1.65	1.59	1.53	1.47	1.39	60
1.91	1.83	1.75	1.66	1.61	1.55	1.50	1.43	1.35	1.25	120
1.83	1.75	1.67	1.57	1.52	1.46	1.39	1.32	1.22	1.00	∞

From "Tables of Percentage Points of the Inverted Beta (F) Distribution," *Biometrika*, Vol. 33 (1943), pp. 73–88, by Maxine Merrington and Catherine M. Thompson. Reproduced by permission of Professor E. S. Pearson.

Table 5 Percentage Points of the F Distribution

$$\alpha = .01$$

Degrees of Freedom

ν_1

ν_2	1	2	3	4	5	6	7	8	9
1	4052	4999.5	5403	5625	5764	5859	5928	5982	6022
2	98.50	99.00	99.17	99.25	99.30	99.33	99.36	99.37	99.39
3	34.12	30.82	29.46	28.71	28.24	27.91	27.67	27.49	27.35
4	21.20	18.00	16.69	15.98	15.52	15.21	14.98	14.80	14.66
5	16.26	13.27	12.06	11.39	10.97	10.67	10.46	10.29	10.16
6	13.75	10.92	9.78	9.15	8.75	8.47	8.26	8.10	7.98
7	12.25	9.55	8.45	7.85	7.46	7.19	6.99	6.84	6.72
8	11.26	8.65	7.59	7.01	6.63	6.37	6.18	6.03	5.91
9	10.56	8.02	6.99	6.42	6.06	5.80	5.61	5.47	5.35
10	10.04	7.56	6.55	5.99	5.64	5.39	5.20	5.06	4.94
11	9.65	7.21	6.22	5.67	5.32	5.07	4.89	4.74	4.63
12	9.33	6.93	5.95	5.41	5.06	4.82	4.64	4.50	4.39
13	9.07	6.70	5.74	5.21	4.86	4.62	4.44	4.30	4.19
14	8.86	6.51	5.56	5.04	4.69	4.46	4.28	4.14	4.03
15	8.68	6.36	5.42	4.89	4.56	4.32	4.14	4.00	3.89
16	8.53	6.23	5.29	4.77	4.44	4.20	4.03	3.89	3.78
17	8.40	6.11	5.18	4.67	4.34	4.10	3.93	3.79	3.68
18	8.29	6.01	5.09	4.58	4.25	4.01	3.84	3.71	3.60
19	8.18	5.93	5.01	4.50	4.17	3.94	3.77	3.63	3.52
20	8.10	5.85	4.94	4.43	4.10	3.87	3.70	3.56	3.46
21	8.02	5.78	4.87	4.37	4.04	3.81	3.64	3.51	3.40
22	7.95	5.72	4.82	4.31	3.99	3.76	3.59	3.45	3.35
23	7.88	5.66	4.76	4.26	3.94	3.71	3.54	3.41	3.30
24	7.82	5.61	4.72	4.22	3.90	3.67	3.50	3.36	3.26
25	7.77	5.57	4.68	4.18	3.85	3.63	3.46	3.32	3.22
26	7.72	5.53	4.64	4.14	3.82	3.59	3.42	3.29	3.18
27	7.68	5.49	4.60	4.11	3.78	3.56	3.39	3.26	3.15
28	7.64	5.45	4.57	4.07	3.75	3.53	3.36	3.23	3.12
29	7.60	5.42	4.54	4.04	3.73	3.50	3.33	3.20	3.09
30	7.56	5.39	4.51	4.02	3.70	3.47	3.30	3.17	3.07
40	7.31	5.18	4.31	3.83	3.51	3.29	3.12	2.99	2.89
60	7.08	4.98	4.13	3.65	3.34	3.12	2.95	2.82	2.72
120	6.85	4.79	3.95	3.48	3.17	2.96	2.79	2.66	2.56
∞	6.63	4.61	3.78	3.32	3.02	2.80	2.64	2.51	2.41

ν_1

10	12	15	20	24	30	40	60	120	∞	ν_2
6056	6106	6157	6209	6235	6261	6287	6313	6339	6366	1
99.40	99.42	99.43	99.45	99.46	99.47	99.47	99.48	99.49	99.50	2
27.23	27.05	26.87	26.69	26.60	26.50	26.41	26.32	26.22	26.13	3
14.55	14.37	14.20	14.02	13.93	13.84	13.75	13.65	13.56	13.46	4
10.05	9.89	9.72	9.55	9.47	9.38	9.29	9.20	9.11	9.02	5
7.87	7.72	7.56	7.40	7.31	7.23	7.14	7.06	6.97	6.88	6
6.62	6.47	6.31	6.16	6.07	5.99	5.91	5.82	5.74	5.65	7
5.81	5.67	5.52	5.36	5.28	5.20	5.12	5.03	4.95	4.86	8
5.26	5.11	4.96	4.81	4.73	4.65	4.57	4.48	4.40	4.31	9
4.85	4.71	4.56	4.41	4.33	4.25	4.17	4.08	4.00	3.91	10
4.54	4.40	4.25	4.10	4.02	3.94	3.86	3.78	3.69	3.60	11
4.30	4.16	4.01	3.86	3.78	3.70	3.62	3.54	3.45	3.36	12
4.10	3.96	3.82	3.66	3.59	3.51	3.43	3.34	3.25	3.17	13
3.94	3.80	3.66	3.51	3.43	3.35	3.27	3.18	3.09	3.00	14
3.80	3.67	3.52	3.37	3.29	3.21	3.13	3.05	2.96	2.87	15
3.69	3.55	3.41	3.26	3.18	3.10	3.02	2.93	2.84	2.75	16
3.59	3.46	3.31	3.16	3.08	3.00	2.92	2.83	2.75	2.65	17
3.51	3.37	3.23	3.08	3.00	2.92	2.84	2.75	2.66	2.57	18
3.43	3.30	3.15	3.00	2.92	2.84	2.76	2.67	2.58	2.49	19
3.37	3.23	3.09	2.94	2.86	2.78	2.69	2.61	2.52	2.42	20
3.31	3.17	3.03	2.88	2.80	2.72	2.64	2.55	2.46	2.36	21
3.26	3.12	2.98	2.83	2.75	2.67	2.58	2.50	2.40	2.31	22
3.21	3.07	2.93	2.78	2.70	2.62	2.54	2.45	2.35	2.26	23
3.17	3.03	2.89	2.74	2.66	2.58	2.49	2.40	2.31	2.21	24
3.13	2.99	2.85	2.70	2.62	2.54	2.45	2.36	2.27	2.17	25
3.09	2.96	2.81	2.66	2.58	2.50	2.42	2.33	2.23	2.13	26
3.06	2.93	2.78	2.63	2.55	2.47	2.38	2.29	2.20	2.10	27
3.03	2.90	2.75	2.60	2.52	2.44	2.35	2.26	2.17	2.06	28
3.00	2.87	2.73	2.57	2.49	2.41	2.33	2.23	2.14	2.03	29
2.98	2.84	2.70	2.55	2.47	2.39	2.30	2.21	2.11	2.01	30
2.80	2.66	2.52	2.37	2.29	2.20	2.11	2.02	1.92	1.80	40
2.63	2.50	2.35	2.20	2.12	2.03	1.94	1.84	1.73	1.60	60
2.47	2.34	2.19	2.03	1.95	1.86	1.76	1.66	1.53	1.38	120
2.32	2.18	2.04	1.88	1.79	1.70	1.59	1.47	1.32	1.00	∞

From "Tables of Percentage Points of the Inverted Beta (F) Distribution," *Biometrika*, Vol. 33 (1943), pp. 73–88, by Maxine Merrington and Catherine M. Thompson. Reproduced by permission of Professor E. S. Pearson.

Table 6 Critical Values of Chi-Square

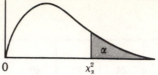

d.f.	$\chi^2$0.995	$\chi^2$0.990	$\chi^2$0.975	$\chi^2$0.950	$\chi^2$0.900
1	0.0000393	0.0001571	0.0009821	0.0039321	0.0157908
2	0.0100251	0.0201007	0.0506356	0.102587	0.210720
3	0.0717212	0.114832	0.215795	0.351846	0.584375
4	0.206990	0.297110	0.484419	0.710721	1.063623
5	0.411740	0.554300	0.831211	1.145476	1.61031
6	0.675727	0.872085	1.237347	1.63539	2.20413
7	0.989265	1.239043	1.68987	2.16735	2.83311
8	1.344419	1.646482	2.17973	2.73264	3.48954
9	1.734926	2.087912	2.70039	3.32511	4.16816
10	2.15585	2.55821	3.24697	3.94030	4.86518
11	2.60321	3.05347	3.81575	4.57481	5.57779
12	3.07382	3.57056	4.40379	5.22603	6.30380
13	3.56503	4.10691	5.00874	5.89186	7.04150
14	4.07468	4.66043	5.62872	6.57063	7.78953
15	4.60094	5.22935	6.26214	7.26094	8.54675
16	5.14224	5.81221	6.90766	7.96164	9.31223
17	5.69724	6.40776	7.56418	8.67176	10.0852
18	6.26481	7.01491	8.23075	9.39046	10.8649
19	6.84398	7.63273	8.90655	10.1170	11.6509
20	7.43386	8.26040	9.59083	10.8508	12.4426
21	8.03366	8.89720	10.28293	11.5913	13.2396
22	8.64272	9.54249	10.9823	12.3380	14.0415
23	9.26042	10.19567	11.6885	13.0905	14.8479
24	9.88623	10.8564	12.4011	13.8484	15.6587
25	10.5197	11.5240	13.1197	14.6114	16.4734
26	11.1603	12.1981	13.8439	15.3791	17.2919
27	11.8076	12.8786	14.5733	16.1513	18.1138
28	12.4613	13.5648	15.3079	16.9279	18.9392
29	13.1211	14.2565	16.0471	17.7083	19.7677
30	13.7867	14.9535	16.7908	18.4926	20.5992
40	20.7065	22.1643	24.4331	26.5093	29.0505
50	27.9907	29.7067	32.3574	34.7642	37.6886
60	35.5346	37.4848	40.4817	43.1879	46.4589
70	43.2752	45.4418	48.7576	51.7393	55.3290
80	51.1720	53.5400	57.1532	60.3915	64.2778
90	59.1963	61.7541	65.6466	69.1260	73.2912
100	67.3276	70.0648	74.2219	77.9295	82.3581

$\chi^2 0.100$	$\chi^2 0.050$	$\chi^2 0.025$	$\chi^2 0.010$	$\chi^2 0.005$	d.f.
2.70554	3.84146	5.02389	6.63490	7.87944	1
4.60517	5.99147	7.37776	9.21034	10.5966	2
6.25139	7.81473	9.34840	11.3449	12.8381	3
7.77944	9.48773	11.1433	13.2767	14.8602	4
9.23635	11.0705	12.8325	15.0863	16.7496	5
10.6446	12.5916	14.4494	16.8119	18.5476	6
12.0170	14.0671	16.0128	18.4753	20.2777	7
13.3616	15.5073	17.5346	20.0902	21.9550	8
14.6837	16.9190	19.0228	21.6660	23.5893	9
15.9871	18.3070	20.4831	23.2093	25.1882	10
17.2750	19.6751	21.9200	24.7250	26.7569	11
18.5494	21.0261	23.3367	26.2170	28.2995	12
19.8119	22.3621	24.7356	27.6883	29.8194	13
21.0642	23.6848	26.1190	29.1413	31.3193	14
22.3072	24.9958	27.4884	30.5779	32.8013	15
23.5418	26.2962	28.8454	31.9999	34.2672	16
24.7690	27.5871	30.1910	33.4087	35.7185	17
25.9894	28.8693	31.5264	34.8053	37.1564	18
27.2036	30.1435	32.8523	36.1908	38.5822	19
28.4120	31.4104	34.1696	37.5662	39.9968	20
29.6151	32.6705	35.4789	38.9321	41.4010	21
30.8133	33.9244	36.7807	40.2894	42.7956	22
32.0069	35.1725	38.0757	41.6384	44.1813	23
33.1963	36.4151	39.3641	42.9798	45.5585	24
34.3816	37.6525	40.6465	44.3141	46.9278	25
35.5631	38.8852	41.9232	45.6417	48.2899	26
36.7412	40.1133	43.1944	46.9630	49.6449	27
37.9159	41.3372	44.4607	48.2782	50.9933	28
39.0875	42.5569	45.7222	49.5879	52.3356	29
40.2560	43.7729	46.9792	50.8922	53.6720	30
51.8050	55.7585	59.3417	63.6907	66.7659	40
63.1671	67.5048	71.4202	76.1539	79.4900	50
74.3970	79.0819	83.2976	88.3794	91.9517	60
85.5271	90.5312	95.0231	100.425	104.215	70
96.5782	101.879	106.629	112.329	116.321	80
107.565	113.145	118.136	124.116	128.299	90
118.498	124.342	129.561	135.807	140.169	100

From "Tables of the Percentage Points of the χ^2-Distribution." *Biometrika*, Vol. 32 (1941), pp. 188–189, by Catherine M. Thompson. Reproduced by permission of Professor E. S. Pearson.

INDEX

A

Activity:
    definition, 2
    endogenous, 3
    exogenous, 3
Additive congruential generator, 154
Additive congruential method, 154
Advantages of simulation, 2
Analysis of simulation results, 135
Analysis of variance, 146
Arrivals, simulation of, 120
Attributes, 2, 16, 20, 60
Average contents, 102, 106
Average utilization, 101, 106

B

Batch confidence intervals, 132
Bernoulli distribution, 175
Binomial distribution, 176
Binomially distributed numbers, 177
Binomially distributed random numbers, 177

C

Central limit theorem, 171
Chain, 65
Chi square distribution, 170
Chi square test, 148
Choice of distribution, 181
Composite method, 166
Confidence interval, 129, 132, 137
Congruential method, 153
Contingency tables, 156–57
Continuous density and distribution, 167,
    181
Correlation, 132
Correlation coefficient, 137
Covariance, 157
Critical region, 137, 143
Cumulative distribution function:
    definition, 164
    empirical, 180
    properties, 164

Curve:
    power, 143

D

Degrees of freedom, 146, 147, 148
Density function:
    probability, 164
Design of experiments, 120
Deterministic system, 120
Differential equation, 99, 110
Disadvantages of simulation, 4
Discrete distribution, 174
Distribution:
    Bernoulli, 175
    beta, 170, 183
    binomial, 176
    chi-square, 170, 172
    empirical, 180
    exponential, 168, 181
    F-, 173
    gamma, 169, 182
    geometric, 175
    hypergeometric, 177
    lognormal, 174, 183
    normal, 171, 183
    Poisson, 178
    probability, 174
    t-, 173
    uniform, 167, 181
Distribution function:
    cumulative, 164

E

Empirical density, 180
Empirical distribution, 32, 33, 180
Empirically distributed numbers, 32, 33
Endogenous variables, 3
Entity:
    definition, 2, 64
    permanent, 17, 64
Erlang, 169
Error:
    type I, 143
    type II, 143

226

Estimate:
    confidence interval, 137
    point, 137
Estimation, 137
Evaluation of a simulation model, 135
Event, 8
Event notice, 10
Event trace, 127
Examples, 135, 188, 200
Exogenous variables, 3
Expected value, 135, 137, 201, 205
Experimental design, 135
Experiments, random, 132
Exponential distribution, 168
Exponentially distributed numbers, 168

F

F-distribution, 173
F test, 146
FIFO queues, 19, 100
Freedom, degrees of, 146–49
Frequency test, 156
Functional approach to subsystem modeling, 127
Functions:
    common simulation, 163
    cumulative distribution, 164
    GPSS, 66, 68
    SIMSCRIPT, 31, 32

G

Gap test, 159
Gamma distribution, 169, 182
Geometric distribution, 175
Geometrically distributed numbers, 175
GPSS:
    action time, 66
    block type table, 61
    block types,
      ADVANCE, 66, 86
      DEPART, 66, 85

      ENTER, 66, 85
      GENERATE, 65, 68, 90
      LEAVE, 66, 85
      MARK, 61
      QUEUE, 66, 85
      RELEASE, 66
      SEIZE, 66
      TABULATE, 68, 72, 84
      TERMINATE, 65, 90
      TEST, 90
      TRANSFER, 73
    control statement table, 66
    control statements,
      CLEAR, 66
      END, 63, 66
      FUNCTION, 68
      RESET, 68
      SIMULATE, 63, 66
      START, 68, 90
      STORAGE, 85
      TABLE, 68, 86, 94
GPSS random number generator, 68

H

Hypergeometric distribution, 177
Hypothesis:
    alternate, 143
    null, 143, 144, 145, 146, 147, 148
    statistical, 143
Hypothesis testing, 143

I

Independence, 132, 171
Initial bias, 130
Interarrival times, 179
Inverse transformation method, 164

J

Jackson's Theorem, 111

Random variable:
  continuous, 167
  discrete, 174
Rejection method, 165
Replication, 133
Routing, 113
Runs test, 158

S

Sample space, 143
Seed, choice of, 153, 155
Seed of a generator, 154
Serial test, 157
Server:
  parallel, 103, 104
  single, 100
Significance, level of, 143
SIMSCRIPT:
  activity, 8
  attributes, 8, 16, 17, 22
  entities, 8, 16, 17, 22
  event notice, 12
  event routine, 8, 9, 10
  exogenous event, 8, 33
  permanent entity, 17
  pointers, 17, 22
  sets, 18, 20, 22
  statement table, 9
  statements,
    ACCUMULATE, 25
    ALWAYS, 14
    AT, 10, 12
    CANCEL, 27
    COMPUTE, 30
    CREATE, 17
    DEFINE, 13
    DESTROY, 17, 20
    DO, 28
    ELSE, 14, 28
    END, 10
    EVENT NOTICES, 10, 12
    EVERY, 16, 18
    FILE, 19
    FIND, 29
    FOR, 18, 28

    IF, 13, 14
    IN, 10
    MAIN, 8, 10
    PERMANENT ENTITIES, 17
    PRINT, 24
    REMOVE, 19
    RETURN, 14, 15
    SCHEDULE, 12
    TALLY, 25
    TEMPORARY ENTITIES, 11
    UNLESS, 29
    UNTIL, 29
    WITH, 29
Simulation:
  advantages, 2, 4
  disadvantages, 4
  terminology, 2
  time, 34
Simulation clock, 11
Standard deviation, 131
Standard normal distribution, 171
Standard uniform distribution, 167
State of a system, 125
Statistics gathering, 27, 30, 60, 68, 132, 194, 204
Status attribute, 38
Steady state, 130
Stochastic, 3
Stopping rules, 134
Structured programming, 127
Student's t distribution, 173
System:
  boundary of, 3
  state of, 4
  stochastic, 3
System environment, 3
System methodology, 120

T

t-distribution, 173
t-test, 147, 148
Tests:
  chi-square, 148
  F-, 146
  frequency, 156